UPSTATE

NEW YORK CLASSICS

FRANK BERGMANN, SERIES EDITOR

EDMUND WILSON

Upstate

Records and Recollections of Northern New York

Foreword by Richard Hauer Costa

SYRACUSE UNIVERSITY PRESS

Copyright © 1971 by Edmund Wilson

Foreword © 1990 by Syracuse University Press
Syracuse, New York 13244-5160

First Syracuse University Press Edition 1990
95 96 97 98 99 00   6 5 4 3 2

Publication of this book is through arrangement with
Farrar, Straus & Giroux, Inc.

A considerable portion of this material first appeared in *The New
Yorker*. "Conversing with Malcolm Sharp" (page 169) first appeared in
the University of Chicago *Law Review*, copyright © 1966 by the
University of Chicago.

This book is published with the assistance of a grant from the
John Ben Snow Foundation.

Frontispiece: The Stone House *(Carl E. La Tray)*

The paper used in this publication meets the minimum requirements of
American National Standard for Information Sciences—Permanence of
Paper for Printed Library Materials, ANSI Z39.48-1984. ∞™

Library of Congress Cataloging-in-Publication Data

Wilson, Edmund, 1895–1972.
    Upstate: records and recollections of northern New York/Edmund
Wilson; foreword by Richard Hauer Costa.
        p.   cm.—(New York classics)
    Reprint, with new foreword. Originally published: New York:
Farrar, Straus, and Giroux, 1971.
    ISBN 0-8156-2499-9 (alk. paper)
    1. New York (State)—Description and travel—1951–1980.
2. New York (State)—Social life and customs.   3. Wilson, Edmund,
1895–1972—Homes and haunts—New York (State)
4. Wilson, Edmund, 1895–1972—Diaries.   5. Wilson family.
6. Baker family.   I. Title.   II. Series.
F124.W726   1990
917.47'610443—dc20   90-35158

Manufactured in the United States of America

To the Memory of My Grandfather,
Walter Scott Kimball
1828–1890

Some of this material in a much abridged form has appeared in the *New Yorker* magazine.

I am indebted to Mr. Joseph Alsop, who knows this part of the country well, for suggestions and directions in visiting the old houses, and to Mr. Douglas Kent, an authority on Hyde-Clarke Hall, for information about the family and the house. I am grateful for the kind collaboration of most of the persons mentioned in the text.

CONTENTS

ILLUSTRATIONS

Foreword

Readers who know Edmund Wilson only through his *magna opera*—books like those early "translations" in *Axel's Castle* (1931), which helped get many of us through Joyce and Eliot in graduate school, or like *Patriotic Gore* (1962), subtitled by Wilson "studies in the literature of the American Civil War," but actually, as Norman Podhoretz has written, "a study in the spiritual history of American civilization"— may be unprepared for the less-severe Wilson, the benevolent village-squire figure who emerges from *Upstate* (1971), his twenty-fourth book and the last published during his lifetime.

For the reader gratefully accustomed to expect of any subject Edmund Wilson tackled, however complex, a distillation, the reading of *Upstate* will prove a challenge. Wilson complained in a letter to me about the large portions the editors of *The New Yorker* had left out ("it comes out sounding like *Wilson or Life in the Woods*"). *Upstate* consists of mounds of entries from Wilson's diary—notebooks, with occasional interpolations, covering the period from 1950 to 1970. Having inherited from his mother upon her death in 1951 the "old stone house" in Talcott-

ville (in Lewis County, forty miles north of Utica,
N.Y.), he made frequent visits and spent a large part
of his summers at "the only place, perhaps, that I
feel I belong [where] everybody knows me—and,
quite unlike the general attitude in New England,
where anyone from two miles away is 'a foreigner'—
[where] everybody seems good-natured and comfortable [and] even the dogs are not yappy and snappy,
as they are likely to be in Wellfleet [on Cape Cod]."

It is not only that *Upstate* might appear to an un-
neighborly reader nothing but two decades' worth of
diaries about a 170-year-old summer house, with the
names of every person—famous and unknown alike
—who visited Wilson there tossed in, but that the
real treasures for Wilsonians are drowned in this
deluge. Thus, among the entries of 1955, a priceless
anecdote on Hemingway's false bravado (relayed to
Wilson by his friend the Canadian novelist Morley
Callaghan—a story not so fully told even in Carlos
Baker's biography of Hemingway) is sandwiched
among local items about nearby Hamilton College
and a reigning campus family there, the history of
the experimental Oneida Community, and a visit to
the Lowville Fair. Later (1957), Wilson tells of having his poet friends—Saint-John Perse, John Wain,
Spender, Nabokov, Dorothy Parker (bibulously)—
use a diamond-point pen to write verses on the win-
dowpanes of the old house. But his diary breaks off
to present an account of a neighbor's pet fox. Always
one to consider his readers—nearly all of Wilson's
hardbound books are sized to fit into a man's coat-
pocket or a woman's handbag—he has uncharacter-
istically omitted an index. Even his essay collections
contain one.

In his sixty-fifth year (1959), he devotes a long

diary entry to "discovering" with Boonville friends a
sylvan retreat at Dry Sugar River where he had picnicked many times as a youngster. And he—not un-
intentionally, I suspect—pairs the entry with a
description of the verve with which he reads English
memoirs of the late nineteenth and early twentieth
centuries, the period in which he feels most at home.

He gives exactly twice as much space to the "Discovery of the Showy Ladyslipper" at age seventy
(1965) as he had given to the "Death of Hemingway"
four years before. To have even one of these rare
June-blooming orchids is to hold a key to some secret
place of the heart. No one of the blessed dares reveal
where they grow naturally or how they got there even
if the locales were known. Wilson uses the incidence
of such a discovery for bucolic relief and mystery just
as he uses the retired farmer and occasional chauf-
feur Albert Grubel, with his catalog of holiday-
accident deaths and gruesome suicides, for another
kind of relief.

When Upstate, Wilson had an Upstater's interests
—at times those of a gentryman, at other times those
of a regionalist. On those occasions when he took
long drives with his amanuensis and *ezermester* (Hungarian for "master of a thousand arts") from West
Leyden, Mary (Horbach) Pcolar, he often sought to
satisfy his insatiable curiosity—about such enigmas
as the origin of Sodom, New York, a village east of
Speculator in a remote part of the Adirondacks; about
the nature of the place, Palmyra, where Joseph
Smith was supposed to have been visited by his angel.
In Sodom, he met an old woman who told him nothing was amiss in Sodom, but "what I call Gomorrah
is down the road." Gomorrah proved to be a house
whose new owner had allowed it to run down. Until

angina ruled out walking, he went fishing with
George Pcolar and attended the firemen's fair and
parade in Boonville mainly to see the Pcolar children
perform.

Of special importance to the author of *Apologies to
the Iroquois* were his tours of the Iroquois Confeder-
acy with New York State Indian historian William
N. Fenton of Albany. He witnessed ceremonials at
the Cattaraugus, Allegany, Tuscarora, and Onondaga reservations. Once he and I compared notes on
a mini-Iroquois-nationalist movement on Schoharie
Creek, near Amsterdam. A band of Mohawks pitched
camp on some land they claimed had been assigned
to them by the United States in the Treaty of Fort
Stanwix, 1784. For months they refused to leave. I
covered the story for the Utica *Observer-Dispatch* in
early October 1957, just missing by days Wilson's
appearance at midmonth.

Put most simply, the region captivated him, the
place where he felt the first intimations that, if he
was not destined to become a poet, he would be
"something of the kind." Wilson liked to recognize
others and be recognized on Main Street, Boonville,
during forays for his favorites, Molson's and Johnny
Walker Red. If anything, the longer he lived, the
more he chose summers and early autumns "in the
country" over being a showpiece—a writer among
many writers—at Wellfleet, an elder in the international set of literary statesmen. He wrote his books
on Cape Cod, but in the end it was not, as Leon Edel
writes in his prefaces to the diaries, "the corner of
America he loved best."

One summer's night, when he was seventy, Edmund was rebuking me on one of my missing cir-
cuits. He could not understand how anyone could be

so wholly wanting in ties to family and origin. He spoke in words similar to those I would later read in *Upstate:* "There is all the difference between a place where one feels the fibers of family and a place in which one is totally unaware of other people's similar fibers." I will never forget his next words, for whose exactness I cannot vouch but whose sense I have indelibly: "You, Dick, don't appear to know or care about such things, but the fact is my life would have been altogether different if my mother had given me the house in my forties instead of my sixties. I'd have settled Upstate here as a landowner, a family man, and the entire direction of things would have been different."

We had been talking, I believe, about his close friend John Dos Passos and that writer's sudden veer, in middle age, to the Right. Most accounts charge disillusioning experiences with Communist-front activity in the Spanish Civil War for his disenchantment with the Left. But that night in the old stone house Edmund Wilson attributed the shift to Dos Passos's inheriting of a large estate in Virginia.

Suppose, however, that Edmund Wilson had inherited the house well before 1951. How would his life have been different? Could ownership of land in his remote—and favorite—corner have quieted that restless intelligence? And how would life have been better for the man who, as Daniel Aaron puts it, was "the moral and intellectual conscience of his generation"?

I believe the most telling words ever applied to Edmund Wilson were those of an epigram drawn from Alfred Kazin's autobiography. He notes that, for Wilson, "life was one elaborately constructed sentence after another, and he had been sentenced to the sen-

tence." Wilson joked about his bondage to syntax
when, in an imaginary interview conducted with
himself, he asks himself to what he attributes his
success as a writer. Wilson questions back, "Am I a
success as a writer?" and then answers: "I attribute
such success as I have had to my mastery of the
periodic sentence."

In its syntactical definition—"a usually complex
sentence in which the principal clause comes *last* or
which has no trailing elements following full statement of the essential idea"—the periodic sentence
bears a curious analogy to its practitioner. Edmund
Wilson's life, a seventy-seven-year-old periodic sentence, paid off its promissory note. When he came
up to the country for five or six months annually,
especially when he came to the old stone house in
June 1972, a dying man wearing a McGovern button,
it was to drop anchor once again, to settle in, and be
—as he writes in *Upstate* (my favorite Wilsonian periodic sentence)—that person who, "although I embody different tendencies and remember that, in
early life, I was sometimes in doubt as to what kind
of role I wanted to play, I have never had much doubt
about who or what I was."

Edmund Wilson's destiny—his being "something
like a poet"—was to write essays, fiction, verse, and
plays out of a civilized interest and inquisitiveness
about human affairs. He had, as George Steiner puts
it, a formidable appetite for difficulty and saw as his
job the making of the inaccessible accessible.

And he, in his redoubt Upstate, was the most accessible of all.

· · ·

For further reading, the publication late last fall of
a memoir by Edmund Wilson's oldest daughter

should not be overlooked. The final one hundred pages or so of Rosalind Baker Wilson's *Near the Magician: A Memoir of My Father, Edmund Wilson* (Grove Weidenfeld, 1989) dramatically convey, from his daughter's caring vantage, why and how Edmund Wilson considered Upstate and Talcottville his spiritual home to which he returned, a dying man, in June 1972. Those pages may stand as a corrective to the rest of the memoir which is a catalog of complaints about her father and most everyone else who crossed her path earlier, until at the old stone house, she learned to enjoy, as well as to judge.

Kinder pictures of Edmund Wilson are revealed in my book *Edmund Wilson: Our Neighbor from Talcottville* (Syracuse University Press, 1980) and Frederick Exley's *Notes from a Cold Island* (Random House, 1975). The four volumes of his diaries and notebooks, *The Twenties, The Thirties, The Forties,* and *The Fifties,* edited by Leon Edel, contain Upstate material. Roger Straus, president of Farrar, Straus & Giroux, wrote me that *The Sixties* would be published early in 1990. The excellent collection of Wilson's *Letters on Literature and Politics, 1912–1972,* edited by his widow, the late Elena Mumm Wilson, was published by Farrar, Straus & Giroux in 1977. Also revealing of the Talcottville Wilson is a much-anthologized essay, "The Old Stone House," in his collection *The American Earthquake* (Doubleday, 1958). Three critical studies, published in the eighties, provide fine introductions to his work: *Edmund Wilson's America* by George H. Douglas (University of Kentucky Press, 1983), *Edmund Wilson* by David Castronovo (Ungar, 1984), and *Edmund Wilson: A Critic for Our Time* by Janet Groth (Ohio University Press, 1989). *Edmund Wilson: The Man and*

His Work, edited by John Wain and published by New York University Press in 1978, contains memoirs written especially for the book. Major libraries will have a powerful comparison of Edmund Wilson with F. R. Leavis and Lionel Trilling in *Three Honest Men* (Manchester, England: Carcanet New Press, 1980).

Sylvan Beach, N.Y.   RICHARD HAUER COSTA
November 1989

UPSTATE

I

Prologue, 1969

I sit here in this old house alone. The little village was years ago a kind of family center, to which my parents and my cousins from all over the country were in the habit of returning in the summers to see one another again, when, after the emigration of our families from New England at the end of the eighteenth century, the members had further scattered to work or marry in other places. When my mother died in 1951, after not having been able to live in it for eleven years, she left the place to me, and I made it a habit, as she had done, to come up here for the summer. I also, in an attempt to revive the old reunions, induced some of my long-absent cousins to join me. But now my parents' generation have died, my own generation are growing old, and my younger cousins who still live here have become rather remote from the rest of us. My own children do not much like it here because they do not have the swimming or the companionship of the beaches of Cape Cod, on which I have been living for some thirty years. The croquet set which I had hoped would occupy them—we always used to play croquet—is still standing by the front door, with

3

nobody ready to set it up. The fishing rods that were once my father's and which I have not made use of for years are also standing untouched in the hall by the old hat rack. Every year I have to make more repairs on the house. It took them five years to build and was finished about 1800. Though it's still solid with its thick walls of stone, it is full of rotted beams and bad leaks. This region had enchanted me in my childhood. With its green hills and its wild rivers it was so much more attractive than the New Jersey town, Red Bank, already become suburbanized, in which I had been born, and I always felt excitement at coming here. It is associated in my mind with the first moments of my being conscious that I was capable of imaginative activity and some sort of literary vocation. When, before I was able to read, I was being read a bedtime fairy tale which had to be dropped because guests arrived, I invented, lying in the darkness before I went to sleep, the rest of the story for myself; and when being driven one day from Boonville to Talcottville, I said suddenly to myself, "I am a poet," then after a moment corrected myself with, "No: I am not quite a poet, but I am something of the kind." And there was my pretty dark cousin Dorothy whom I was always hoping to kiss.

Later, the place came to bore me. My favorite cousins were never there; and the much more stimulating experiences of prep school and college and travel had rescued me from Red Bank. But after I had reached my fifties and was in possession of the house myself, it became a refuge in the summers, where I thought that it was possible, as my parents had done, to get away from everything else. Now, it is true that this part of the United States has changed very much less since I first knew it as a child than any other part of this country I knew, but, nevertheless, all the things that make everywhere

else unpleasant have been cropping up around me here.
There are an air base at Rome, not far from me, from
which planes start out every morning to make a flight in
the direction of Russia before turning back to the base,
and a nearby radar station which in the event of a Russian attack would of course be a prime target. The town
of Talcottville—which at its peak, I understand, had a
hundred and twenty-some inhabitants, and has dwindled
to eighty-some—was in my youth a clean and trim little
settlement; but today it looks partly disreputable with its
tumbledown squalid houses whose inhabitants hardly get
along by working in the Boonville chair factory or who
cannot go to work at all in order not to lose their unemployment relief. There are many delinquent young people, one of whom, I am told, has announced that he is
going, like his parents, to live on relief and make a point
of having plenty of children in order to get plenty of this.
These break into garages to steal and into unoccupied
houses simply to mess them up. The Birch Society plas-
ters the town with posters saying "Impeach Earl Warren"
—I found one on my own property. When one of these
posters disappeared, I assumed that a liberal spirit had
been roused to action in Talcottville; but this turned out
to be the work of the delinquents, who undoubtedly had
no idea who Chief Justice Warren was.

One side of my stone barn fell down—it was built at
the same time as the house—and I had to have much
masonry rebuilt. Of my mother's once considerable garden, only the clumps of peonies and the plantings of
currants and gooseberries are left—I have tried to keep
them weeded out—and my great-aunt Rosalind's straggling roses. A white rose by the front porch, in spite of
the weather and the insects, has by care been made to
survive. At first, after my mother's death, I filled shelves
with the books from her Red Bank house—from her girl-

hood favorites, with signatures of the eighties, the stories of Juliana Horatia Ewing, which I never quite liked or understood, but, since her death I have had rebound; to W. W. Jacobs, which I read with her, and Somerville and Ross, which I didn't; and my father's collection of travel books, about Africa and Tibet, the Arctic and the Antarctic, which last explorations have always peculiarly bored me; and my own childhood favorites: Raffles and Sherlock Holmes, Frank Stockton and William De Morgan, with my later prep school reading: George Borrow, Francis Thompson, the Everyman *Ring and the Book*; complete family sets of such by now almost unreadable nineteenth-century writers as Wilkie Collins, Bulwer-Lytton, Disraeli, Charles Kingsley and Ruskin; complete Dumas and Hugo and Balzac. But I soon came to see that this was not enough, and added Pushkin, Chekhov, Swift, some Henry James, a number of the Pléiade volumes, the new complete edition of the Goncourt diary, Skelton and Beaumont and Fletcher together with a number of books—*Clarissa*, Hazlitt, Gioacchino Belli, Milton's complete prose, which I laid in for the dismal and impassable winters which I have always made sure not to spend here, so never had read these books. There are also bound files of *Harper's Monthly* in the fifties and sixties, *Littell's Living Age* for the seventies, *St. Nicholas* going back to its beginnings in the seventies, *Harper's Magazine* for the seventies, and the *Century Magazine* for the eighties. I found these magazines very useful when I was writing about the Civil War period and after.

The memories of the past, the still lingering presences of the family, which so haunted me when I first came back here, have mostly evaporated. Although I have made new and interesting friends, my life up here now seems thinner. Here I am in the northern countryside, still

beautiful but now somewhat empty, incapacitated physi-
cally now for bicycling, fishing and exploring—I was in
the habit, in my youth, of walking every afternoon to a
swimming hole called Flat Rock in Sugar River. Much
of the time I am quite by myself in an interior which is
now all my own. It is almost as if no woman's hand has
ever had anything to do with it since I cleaned out the
old Franklin stoves and the stuffy old Victorian portières.
My housekeeper, Mrs. Hutchins, keeps everything polished and clean: the pewter and crystal and silver. And
every summer she seems to find something new: some
object, quite blackened from disuse, that had been lying
in an old drawer or closet: copper candlesticks, a brass
oil-lamp on a long spiral stem, a silver napkin ring, silver
salt and pepper shakers, a silver-topped inkwell with my
great-aunt Rosalind's monogram—which have all now
been made to shine. I had already rescued myself the little
silver smelling salts bottle, with pretty winged cherubs
on one side and my mother's married monogram on the
other—for Helen Mather Kimball Wilson: she never
wanted to drop the Mather, of which she was rather
proud—that I am told was the first post-marital gift that
was given by my father to my mother.

Is the writing of this Talcottville book a last effort to
fill a vacuum? Though I spend much of my time in
Massachusetts, I am legally a resident of New York, and
my relations with Lewis and Oneida Counties are still
closer than with Wellfleet on Cape Cod. But what more
is there here for me to do? And yet I find it difficult to
break the old habit—which goes back for me, it must be,
seventy years—of returning to this place in the summer. In
the later years of my mother's life, she imagined every year
that she would be able to come again, but her health, in
her late seventies and her eighties, was never to make
it possible—except on one occasion, when she was going

into the hospital for an operation and she made the effort
involved in a visit of inspection. She spent the night in
Boonville; the house was unfit for habitation. When she
told her sister-in-law, whose family had come from Knoxboro not far away, about going in at night to the Stone
House, now become rather spooky, my aunt Caroline
advised her, "Nelly, when you go into those old houses,
you ought always to take a flask of brandy." My mother,
being very deaf, had to have this repeated, and, when
she understood—she did not much approve of drinking
—her only comment was "Oh." I eventually became worried about the old place and without letting my mother
know, for she did not like other people to meddle with
her property, came up here and found it in deplorable
condition. I have spent, in the years since her death, as
much time as possible here, excavating the old drawers
and attics and having something repaired every year. And
now I am sitting alone here, and all the old ghosts are
gone.

II

In the summer and autumn of 1802, the Reverend
John Taylor of Deerfield, Massachusetts, explored, on "a
missionary tour," by horseback and stagecoach journey,
"the Mohawk and Black River countries." His diary of
this journey was published after his death by his son in
some periodical or collection of papers which, since the
copy I have is clipped out of it, I cannot identify.

Dr. Taylor, who had been to Yale, was evidently a Con-
gregationalist, and he believed that the Methodists and
Baptists were personally undesirable as people and theolog-
ically dangerous influences. The Methodists, very pious,
would "fall down . . . and, after lying twenty or thirty minutes, rise, crying glory to God. Some of them appeared to
be senseless—others in great agitation." After preaching to
about forty people, mostly Baptists, he writes that "they
are, a few excepted, extremely ignorant, and the ignorant
Methodist preachers are leading them into errors and
all kinds of disorder . . . General Floyd thinks that many
of the best characters among them, when they have had
time to reflect, and when their passions are a little sub-
sided, will fall off from that sect, and will become Pres-

9

byterians or Congregationalists. At present he thinks that
they ought to be treated with great tenderness." The people [in Sandy Creek] are Baptists from Rhode Island,
and are a most wretched people—the filth of the world
. . . [They] are in general nothingarians or fatalists—or
Methodists and Baptists, who are the worst of all." Of
Remsen, he writes, "This is a broken society. The people
are very ignorant and very wicked—about three months
since a stranger came into town, who appeared to be a
pert coxcomb, about twenty-eight years of age, who calls
his name Alexander. He soon obtained a school, and in
about a fortnight set up preaching, and he pretends to
preach every Sunday. Who and what he is they know
not—but that he is some notorious villain I believe there
is no doubt. Most of the people—especially the wickedest
part—are very much attached to him. There is no church
in town, and but one professor [professing Christian],
who belongs to the church in Stuben [Steuben]." "At the
house of a Rhode Island Baptist. Here is a mixture of all
the physical and moral evils that can well be conceived
of. Here may be found filth of all kinds, such as dust,
mud, fleas, bedbugs, rotten meat, and sour bread; and, as
to moral evils, you may here find ignorance, self-will, self-
sufficiency, ill manners, pride, boasting, fanaticism, and
witchcraft; and this description, I believe, will apply to
all the families in the town, Mr. Hackley's excepted." It
is interesting to know that among the sects that Dr. Taylor
regarded as competitors were the eighteenth-century
Deists, who would not have a Bible in the house. "They
[a school of about forty-seven children] have a deistical
instructor, to the great grief of some pious persons."

He is, nevertheless, impressed by the prevailing atmosphere of hopefulness: "Poor people have, in general, been
the first settlers. They have bought farms of about a
hundred acres—have cleared ten or twenty—built a log-

house—and then sold to others, for a sum as much greater
than they gave, as to purchase them another hundred
acres—and by this means have placed themselves in a
short time in a good situation. It is considered here but
a small affair for a man to sell, take his family and some
provisions, and go into the woods upon a new farm, erect
him a house and begin anew. Society is here made up of
all characters. It is a mixture of everything that can be
well conceived of, both as to nations and religions. The
great body of inhabitants are, however, from Massachusetts and Connecticut. One thing is peculiar in this
wilderness,—every countenance indicates pleasure and
satisfaction. [The equality of circumstances cuts off a great
proportion of the evils which render men unhappy in
improved societies,] and the influence of hope is very
apparent. I do not know that I have seen an unhappy person for ninety miles on this river. There is no complaining of hard times; but everyone is cheerful and contented
—for they all foresee that in a few years they will have a
great plenty of worldly goods, in a common course of
events."

He emphasizes one of the most important factors in
the development, or lack of development, of this part of
New York: the obstinate feudalism of the landowners.
"It is incredible," he writes of the town of Western, "how
thick this part of the world is settled—and what progress
is making in opening the wilderness and turning it into
a fruitful plain. The land in this town is most excellent—
crops are rich. The same evil operates here, however, as
in many parts of this country—the lands are most of them
leased. This must necessarily operate to debase the minds
and destroy the enterprise of the settlers—altho' the rent
is small—only 19 [dollars] an acre; yet if men do not
possess the right of soil, they never will nor can feel independent. And what is as great an evil, they will always

be under the influence of their landlords." And "from Turin, we came into Leyden [the township in which Talcottville is situated], where [Gerret] Boon made a settlement. This place does not appear to be very flourishing. The people are poor, and too much of the land is leased. The Americans never can flourish when on leased lands —they have too much enterprise to work for others, or to remain tenants—and where they are under the necessity of living on such lands I find that they are greatly depressed in mind, and are losing their animation." I have found in an old county history that the Talcotts were thought to have "adopted a policy adverse to the building up of the village at the point where natural advantages greatly favored," since they "refused to sell village lots to mechanics." The progress of the democratic processes was to some extent impeded here. No town meetings as in New England; the landlords were still in control. And it seems to me that every upstate New Yorker whose family belongs, or once belonged, to this landlord class retains something of this feudal mentality. They have never been able to get over the conviction that they ought to have the say as to what is for the good of the lower orders. Franklin Roosevelt was an obvious example of this: when he declared that he was going to be President of *all the people* of the United States, he spoke in detachment from the business world and meant that, as the lord of the nation, he was going to take responsibility for seeing that all the various ranks of people, as far as was in his power, were going to be given what was good for them. To establish the WPA and other devices for creating employment, to pack the Supreme Court with justices who would be sure to approve his policies, were expedients as to which Roosevelt did not feel the slightest hesitation. And he is said not to have been at home save with people of his own kind of background—

if not well-to-do squires, at least people well established
and educated in a similar way. The technique in which he
had been trained was not good fellowship but a patriar-
chal kindness. An earlier product of New York State was
James Fenimore Cooper of Cooperstown, who was horrified, on returning to the United States after seven and a
half years in Europe, to find that, on Lake Otsego, the
feudal domain of his family was being invaded by "squat-
ters." He very soon closed off to the public a little picnic
ground on the lake which his father had thrown open for
general use. The old buildings had been destroyed and a
new one constructed without the son's permission, and
since the land did still belong to the Cooper estate, he
was able to win a suit which he brought to keep inter-
lopers off it. Though the death in 1839 of the last patroon
—that is, Dutch landowner—Stephen Van Rensselaer, and
the administration of Andrew Jackson 1829-37, put an
end to the feudal era, Cooper, still professing his faith in
democracy, in equal political rights, spent a very large
part of his later life in fighting what was called "the anti-
rent war"—that is the attempts of the tenant farmers to
escape paying for leases on land which they had been
living on and cultivating for years, during many of which
Cooper had been living in Europe and celebrating America to the Europeans. He was in the habit of writing in
his novels as if most of these anti-rent agitators were unscrupulous sharp-dealing New Englanders, who knew
nothing of the seigneurial grand manner of New York,
and he frequently found himself, at home, characterized
as an arrogant aristocrat.

III

New York Religions

The Reverend John Taylor, a rooted New Englander, is already aware of all this and has foreseen that, in a newly settled section of America, a feudal social system could have no future. But what he did not foresee was that the vacuum created there by sloughing off the old religion was not to be filled by his own Congregationalism in competition with Methodism and Baptism but by a great proliferation of entirely new cults that had no Calvinism or even Wesleyanism to restrict them to older theologies. The Methodists and Baptists themselves, Mrs. Fawn M. Brodie says in her biography of Joseph Smith, were in a state of considerable confusion by the second decade of the century. The Methodists "split four ways, and the Baptists became divided into Reformed, Hard-Shell, Free-Will and Seventh Day Baptists and Foot-washers, and other sects." Even the standing of strict Calvinists was dubious. My great-great-grandfather Ruel Kimball (as Reuel was then spelled), born in 1778, a Presbyterian minister married to Hannah Mather, a cousin of Increase and Cotton, came over from Vermont in 1805 and from about 1816 officiated in a church on Leyden

Hill. He also organized in 1826 a First Presbyterian
Church on what was called the Brantingham tract, which
began with twelve communicants and, not having a regular church building, held services in Ruel Kimball's and
other people's houses. The membership of this church
increased in four years to twenty-three, but thirteen years
later had shrunk to nineteen. It was then meeting in a
schoolhouse, and did not get a real church, known as
"the Forest Church," till 1854. Kimball carried on the
Calvinist tradition in sermons so full of hellfire that,
according to local legend, the corn never freezes on
Leyden Hill. This was apparently too much for his congregation, who were enjoying their freedom from the
New England theocracy. They put "Priest Kimball" out
of his pulpit—though they afterwards reinstated him. But
other religions were introduced or actually founded in
New York that were quite independent of the New
England sects. Here was a great sparsely settled country,
not ruled by the Calvinist Church, where worship could
take any form.

The zeal that could in those days be manifested by
members of the Presbyterian Church is illustrated by an
anecdote in the *Life of Thomas Brainerd, D.D.* (1870).
Brainerd was a man from Leyden, who later became a
celebrated preacher in Philadelphia:

"When about the age of fourteen, Thomas was walking
with young Reuel Kimball [my great-grandfather], two
years his senior, when their conversation turned upon
preaching. In the bragging style natural to boys of that
age, Thomas said to his friend: 'I can preach nearly as
well as your father, now!' Young Kimball questioned his
ability, and challenged him to the proof.

"Springing upon a stump, in which that newly cleared
land abounded, Thomas rehearsed Mr. Kimball's sermon
of the previous Sabbath, giving the introduction, the

My great-great-grandfather, Ruel Kimball (1778-1847); my great-grandmother Hannah Mather Kimball; my grandfather Walter Scott Kimball

title, the divisions, the arguments, the illustrations, the application, and conclusion, in what seemed to his astonished auditor the *very words,* without variation, in which he heard it preached the day before. Although greatly surprised by this exhibition, young Kimball would not yield the victory. He added: 'Well, you can't *pray* as well anyhow!' Thomas replied, in a lower voice, 'I haven't tried that!'"

Ann Lee, for example, the daughter of a Manchester (England) blacksmith, had joined an evangelical sect known as the Shaking Quakers, which profaned the Sabbath by shouting and dancing. She was punished for this by being sent to jail in 1774, but she had had a divine vision in which a voice told her to go to America. She managed to get some land near Albany and there founded her own branch of this sect. Having lost all four of her children, she led a crusade against marriage. As a substitute for sexual activity, the Shakers made a ritual of their shaking, which was a strange kind of non-sexual orgy. They marched and whirled about, but the women kept apart from the men. They pretended to play on invisible instruments and became possessed by tribes of Indians or George Washington and the Founding Fathers. Mother Ann announced herself as the second incarnation of Christ. They were organized in a communist economy, and wore linen, knitted their underwear and made slim and austere furniture. Mother Ann was succeeded by another able woman, and as late as the nineteen thirties there were still a few Shakers left.

The example of Mother Ann was followed by another somewhat younger woman prophet, Jemima Wilkinson of Providence, Rhode Island, who called herself the "Public Universal Friend" and who was also believed by her followers to be the second incarnation of Christ. She said

that, in the course of a fever, she had fallen into a trance
and waked up believing she had died and that her soul
had gone to Heaven. She was now possessed by the Spirit
of Life, which had come "to warn a lost and guilty, gos-
siping, dying world to flee from the wrath to come."
Jemima Wilkinson was said to be handsome: she had
black hypnotic eyes. She was better bred and educated
than Mother Ann, who could not read or write, and she
appealed to a somewhat better class of disciples. They
followed her on horseback, riding two by two; and
Jemima rode ahead, wearing men's clothes under a long
woman's robe. But she aroused such resentment in New
England, and later in Philadelphia, where Mrs. Wilkinson was stoned by a mob, that in 1790 she fled and took
refuge in western New York, near Seneca Lake, "where
no intruding foot could enter." The settlement she assembled was called Jerusalem. The Treaty of Fort Stanwick
(now Rome) with the Iroquois Indians in 1784 had only
just made that region safe for settlers. It was a rough
forested country. Even the Iroquois had come there only
in order to hunt in the forests. Jemima established good
relations with the Indians, who called her Squaw Shin-
newanajistawge, Great Woman Preacher. But she eventually fell out with her companions. She had appropriated
twelve thousand acres and lived in what was thought to
be luxury. "As she grew older"—I am quoting Ernest
Sutherland Bates in the *Dictionary of American Biography*—"she became more dictatorial in her methods and
developed a penchant for degrading forms of punishment
for infraction of the society's rules, such as compelling
one man to wear a black hood for three months and
another to carry a little bell fastened to the skirts of his
coat."

    The Indians themselves at about this time had a new
religious movement. A Seneca named Handsome Lake,

notorious for hard drinking, was frightened in 1799 by a drunken brawl which caused the deaths of several persons, and in the course of an illness had a vision in which divine messengers appeared to him and ordered him to preach against the alcoholic habits that were ruining his people. Influenced perhaps by the Quaker missionaries, he formulated a code of morality which is recited once a year in the Iroquois Longhouse—that is, temple and council house—and which is now an integral part of the national religion that is an element of their nationalist movement.

The Mennonites arrived in New York in the thirties and invaded the unsettled wilderness near Lowville which is now the town of Croghan. The sect had been founded by a Friesland priest who, at the time of the Reformation, had become a kind of Reformer but one who was not accepted by either the Protestants or the Catholics. They dispensed with an official priesthood, repudiated the obligation to take oaths and refused to serve in the constabulary or be liable to military service. They left the state church and set up in Zürich from 1525 as an independent sect. They were mostly Alsatian or South German or German Swiss, and they did not learn to speak English till 1916, at the time of the first World War. Having crossed the Atlantic in a sailboat, they came to Germantown, Pennsylvania, in 1683; but some penetrated the New York forests. There was nobody here then but the Indians, and they were surrounded by bears, wolves and panthers. They built log cabins or slept under the trees. In time they organized a community, and this community is still thriving. They now have four churches, and six hundred communicants. They have abandoned their old details of costume, the special hat and jacket, the hooks and eyes which were substituted for buttons, because these were regarded as finery, and razors are no longer

outlawed as they were when the Mennonites were obliged
to wear beards. But a Mennonite Church I once visited
had nothing so frivolous as a steeple, and was primly
simple and bare. Outside, the neat and trim cemetery
consisted of rows of little white stones, all with Germanic
names and all exactly alike, in harmony with their rule
of equality. They still maintain their principle of refusing
to kill and will not take part in a war. Our government
allows for this by letting them off with two years of
working without pay for a government service: building
projects or protecting animal life. Their ministers and
bishops are not paid. They had no motorcars till 1963.
They are trusted and liked by their neighbors. But I
cannot be sure that their continued discipline was in
every way desirable. Their complexions seemed rather
unhealthy, like those of the Pennsylvania Dutch, many
of whom are Mennonites; and I thought the young girls
might be happier if they were allowed to wear gayer
clothes than the rigorously plain and unenticing ones
which the Mennonite system imposes. There are 300,000
Mennonites in North America.

The most successful of all these new cults, Mormonism,
which called itself the Church of Latterday Saints, was
born in Palmyra in the eighteen twenties, but did not
have its full development there. Joseph Smith was
brought as a child from Vermont to just north of the
Finger Lakes. He had a lively megalomaniac imagination,
and at the age of twenty, in 1827, among those exalting
hills, over which the thunder hovered, he asserted that
an angel called Moroni had appeared to him and given
him a stone box in which were to be found revelations
written in "reformed Egyptian" and inscribed upon gold
plates, together with a pair of magic spectacles which
enabled him to translate them into English. In 1830, he
founded a church of which the congregation in a month

increased from six to forty. But he was also mobbed and arrested by persons who thought him an impostor, and to escape from the hounding he invariably provoked, he was forced to go further and further west till, at the age of thirty-nine, he was shot while in an Illinois jail. Smith's henchman Brigham Young led his followers to the wastes of Utah and, with steady tenacity of purpose and very shrewd practical ability, consolidated the Mormon state in the mountain-hemmed desert of Utah. I find that a distant Kimball relative of mine, Heber Chase Kimball, whose family like so many others had moved from Vermont to New York, where his father and he were blacksmiths, was converted in 1832 from the Baptist to the Mormon Church. Now, according to the *Dictionary of American Biography,* having "a strong religious fervor, a ready belief in the existence of miracles," and a gift of prophecy of his own, he was "ordained one of the twelve apostles who, in the early days of the church organization, stood next to Joseph Smith in rank and authority." He was sent as a missionary to England, where, according to varying reports, he was either extremely successful or extremely unsuccessful. In Utah, in 1847, he became, with Brigham Young, one of the members of the triumvirate, known as the "first presidency," who ruled the Mormon community. "Though he suffered some mental anguish on first receiving the doctrine of plural marriage, he in time accepted it wholeheartedly and practised it fully, attaining to forty-five wives and sixty-five children."

It will be noticed that common features of several of these religions were the attempts to come to terms with the coexistence of the Red Indians; with the second coming of Christ; and with the problem of regulating sex. In the first of these cases, Joseph Smith, who had been led by the Indian burial mounds to believe they were the graves of two hostile races—a white and a red people, who had fought one another for a thousand years, with the result that the whites were wiped out, included in his Book of Mormon an account of the origin of the Indians in Jerusalem. This is still used by Mormon missionaries for their proselytizing among the Indians. In the case of dealing with sex, which Mother Ann and Jemima Wilkinson had determinedly attempted to discourage, the polygamous solution of Joseph Smith was originally not inspired, it would seem, by any social considerations but simply by his own sensuality, which extended to stealing his colleagues' wives; and was established by Brigham Young as an accepted institution that served certain useful ends. Women in the early nineteenth century, before contraceptives were common, were likely to be worn out by childbearing—the men often married second wives and produced a second brood after the first wife had given out; and before Ignaz Semmelweis and Oliver Wendell Holmes in the forties had discovered the antiseptic methods for preventing puerperal fever, an appalling number of mothers died of it. It was important both to have more potential mothers and to distribute the begetting of children among them. In the case of Mother Ann Lee and Jemima Wilkinson, they tried to avoid the problem by refusing to have children at all. In the system of the next great leader who emigrated to New York from New England, both the second coming of Christ and the reorganizing of sexual arrangements played very important roles. John Humphrey Noyes, also from Vermont, born in 1811, who had studied for the ministry at Yale, was the prophet of a heresy called Perfectionism. Noyes's doctrine was that Christ had already come again, and that there was no longer any excuse for not getting rid of sin in this world—which meant getting rid of Calvinism, with its unalterably predestinated damnation. On a visit to New York City, he had been

tormented by the temptations of sex and had gone to
preach in the brothels; but later, in the town of Putney,
Vermont, he trained a group of highly respectable Ver-
monters to practice a kind of "bundling," as embracing
without actual intercourse had earlier been called in New
England, which was intended to muffle the passions and
prevent irrelevant children. The women could experience
any number of orgasms but the men were supposed to
forgo them. What was known to Noyes's followers as
"complex marriage" first began to be practised in Putney
in 1846, and this was accompanied by "Bible Communism"—another feature of these early communities. These
two innovations caused so much scandal that eventually
Noyes and his followers, like the devotees of many of
these unconventional cults, found their way to western
New York and established the Oneida Community. I
visited this first as a child when the curiosity of my father
induced him to look it up—I do not remember anything
except staring at the entrance of the "Mansion House,"
a large impressive building, which had the air of a re-
pository of some kind of authority. In later years, I got
to know the descendants of the founding families, including the son and the granddaughter of John Humphrey Noyes. But what concerns us at this point is that
for thirty years Noyes was able to maintain a eugenic
experiment that completely disregarded the accepted system of marriage in the interest of producing a higher
breed. There were some forty families involved, selected
by Noyes from the best New England stock, and their
mating was subjected to a rigid discipline. The women—
fifty-nine of them—were obliged to sign the following
pledge:

1. That we do not belong to ourselves in any respect,
but that we do belong first to *God,* and second to Mr.
Noyes as God's true representative.

2. That we have no rights or personal feeling in regard
to child-bearing which shall in the least degree oppose
or embarrass him in his choice of scientific combina-
tions.

3. That we will put aside all envy, childishness and
self-seeking, and rejoice with those who are chosen
candidates; that we will, if necessary, become martyrs
to science, and cheerfully resign all desire to become
mothers if for any reason Mr. Noyes deem us unfit
material for propagation. Above all, we offer ourselves
"living sacrifices" to God and true Communism.

The men had to subscribe to equivalent submissions,
and each, if he wanted to mate, had to apply to a Central
Committee in order to impregnate a given woman; and
one's partner, whether man or woman, had to be older
than oneself, so that he or she would know better than an
inexperienced person how to handle the relationship—
two young people would be too impulsive—and it was
essential that one of the partners should be spiritually
superior to the other: the stock must not be made to
degenerate. The proposal of the applicant, if granted, had
always to be conveyed through a third person. If the
Central Committee should calculate that the union of
two persons, on account of their qualities, was likely to
be specially desirable, they could be ordered to breed
together. What was called "Special Love"—that is, what
we call falling in love—was dreaded and always discouraged: the lovers would be separated and sometimes
punished. The number of children was limited, and there
were very few unplanned births. In thirty years, there
were fifty-eight children—at least nine of them John
Humphrey Noyes's—and only four miscarriages. These
children soon entered a nursery, and the parents were
not supposed to show special concern or affection for
them. The Community prospered thus for three decades:

they manufactured a trap for wild animals that had been invented by one of its members, and also sold preserved fruits, which they had been among the first to put up in glass jars. It disintegrated in the seventies, though it was not destroyed, as the result of two fatal events: a moral crusade against it conducted all over the state by a professor at Hamilton College, next door to them, and a revolt of the younger members, who complained that Noyes and his elders, now aging, had made a practice of assigning to themselves the most desirable of the young girls. There were also the advanced Darwinian ideas which the young men were bringing back from Yale. These were undermining their faith in Perfectionism, which Noyes had established as the official cult, with its own theology and ritual. The women appear to have been discontented with the ban against personal property. One is shown at the Mansion House today one of the miniature chests of drawers that this restriction was so far remitted as to allow the ladies to own and which thus became the first small triumph in a more general conquest of possessions. The founder at this point resigned and put himself beyond legal action by going to live in Canada. But he continued from a distance to dominate the community, and some of his loyal disciples followed him. He died just over the line on the Ontario side of Niagara Falls. The Community gave up the old breeding system and began to have legal marriages. It continued to be profitable and self-supporting, and in 1881, it incorporated itself. Today, with factories in both Oneida and Canada, it manufactures the tableware called Community Plate. It still holds to the communist ideal to the extent that—although the administrators are allotted higher pay than the factory workers—it does not allow anyone to become either very rich or very poor. The huge Mansion House—finished in 1871—which looks rather like a cross between an old-fashioned hotel and an old-fashioned sanitarium, is still, with its ample and well-mowed lawns, its majestic trees, planted long ago, kept up to a proud standard which has never been abandoned. It is headquarters for the managers of the business and the survivors of the old group, and it provides accommodations, as Peterboro and Yaddo do, for a number of artists and scholars. All the younger people eat from Community Plate in a common dining room, and the atmosphere is informal, with the conversation of serious cultivated people. Like the Mormon church and center at Palmyra and the monument to Joseph Smith, with the golden Angel Moroni at the top of its marble shaft, towering above the sheer cliff, the Mansion House is still here to affirm the enduring heritage of some of this late growth of religions.

Certain members of the clergy of the established churches seem to have been affected by the atmosphere of religious exaltation.

Charles Grandison Finney, 1792-1875, who had been brought from Connecticut at the age of two to Hanover, Oneida County, discovered the Bible while studying law and underwent a dramatic conversion. "He seemed to see the Lord standing before him; he received a 'mighty baptism of the Holy Spirit,' and wept aloud with joy and love; wave after wave came over him, until he cried, 'I shall die if these waves continue to pass over me!' At another time, he beheld the glory of God about him, and a light ineffable shone into his soul. He saw all nature worshipping God except men, and broke into a flood of tears that mankind did not praise God" (*Dictionary of American Biography*). He became a Presbyterian, and though he refused to go to the Princeton Seminary—at that time the most unyielding stronghold of the Calvinism which he was later to criticize—he was licensed by the

Presbytery to preach. He conducted revivals in the East and Middle West which "attracted attention all over the country. . . . Violent physical manifestations resulted from his preaching; people burst into tears, shrieked, fainted and fell into trances." He eventually became President of Oberlin College and pastor of a church in Oberlin. Charles Finney's popularity was no doubt partly due to his rejection of old-fashioned Calvinism. He preached the possibility of repentance and of rising superior to one's weaknesses. He called himself a New School Calvinist and was much disliked by those of the old.

William Miller went a good deal further. He had been brought at four from Pittsfield, Massachusetts, to Hampton, New York, just over the border from Vermont, in Washington County. He was largely self-educated and first became a Deist; but, after serving in the War of 1812, joined the Baptists, with a license to preach. He had become convinced from a study of the Bible that the prophets had foretold the Second Coming as to take place in 1843 or 1844. This belief was made the basis of what was later to be known as the Adventist Church, which had adherents in New England and even in Canada. "At least a hundred and twenty camp meetings," says the *Dictionary of American Biography*, "were held during the summer months of 1842, 1843 and 1844, with an estimated attendance of half a million. . . . Signs in the heavens . . . were reported; and a great meteoric shower which occurred in 1833 was regarded as an omen; strange rings were seen around the sun; crosses were discerned in the sky; and a great comet appeared at high noon and for days hung ominously over the earth like a huge sword threatening a guilty world. The entire country was astir. People began to lose their reason. Expectation became fixed on a specific date, October 22, 1844." This was the date of the sixteenth birthday of my grandfather Walter

Kimball, and he used to tell of how the Adventists would not harvest or lay in provisions for the winter of the Last Day, with the result that when the Second Coming did not occur, their neighbors had to supply them through the winter. They had been up on their roofs and haystacks in order to be nearer Heaven, and had sometimes assembled in the cemeteries in order to be close to the resuscitated dead. The story that they equipped themselves with robes for ascension is doubted by Whitney R. Cross, the author of *The Burned-over District*, a careful but rather drily academic study of what he calls in his subtitle "Enthusiastic Religion in Western New York." But the Adventists, when their Advent had failed to take place, of course became the butts of their neighbors and for a season endured persecution. "Mobs stormed the Adventist meeting places"—I quote Professor Cross—"In Loraine, thirty black-faced ruffians, egged on by the Methodist minister, attacked the congregation with clubs and knives. Tar and feathers abounded in Toronto, Canada." Some of the Adventists joined the Shakers or went back to the older churches. Some concluded that the Reverend Miller had simply made an error in calculation; others thought that Christ *had* come but not in a spectacular way. Some set themselves up as an élite who had been subjected to a test of faith and who, having proved themselves, were unique in being sure of salvation. The Adventists split up into several sects. Some of the preachers who had been most fervent were accused of having fallen into evil practices—one of receiving stolen goods and keeping "a very bad house." Certain of these "spiritualizers," "in addition to kissing and embracing . . . practice promiscuous lodging. . . . We have heard them say they are immortal, cannot die, and have got to raise up spiritual children." A religious conference in Rochester "engaged in footwashing and indiscriminate kissing." At

a gathering in Springwater, "one of the members was
testing his hostess's consecration to God by making 'licentious advances.'" Whitney Cross believes that the Adventists were recruited from a discontented class of settlers,
who seized upon the hope of being rescued from the hard
impoverished life of western New York. The Adventist
Church still survives.

Somewhat akin to these dedicated founders of cults
were the Fox sisters of Hydesville near Rochester and the
Davenport brothers of Buffalo. The Fox family had in 1841
come to live in a house that was supposed to be haunted
by the ghost of a murdered peddler whose body had been
buried in the cellar, and Margaret and Katherine Fox,
already when they were eight and six, had been in the
habit of scaring the other members of the family at night
by bumping apples on strings on the floor and then pulling them under the bedclothes. From this they went on
to rappings produced by cracking their toe-joints. The
neighbors came in to hear this, and their questions were
answered by the rappings. The newspapers reported these
manifestations, and the Foxes began charging admission.
They took their show on to New York, where a religious
element was added. Hymns were sung, and the Fox
sisters became a popular sensation. Eventually they toured
the country. Horace Greeley, the very influential editor
of the New York *Tribune,* became so much interested
in them that he sent little Katherine to school. It was at
that time, from the fifties and through the seventies, that
the interest in spiritualism was at its height, and extended
to Europe and Russia. Spiritualist circles were sometimes
called "churches." But when a serious investigation was
made in 1884, the results did not bear out the Foxes'
pretensions: it was found that Margaret could produce
no raps if her feet were put under control. In '88, having

now become a Roman Catholic, she publicly confessed her fraud: "My sister Katie and I were very young children when this horrible deception began. . . . We were very mischievous children and wanted to terrify our dear mother, who was a very good woman and very easily frightened." She now exploited public exposures instead of pretended séances, and her sister confirmed her statements. But this made no impression on her devotees, who insisted that the phenomena had been authentic, and that Margaret had been under the influence of liquor when she asserted that they had been fraudulent. Eventually, needing money, she was driven back to giving séances, though she was scrupulous in warning her audiences that she "did not claim any spirit power; but people must judge for themselves." In the meantime, the Davenport brothers, who had learned to untie the knots of the ropes that were supposed to restrain them, had been making a name for themselves by producing manifestations in a darkened cabinet. They gave performances in France and in England, but were exposed by the professional magicians, Nevil Maskelyne and Robert Houdin. Back at home, Harry Kellar, then twenty-one, became their advance agent and manager, but he later dropped the pretense of their possessing supernatural powers, and in his career as an independent magician, would show that he could duplicate the Davenport performances.

But spiritualism still persists in the town of Lily Dale in Chautauqua County. Mr. Carl Carmer, who visited Lily Dale at some date before 1936, reports that he had to pay admission in order to enter the town, and that the mediums who were supposed to be able to communicate with the other world invariably gave wrong information. (I shall later describe my own visit to Lily Dale.)

An odd attempt to produce not a spiritual but a tangible

wonder was that planned gratuitous imposture known
as the Cardiff Giant. A man named George Hull, a kind
of imaginative charlatan on a lesser scale than Joseph
Smith, an atheist who had been attracted by the theory of
Evolution but had also been experimenting with alchemy
as well as manufacturing cigars at Binghamton, New
York, went to the trouble of having carved in Chicago
from a gypsum block quarried in Iowa a huge statue, ten
feet four inches tall, designed to resemble himself. (I am
indebted for my information to a paper by Miss Barbara
Franco, in the October 1969 issue of *New York History*,
published by the New York Historical Association; and
to a pamphlet, *The True Moral and Diverting Tale of
the Cardiff Giant*, by James Taylor Dunn, also published
by this Association.) Hull was said to have been provoked by an argument with a fundamentalist minister,
who took seriously the statement in Genesis 6.4 that is
translated in the King James Bible as, "There were giants
in the earth in those days," but one fails to understand
how so elaborate a hoax can have followed from such a
disagreement, and I am inclined to believe that just as
George Hull combined alchemy with an interest in
Evolution, he may have wanted, as some forgers do, to
create something non-existent—that is, to produce a
miracle which in its grotesque way would contribute to
filling the religious vacuum of western New York. And
by having the giant formed in the likeness of himself, he
may perhaps have wanted to attain to a superhuman personality. At any rate, together with an accomplice, a
farmer in Cardiff, near Syracuse, he arranged to have
the statue buried by night very close to the farmer's barn.
To put this image over on the public became the great
ambition of George Hull's life, and he spent on the whole
operation $2,600. A great deal of care and precaution had
been taken to ensure a successful deception. Hull rough-

ened the surface with a sponge filled with water and sand;
he produced artificial pores by hammering it with a block
of wood studded with darning needles; and in order to
make the figure look old, he drenched it with sulphuric
acid. A year after the giant had been buried, October,
1869, his accomplice, the owner of the farm, hired men
to dig a well at that spot, and their spades, about five
feet down, hit on the stone giant. The owner of the farm
put it under a tent and charged first a quarter, then fifty
cents, for admission. It drew crowds from Syracuse and
elsewhere. The imposture was made to seem more plausible by the many fossils found in that vicinity, and the
Onondaga Indians were reminded of their legendary stone
giants that they had been sometimes able to trap in pit-
falls. Cardiff was a little village which, like my own little
village of Talcottville, had been left with no chance of
development on account of having been skipped by the
railroad and which welcomed this stimulus to its trade.
In a very few days after the giant was exhibited, a group
of businessmen of Utica and Syracuse bought a three-
quarters interest in the figure for $30,000. They moved
it to Syracuse, and the giant became a factor in promoting
the fame and success of that industrial city, as the Syracuse press had a stake in upholding the authentic an-
tiquity of the giant, which was soon being denied by
academic experts. Despite the public confession of the
hoax by the two sculptors who had carved it in Chicago,
people still paid money to see it when it was moved to
Albany and Boston. P. T. Barnum had a plaster replica
made, and showed it in New York as genuine. When the
original was brought on and publicized, it attracted far
less attention. When it was later exhibited in Boston,
Oliver Wendell Holmes bored a hole behind its ear to
prove that it was merely a statue, but Emerson declared
it "beyond his depth, very wonderful and undoubtedly

ancient." Carl Carmer found people in the neighborhood
of Cardiff who still thought the giant was a petrified man.
Eventually it was acquired by the New York Historical
Association, and was exhibited in a pit, where it lies as
if stiffened by death, with its immense square skull and
imposing penis, the product, it seems to me, of an overwhelming compulsion to create some superhuman being
to walk those New York State hills, where the Word of
God had not been spoken. I visited it not long ago and
found it in a state of deterioration. In the course of its
traveling and being displayed at one county fair after
another, its legs had already been broken off at the knees,
and now, while exposed in the coverless pit, it has suffered from the terrible winters: the genitals and toes are
eroded. It is now protected by a shelter. Poor old giant!
One can't help pitying him. Like all statues, he represents
the desire of human beings to transcend their human
limitations.

The Reverend John Taylor in 1802 found that a Mr.
Ely, who had "formed a church," preached every third
Sunday to the inhabitants of Leyden, which is still
the official name of the township that includes Talcottville. My cousin Dorothy Mendenhall says, in her autobiography, that the Talcottville she knew as a young girl
in the eighties, a hamlet of twenty houses, had three
buildings intended as churches; but the Methodist
Church was rarely used, the Baptist Church was visited
by a minister from outside, who came only on alternate
Sundays, and the Presbyterian Church was used as a
roller skating rink. There is today only one church, with
a meager congregation composed mostly of old people and
a visiting minister from elsewhere. It has been vandalized
lately by the local hoodlums.

IV

Hardships and Dream Pockets

The early settlers in upper New York State invested in enormous tracts of land, which they were sometimes unable to cultivate. The family of my Munn cousins owned fifty thousand acres, which included a good deal of forest land and two Adirondack lakes. Turning such land into pastures meant uprooting all the trees, and was a backbreaking disheartening job. The temptation was great to sell it for timber. The defeat of the farmers by their acres sometimes had tragic consequences—as in the case of the "John Brown Tract," which presented a problem that was never to be solved.

This John Brown was not the Civil War fanatic, but a rich Rhode Island merchant, who had fought in the Revolution and served in the Continental Congress. He laid the cornerstone of Brown University, which was named after his family, and had acted as its treasurer for twenty years. In 1798, he bought for $33,000 a tract of two hundred and ten thousand acres of what was then known as "the Great Wilderness," a tract that covered the northern part of Herkimer County and extended on either side into Hamilton and Lewis Counties. He divided

35

it into eight townships: Enterprise, Perseverance, Una-
nimity, Frugality, Sobriety, Economy and Regularity.
He cut a road, built a gristmill, a sawmill and a handful
of log houses, and he sent an agent to live there. He made
occasional visits to the tract, but he died in 1803 (or, as
one source says, 1806). A son-in-law then undertook to
live there and "cleared over two thousand acres"—I quote
from *Historical Sketches of Northern New York and the
Adirondack Wilderness,* by Nathaniel Bartlett Sylvester,
published at Troy in 1877—"built thirty or forty new
buildings, drove in cattle and a flock of three hundred
merino sheep. He built a forge and opened a mine of
iron ore. He spent his own fortune there and all the
money that he could borrow from his friends." He was a
Prussian, over six feet tall, with aristocratic pretensions,
who liked to call his place "The Manor." But his wife
refused to live with him there. He succeeded in making
only one ton of iron and by December, 1819, he was
unable to raise any more money and went out "to a
lonely spot" and shot himself. The buildings now fell
to ruin and were used as a shelter for hunters and trap-
pers, and of the game they hunted and trapped. But in
1832 one of these hunters moved in to stay. He was what
was called in Canada a *coureur de bois,* a man named
Nathaniel Foster, of a prowess and reputation that suggest
those of Natty Bumppo. He was famous for his hatred
of the Indians and for the number of Indians he had
killed, and there was a particularly quarrelsome Mohawk
called Drid already living on the tract. The following
exchange is supposed to have taken place between Foster
and Drid: "There is no law here," said Drid. "If I kill
you, I kill you, and if you kill me, you kill me." "I will
not make any such bargain as that," answered Foster.
Drid soon after this tried to stab him, but two other men
intervened, and he only wounded Foster, though badly,

in the arm. Drid went up the river in a canoe with two white men. Foster went overland and waited for them, then shot Drid as they were paddling past. He was a crack shot like Natty Bumppo and had aimed accurately between the two white men at either end of the canoe. Foster was tried for murder and, the threats that the Mohawk was said to have made not having been accepted by the judge as admissible for a defense, he was found guilty of homicide; but the Common Pleas court overruled this decision, and Foster was then acquitted. He could no longer live on the tract, because he was afraid that Drid's relatives would come to revenge his death—though these simply took his widow and children away and said of Drid, "He was a bad Indian. Let him go." But Foster moved away to Boonville, a few miles from where I am writing this, and there never went out after dark.

Foster was succeeded after a few years by another man of the woods, who kept a sort of forest hostelry. "In 1855, Horatio Seymour, then Governor of New York, stopped there with a visiting party which included a Maid of Honor of Queen Victoria. The Honorable Amelie Murray records that the daughters of their host, who ranged in age from twelve to twenty, regarded the ladies with astonishment, for they had never had a chance to look at any women except their mother and one another: "I could not elicit a word from them. I then remembered that we had met a single hunter rowing himself on the Moose River. 'Where on 'arth do they women come from?'" But this hostel keeper also fell a victim to the violence that was natural to this solitary life. In a quarrel about a dog collar in 1868, he shot and killed a white man, a guide; then, overcome with remorse, he loaded his pockets with stones, hung a large one around his neck and drowned himself in the lake.

The upper part of Herkimer County is still extremely wild. The northeastern part of Lewis County, which must have been part of this tract, has a few scattered summer camps but parts of it are hardly passable. The Independence River, with its stone riverbed and resounding cataracts, to which we sometimes go on picnics, falls through forests which beyond a point are pathless and which seem to be completely uninhabited.

The other side of the hardships of this wilderness and isolation is a certain romantic enchantment which the north country generates for its addicts. The old mansions with their vast tracts of land enabled their masters to live in an independent realm of dream quite aloof from the preoccupations of the growing industrial cities.

One of the most interesting of these baronial places, not far from the town of Mohawk in Herkimer County, was traditionally known as Henderson House, but is now called Gelston Castle. It was built in 1832 in imitation of British country houses, and is said to have taken ten years in the building. The gray limestone blocks had to be hauled to the top of a high hill. The architecture is remarkable for its imaginative good taste and makes a delightful contrast with another building, known as "the Manor," a replica of an Irish Castle, built in the eighteen-sixties, and now turned into a restaurant, which has, both inside and out, walls of rough ugly black stone, and an ornamental fountain, painted blue. The front door of Henderson Hall is flanked by two bulging structures that give somewhat the impression of round towers, for the broken windows of which the present occupants of the "castle" have had to get special curved panes made. Beyond one of these a stone wing, also rounded, extends to the right. There are trimmings of white fancy ironwork: a low fence along the ground and a differently

patterned fringe along the roof. There are high French
windows on the bottom floor. The front steps are single
slabs of stone. The chimneys are crenellated. The great
hall is sixty feet long. The view from behind the house is
the most impressive I have seen here: the enormous bil-
lowing hills of the Mohawk Valley, green when I saw
them in May, below a gray rainy sky.

There is a fascinating account of Henderson Hall by
Joseph and Stewart Alsop in the *Saturday Evening Post*
of January 26, 1957—*Lament for a Long-Gone Past*. It
was built by Scottish Douglases, who had made a fortune
in America, and in the time of the Alsops' youth, the
owner was a Theodore Douglas Robinson, who married
Corinne Roosevelt, a sister of Theodore Roosevelt. She
published several books of poetry that I used to hear
about without reading them in the early nineteen hundreds. The Alsops, her grandchildren, spent their summers here as boys. The family were self-willed and energetic individuals who, detached from any real community,
lived here in an eccentric way that would probably have
been impossible anywhere else in the North. An eighteenth-century relative—the family had already had a
house there then—kept a portrait of George III in his
cellar till long after the Revolution and made a practice
of taking down the younger descendants, unveiling the
portrait before them and saying to them, "Children, bow
to your master!" The Scottish grandfather of the Alsops
regarded it as an extravagance to spend money on gaso-
line for motorcars, and the boys were met at Herkimer by
a "democrat," an old-fashioned kind of two-seated carriage. The collection of objects in the house included a
waffle-iron which had belonged to President Monroe,
a goblet of Walter Scott's, which had been stolen from
Scott himself by a great-great-aunt of the Alsops, whom
Scott described as "plain" and "frightfully red-headed."

The goblet was encased in a silver thistle to protect the
rim from profanation by any other lips. This great-aunt,
when she found some uncomplimentary entries in her
husband's commonplace book, had her marriage bed
sawed in half and the two halves made into Empire
couches. And there were also relics of the pre-war South,
with whose cause the family had sympathized. There
occurred, as was customary in upstate New York, a gathering every summer of "uncounted Roosevelt and Robinson
cousins in the first, second and third degrees. . . . In all,
seldom fewer than twenty and quite often more than
thirty people had to be fed each day at Henderson, above-
stairs and below. . . . Outside the house . . . still another
large human population was needed to work on the farms,
in the stables and in the gardens." The breakfasts were
enormous and were announced by a tune called *Up with
the Bonnets of Bonnie Dundee,* which the senior parlor-
maid had to learn to play on a chime of small gongs in
the pantry, and these breakfasts were sometimes enlivened
by the readings of a set of humorous verses composed by
the poet grandmother. There was a herd of unbroken
Shetland ponies, which were difficult to control but which
the Alsops' sister found out how to manage by breaking
a raw egg on the pony's head. The children dreaded being
driven in a brake down a very steep two-mile hill, drawn
by four equally untrained horses, while the groom blew
a coaching horn, the iron brakes screeched and the youngest of the children wailed. The family liked unruly
animals and were rather given to violence: they slammed
doors and had loud voices. One of the rituals was Sunday
night prayers, to which Uncle Teddy Roosevelt, when it
devolved upon him to preside, did not readily adapt
himself. It imposed a traditional reading from a particularly bleak book of sermons. "Uncle Teddy fingering a
whip, would post, on either side of his chair, two of the

fiercest of his German police dogs, which, at the climax
of the sermon, would fly at one another's throats." He
would "joyfully" lash them with his whip, shouting "Blast
and damn you, get back where you belong!" The departure of guests was solemnized by long "ululations"
from a conch-shell, also performed by the senior parlor-
maid, and by "wildly" waved farewells from the family.

Mrs. Robinson died five years ago. The house was put
on the market, and was bought by a couple of Scottish
origin named Blair, who have turned it into "a home
for the handicapped." Old ladies, rather dim-witted, sit
around in the once-splendid rooms. Almost all of the
furniture has been sold by the family. In the great hall
are left behind only two objects hard to remove: a huge
barrel organ, made sometime before 1820, which the
Blairs have not found out how to work, and a marble
fireplace from Italy, carved with classical figures, which
badly needs to be cleaned; but the Blairs, who have not
occupied the house very long, have not yet been able to
attend to everything. They congratulate themselves, rightly, that they have saved the old place from collapse. The
miscellaneous set of objets d'art, like the contents of a
New York auction room, which they have bought and
installed in the house, somewhat jars with the remnants
of former splendor. A solitary old chandelier still hangs
from the high ceiling. The Blairs discovered in the bathroom, slipped down behind the wash bowl, a quatrain of
advice to guests composed by Mrs. Robinson, the poet:

> "While the 'pump' is all undone
> Do not let the water run.
> Spare the John whene'er you may
> And pray the wind will blow all day."

The only one of my immediate neighbors who at all
maintains this style of living, though on a much more

modest scale, is Walter D. Edmonds the novelist. His
family come from Utica, and the nine hundred and forty-
acre estate called Northland, near Boonville, on which he
lives, was inherited by his father from his grandfather
in 1897. This place has a good deal of charm. A pretty and
lively little brook runs past the low but ample country
house, with a red barn and a caretaker's cottage in the
background. Edmonds's father created an artificial lake,
the black waters of which are indistinguishable from those
of the Black River, which runs very close. The view is
screened by a wooded hill. Walter Edmonds's first novel
Rome Haul, is a more or less picaresque story of the days
of the Erie Canal, though he says he never made the
canal trip and that almost the whole story was imagined.
His novels since then have all been historical and all
have dealt with upstate New York. They have, I think,
come out of the fantasies of a boyhood imagination
under the influence of the peculiar spell of the country
in which he lives. He depended, in these novels, very
much on conventional patterns, and his books became
best sellers; but the forests and fields and snows, the
unexpected changes of weather, the rural speech of the
people and the behavior of the wild and domestic animals, are recorded with perfect accuracy from intimate
observation. This is a vision of a past now remote on the
part of one remote from the truck-laden highways and
even from the shopping centers.

Another case that, although quite different from these
residences of lords of their acres, I would assign to the
category of dream realms, is the Oneida Community of
which I have spoken in connection with the local cults
and of which I shall have more to say later. The great
"Mansion House" still dominates its lawns and trees and
still has something otherworldly about it. Mrs. Constance
Robertson, the granddaughter of the founder, has de-

scribed to me her childhood memories of playing in the labyrinth of the cellars, memories which evoked for me an atmosphere almost Gothic. Like Edmonds, she has written historical novels which deal with this part of the world; but only one of them, *Seek-No-Further*, derives in any way from her experience of the Oneida Community. I think that, in conceiving this book, Mrs. Robertson made an error in combining the Oneida Community, morally and intellectually the most dignified of these cultist organizations, with the fantastic Spiritualist communities which cannot command such respect. The mesmeric influence of the charlatan Messiah, amusingly combined with the awe of the newly invented machine—which the Messiah uses as an aid to seduction—does render a genuine phenomenon of those days of the Civil War period when people felt close to the supernatural; but this sinister and unpleasant character has nothing whatever in common with the high-minded John Humphrey Noyes.

The fascination that upper New York State could exercise upon me from my earliest summers—so long ago now that I cannot remember when I was first brought to Talcottville—makes it possible for me to understand its attraction for the people I have mentioned. One felt on the sleeping car in which we first travelled, on the morning train from Utica to Boonville, and in the carriage by which we were met, that one was entering a different world. The world of Red Bank, New Jersey, to which both my grandfathers had come from New York, was partly the old-fashioned village life of Shrewsbury, where my Wilson grandfather was Presbyterian minister, and of Eatontown, where my Kimball grandfather had for many years been a doctor; partly the suburban town life that was spreading from New York and Philadelphia; and

partly the leisured life of summer cottages and big places
on the Jersey Coast, among which, in his more prosperous
years, my grandfather had had his practice. In this last
milieu, the importance of money, in the early nineteen-
hundreds, was obtrusive and rather disturbing. But, in
Lewis and Oneida Counties, this importance seemed not
to exist. Some of my relatives in Utica belonged to the
well-to-do class who lived in the big square houses, but
Utica as an industrial center, mostly dependent on the
"knitting mills," was already then in its decline and was
never to grow to the size and the prosperity of Syracuse,
Buffalo and Rochester. Leyden, as we always called it
then, was a widely strewn community of dairy farmers,
where there were only two social classes, the well-estab-
lished educated landowners, predominantly of English
descent, and what had originally been known as the
"mechanics," mostly German and Irish, who had been
driven to the United States by the potato famine or by
the '48 revolt in Germany, with whose children, a cousin
tells me, we were not allowed to play. I don't remember
this as constituting a problem. We had otherwise the
utmost freedom and thoroughly enjoyed ourselves in
Sugar River, with its Big and Little Falls, and its flower-
and-fern-hung high stratified sides; or among the fields
of long grass, with their concealed and untroubled ponds.
My father would take us on long trips to Canada or visits
of exploration to such nearby towns as Rome and Carthage, to which we travelled in two large carriages. I
wonder at the pitch of excitement to which, although we
had had experience of the sights and entertainments of
New York and Boston, we could be stimulated then
by these very mild adventures. Once installed in the
local hotel, my father ordered drinks for the grown-
ups, then took us to whatever amusement, usually meager
in summer, the little provincial towns or Canadian cities

Our friend Huldah Loomis as a young girl; Martha ("Min-nie") Collins, at whose house we used to stay in my youth; and her father Chester Munn

afforded. I remember Halifax as a blankly dead and depressing place, where there was nothing to go to see except a show of performing horses. Leyden, in which we stayed, was a country of very high skies with white clouds that reduced the proportions of everything else, even the rising hills; of orange sunsets and menacing thunderstorms; a place that was strange and liberating, yet a place where one was perfectly at home. I still felt, coming back here at thirty-five, after many years of almost total absence, that I was visiting a foreign country but a country to which I belonged. Everybody was related to everybody else or, at no matter what distance from one another, were neighbors or very old friends. They had grown out of the country like the elms. Three houses in this little village belonged to the family connection, and "the Stone House," which I have inherited, was in some sense the center of the town. In my childhood it was inhabited all the year around by a great-uncle and a great-aunt, and a family of cousins spent their summers there. I have been struck, in coming back, by the extent to which the hierarchy of the smallest social unit, if sufficiently isolated, may assume the degrees of prestige of a capital or a nation. Our position was so unquestioned in this little corner of Lewis County that I have never ceased to derive from it a certain conviction of superiority, which was somewhat eclipsed when I lived in New Jersey surrounded by people who were richer than we. There is little of that old life now left, and the glamor has largely vanished. But one aspect of this country does still seem strange: it is true that in modern America it presents itself as something of an anachronism, but, unlike most old things in America, it is an anachronism that still flourishes, that is still more or less of a going concern.

V

Talcottville

The Talcotts first came to this country from Warwick-
shire in 1632 and established themselves in Connecticut,
near what is now the city of Hartford, of which they
built the first house, in what is now the town of Talcottville. The motto on the Talcott crest was *"Virtus sola
nobilitas."* I have visited the Connecticut Talcottville,
where the Talcotts still own a mill and seem to have
dominated the town. A cemetery is full of Talcotts. The
son of the original Talcott, Lieutenant Colonel Sir John
Talcott, led the forces of Charles II against the forces of
the Wampanoag Indian who called himself King Philip.
The first Talcotts came to America with those who were
to be the members of the Massachusetts Bay Colony,
and one of Sir John's sons served for seventeen years as
colonial governor of Connecticut. His great-grandson
Hezekiah, after fighting on the Tory side in the American Revolution, bought a tract of sixteen hundred acres
in northern New York. It was called the Inman Triangle, and was bounded by Sugar River, by what is now
"the West Road" and by some borderline east of our
house which I have not been able to determine. It had

been confiscated from royalists who had never seen it.
Hezekiah, with his two sons, went up there by oxteam
in 1798 and found forests, sites for mills and a quarry.
He built a mill and a small log house and started what,
for that time and place, was to figure as a quite impressive
mansion built out of the gray limestone from the quarry.
But the loghouse burned down before the mansion was
finished—it took four or five years in the building—and
the family moved into the Stone House. The first recorded
event in connection with this house is a memorial service
for Washington, who died at the end of 1799. It was at
first the only such house in that locality and was the center
of the meager community that consisted chiefly of the Talcotts and the hired people who worked for them. They
all ate together, to the number of twenty, in the big
dining room at two separate tables. There was a post
office, which is now our china closet, and meetings were
held in the house, at one of which the line was decided
on that would divide Oneida from Lewis County.
There were outbuildings made of wood: a spinning room
in which three maids were kept at work till the light
gave out; and, behind it, a smokehouse and dairy, above
which the three millers slept. A ballroom was eventually
added, above a shed where horses were kept, which extended to a stone barn from the south side of the house.
In these very early days, the kitchen was the only heated
room. The men made two trips yearly to Utica, which
was about fifty miles away, with long lists of purchases
for the ladies. This took them several days. The families
in that country lived so far apart that friendly visits, paid
and returned, were likely to last for weeks. The visitors
went on horseback, with the ladies riding pillion. The
Talcotts had been landed gentry in England, and they
continued the feudal tradition by refusing to sell lots

to "mechanics" or to relinquish the water power of Sugar River.

Thomas Baker, my great-grandfather, was to change all this. He was a descendant of a Reverend Thomas Baker who was settled in Newport, Rhode Island, by 1653. My great-grandfather was born in Hoosick, New York, at the end of 1799. He came to Talcottville in 1825. He first set up a general store, then sold out and became a cattle dealer. He married Laura Shaw, a girl from Trenton, New York, by whom he had eight girls, most of them said to have been attractive, and one son, the last of the children, who had a harelip and cleft palate. Their mother died at his birth. By this time, the Talcotts, who had not prospered, were pretty well depleted in that part of the world, and there were only two Talcott women living in the house alone. Thomas Baker was town clerk and supervisor. Unlike the Tory Talcotts, he was a Jacksonian Democrat and sat as an Assemblyman in 1844. He was something of what is now called an "operator." He worked the farm and shipped the stone from the quarry to market by way of the new canal. He charged the neighbors for the use of his well. But he is said to have been generous and not unamiable. One of my aunts remembers him as "an old man with a round rosy face, who would come in and give me big brown pennies or braided bags and slippers that he'd gotten from the Indians in the West." He would burst into tears when she left. My uncles used to joke about him, and the Talcotts regarded him with a certain scorn. The original members of the family had abandoned the New York Talcottville, and I find in the county records that Thomas Baker acquired the house in 1832 from Jesse Talcott, the inheritor by primogeniture and the last of the male Talcotts who had remained in that region. He was dissipated and generally accounted a rather good-for-nothing character. Their descendants never forgave Thomas Baker for breaking up the feudal unit by freely selling lots to mechanics and so creating the little village whose name he changed from Talcottville to Leyden. It is still included legally in the Town of Leyden. Later, in the early nineteen-hundreds, my cousin Grace Reed, a Talcott, who lived in the Stone House in the summers, circulated a petition in the village and got the name changed back to Talcottville. There had been a terrible family feud. Thomas Baker, after his first wife's death, married Sophronia Talcott, a spinster, and moved with his family of daughters into the Stone House, supposedly on March 10, 1851. (It is hard to reconcile this date with the transfer of the property in 1832.) Sophronia's sister Jannett had married a Baltimore architect, who had died in an epidemic of yellow fever, and she had come back to Talcottville to live with Sophronia. When Sophronia died, it was found that she had left the Stone House to her husband instead of, as Jannett expected, to her. Jannett attempted to break the will on the ground that it had been made under undue pressure when Sophronia was too old and weak-minded to understand what she was doing and that she had made a later will, leaving the property to her sister. I have looked up these wills in the county records and read a transcript of the hearing at the county seat on March 7, 1877, and I find that there were actually four wills, two of which do not exist in the Talcott version of the case. The first was made in 1869, when Sophronia was certainly not in eclipse: it leaves the property to the Bakers, and it is witnessed by two of Sophronia's sisters, Rosalind and Laura Ann. The second, made in 1874, again leaves the property to the Bakers, but disposes a little differently of some of the items that are left to her sisters. The third will, not drawn up in the Stone House but in the Collins house, where she then was

My great-aunt Adeline (Mrs. Thaddeus Munn); my great-aunt Rosalind Baker; my great-aunt Laura Ann Baker

staying, transfers the property to Sophronia's sister. But the fourth, made in 1875, again leaves the property to the Bakers. The possible vulnerability of this last will was due to the fact that Sophronia, in the year before her death, was said to have "had a fit" at the breakfast table and never thereafter to have left her room. She had signed the will with an X. But the witnesses to this last will testified that Sophronia was still able to talk and make sense, to understand what she was doing. There were thus three wills against one, and it was no doubt possible for the Bakers to convince the conductor of the probate hearings that it was the only one of the wills which left the house to the Talcotts that was the product of undue influence— but on the part of Mrs. Daniels (Jannett Talcott), since from 1869 to 1874, Sophronia had had other intentions. It was, oddly, a Talcott, a Lowville lawyer, who defended the Bakers in the case. Jannett Daniels and her allies dropped their depositions, and the house became the property of the Bakers. The Talcott version is that Thomas Baker bought them off. The record of this hearing is amusing. Witnesses were called to testify that, before taking part in the ceremony of signing the final will, they had been bribed by Thomas Baker by being asked to dinner.

This verdict split the village in half—though one of the Baker daughters had already married a Talcott—between those who sympathized with the Bakers and those who sympathized with the Talcotts. The latter would not pass the Stone House but went to the trouble of circumventing it; if one of the women met a Baker, she would step off the village sidewalk so as not to have to brush past. A young Talcott-Kimball cousin of mine, who had lived much in the Stone House and come to prefer the Baker daughters to what she called "the rather forbidding Talcott women," remained—though at the cost of a certain hypocrisy in her relations with the Talcott supporters—on excellent terms with the Bakers. Because she still lived in the Stone House, she was ordered off the Munn and Collins property. Her mother, she says, endeavored but did not succeed in being friendly with both parties. This unpleasantness lingers as a family joke, though there is still a rankling touch of bitterness.

The record of Thomas Baker in the *Genealogic and Family History of Northern New York* asserts that two Talcott brothers had already made the house a hotel, but this may merely be due to their having complied with a government regulation according to which, I am told, the new settlers in that part of New York State must have adequate accommodation provided by those already settled there. Among the pioneers, during the winters, many cattle had not survived and the women had acutely suffered. It had been stated that anybody who bought land here would have to supply grist for the cattle and shelter for the new settlers. Talcottville had really been a land speculation, based on the Talcotts' hopes that a railroad would run through the town, and, I have heard, on its being one of the proposed ports for the Erie Canal. It was planned to have a village green such as one finds in New England towns and in some other larger New York State towns, around which the community would have centered and beside which our house would have stood; but these other New York State towns have had a more satisfactory growth: the railroad did not run through Talcottville, and the Talcotts were left high and dry. It is unquestionable, though both sides of the family have tried somewhat to minimize this, that Thomas Baker for some years exploited the Stone House as a hostelry. This is indicated in an *Atlas of Lewis County* published in 1875 and it is so described in Hough's *History of Lewis County* of 1883. One of my aunts once told me that Thomas

Baker's daughters objected to having the place so used. He died in 1883, and it could not have continued after this. In my youth, I never heard the subject mentioned.

The young girl I have spoken of above who lived in the Stone House when nobody was left there but two Baker ladies and Thomas Baker, Jr., was my cousin Dorothy Reed, later Dorothy Mendenhall. She had a remarkable career as a woman doctor at a time when women doctors were discouraged, beginning as a pathologist and later becoming an authority on child welfare. I owe a good deal of my information to conversations with her and letters from her, and to a remarkable autobiography, which I hope to see published. I do not think she is quite always reliable, as when she seems to imply that the Stone House cannot be described as a real hotel because Great-Grandfather Baker did not put travellers up overnight. In her whole account of Talcottville, I feel that the tradition of feudal grandeur—which she mostly associates with the Talcotts—has somewhat colored her account. Thomas Baker is regarded as an interloper. She describes him in letters to me as a "gentleman (?) adventurer" and "a dreadful old man." Yet she says that one of his daughters, my "Aunt Lan," Laura Ann Baker, was "one of the truly great women I have known and influenced my life and all who knew her." Dorothy Reed's grandmother had been married to a Talcott and had, Dorothy writes, "gone by oxcart through wilderness into unbroken forest—the foothills of the Adirondacks with her husband" in 1805. Her great-grandfather was a Richard Kimball, brother of my great-great-grandfather, Ruel Kimball, the preacher. (I may mention that the Kimball genealogy contains a delightful crest for the Kimballs: two lions rampant, one red and one with a dagger, and a motto, *Fortis non ferox*. The compiler, himself not a

Kimball, says that he can find no evidence that this coat of arms is authentic, but that a Kimball may use it if he chooses.) Richard Kimball had published an English grammar and had served in a surveying crew sent out by the State of Pennsylvania to cover the whole of Ohio. He had been paid by a grant of land there and left New York to live in Ohio, and his daughter, my cousin Grace Reed, the mother of Dorothy Reed, married William P. Reed, a well-to-do manufacturer of shoes in Columbus. Reed came from a New England family, who prided themselves on their direct descent from the seventeenth-century poet Anne Bradstreet. Dorothy liked to establish the link between her and me that Anne Bradstreet had been praised in *Magnalia* by my collateral relative Cotton Mather. After William Reed's death, his widow reverted to Talcottville and rented it for the summers from the surviving Thomas Baker, Jr., and his two surviving sisters. Aunt "Lan"—I quote Dorothy (Reed) Mendenhall—"was a remarkably handsome tall woman, who must have been beautiful in her youth—of force and elegance—cultivated, although rarely out of this hamlet. . . . She worked all day like a slave, seeing to provisions and meals for a family that waxed and waned unexpectedly." Aunt "Lin" (Rosalind), who was older than her sister, was a professional fading lily and exquisitely ladylike. A fiancé was supposed to have been lost at sea, and she kept up the role of an invalid and bullied Lan with her invalidism, "leaving all the work to be done by others"—except for one day in the year, when she suddenly rose from her chair and made delicious apple jelly. To call on her in my childhood was a kind of august ceremony. An appointment had to be made, and she received you in her invalid's chair and talked like the people in old novels. She patronized the people in the town. She, too, even though a Baker, was infected with the Tory legend. It was said that the great-grandmother of Great-Grandmother Baker, had been a daughter of one of the Earls of Essex, who had eloped with a gardener to America. A Kimball aunt of mine, the genealogist of the family, discovered that another branch of the Shaws, with which we had had no communication, had been cherishing the same legend; and, on looking up the Essex family, she found out that there had indeed been a Lady Anne for whom no marriage or death was given. My family used to joke about this snobbery based on so tenuous and distant a connection.

Cousin Grace Reed, also, had something of the air of a *grande dame*. She wore a pince-nez on a gold chain and a high tortoise shell comb at the back of her head. She imposed on her granddaughter Dorothy Furbish—I remember her always forbidding her to go places or do amusing things—a propriety that must have been frustrating. It was she who had the name of the village changed back from Leyden to Talcottville. She spent the summers in the Stone House, which she leased for twenty years from Uncle Tom, and took her daughters to Germany in winter. Her insistence on maintaining her superior status had certain advantages for her family but it also had certain dangers. One of these daughters, Dorothy exhibited from girlhood a very strong character and a decisive practical intelligence unusual for a girl of that age. She had no schooling but had been educated by a governess provided by her mother, who had equipped her for entering college and whom she always remembered with gratitude. She took steps while still in her teens to avert the looming consequences of her mother's insouciant improvidence. She learned from a family adviser who had been looking out for their investments that her mother was spending her capital, and she succeeded in putting Cous-

in Grace on a budget. A certain disapproval of her
mother for her incompetent conduct of her life is evident throughout her autobiography, together with a
constant solicitude for keeping Cousin Grace solvent,
which eventually resulted in Dorothy's having to make
over her own inheritance to her mother and to depend
entirely on her earnings. She was also burdened with the
responsibility of providing for her sister's three children.
Dorothy was capable, handsome and, though in her youth
she had at one time shown signs of tuberculosis, physi-
cally pretty strong; her sister Bessie was frail and so win-
ningly beautiful that everybody loved her, but she, too,
had tuberculosis and eventually died of spinal meningitis.
My uncle Paul Kimball was in love with Bessie. He
was very attractive to women, but his engagements and
love affairs never resulted in marriage. He had com-
menced as a promising surgeon; but had himself developed tuberculosis and had been sent to a sanitarium
at Saranac. He had also, having at one period taken to
drink, had to resort to the "Keeley Cure." Bessie Reed, in
the meantime, had been taken by her mother to study
music for three years in Berlin. (I have the old libretti of
their Wagner operas, with the unfamiliar words written
in.) And there she became engaged to another student
of music named Willard Furbish, the son of a paper
manufacturer in Winchester, a suburb of Boston. (The
group of boarders at their pension turned out to have
several connections with my family. Besides Furbish,
there were the father of Malcolm Sharp, who married
his daughter, Dorothy Furbish, and my teacher of Greek
at the Hill School, the distinguished old humanist Alfred
G. Rolfe.) Willard Furbish was very much disliked by
the family: he was thought to be "spoiled" and "disagreeable."

When Bessie had announced her engagement and re-

My cousin Grace Reed; her daughter, my cousin Elizabeth
Reed (Furbish); my maternal uncle Paul T. Kimball

turned to the United States, Paul Kimball, now recovered
from the worst of his afflictions, made a trip to Talcottville in order to remonstrate with her. A painful scene,
I am told, took place in the big room which is now my
study. It is as if its vibrations still reach me in this room,
in which I am writing. Bessie said that she had given
Willard her word and that she could not go back on it
now. Her strong-minded sister Dorothy, then eighteen,
was away at Smith College, and she says in her memoirs
that, on that account, it was impossible for her to do
anything about the situation. It was evident when she
told me about it, that she hadn't the slightest doubt that
if she had only been there, she would have been able to
set Bessie right. Paul Kimball never married: he had a
modest but smart career as a physician to the rich, with
whom he spent a good deal of time on their yachts and
on hunting expeditions. I believe that his attachment to
his mother, my grandmother, may have prevented him
from founding a family: it is plain from her diary how
much she adored him. Bessie did marry Furbish and at
first went to live with him in Winchester. She had three
children: one girl and two boys. But the Furbish mill
burned down, and Furbish was left with no money, no
industrious habits and no training in anything but music.
The conscientious and practical Dorothy, who liked to
manage everything herself, went to the mat with her
brother-in-law and made him agree to have her bring up
the children. Their mother came back to Talcottville and
died in the west room in which I now usually sleep.

The family had as little as possible to do with Willard
Furbish. I had a most unpleasant impression of this.
When I saw the children in summer—I was on very
friendly cousinly terms with them—they were always with
their aunt or their grandmother. I remember only one
occasion on which their father came to see them. Young

Dorothy has since told me that when he had brought them some fireworks for a 4th of July, he had taken them down to the river in order to set them off. I suppose that he did not want to run the risk of setting fire to barns or houses; but since nobody else went with them, the celebration seems rather forlorn. I have always felt it very unfair that young Dorothy should have gone through life under the shadow of her mother's family's relentlessly maintaining the attitude that she ought to have been the daughter of someone else. I may say that though I so much admired young Dorothy, she told me in later years that she never had much use for me. When I said that I thought she had had a crush on a handsome farmer friend of ours, with whose family she had sometimes stayed, she replied that it would be much nearer the truth to say she had a crush on my father, who was tall, good-looking, quite unrural, and had a certain worldly air of superiority.

VI

Dorothy Mendenhall

Dorothy Reed had intended to be a journalist, but she was later diverted to medicine—influenced, I imagine, by the family examples of my Kimball grandfather and by her cousins, his two sons, who were to help her in her career. She was thoroughly depressed about her own immediate family. Her sister Bessie, who she thought had made an undesirable marriage, was now dying at Talcottville, and her brother had turned out to be a casualty that his sister at last gave up. He went West and was always writing for money. Dorothy, with characteristic trenchancy, finally refused to send him any more, and never saw him or heard from him again. The beauty whom everybody loves and who pathetically dies young, and the son who does not prosper and vanishes in the West seem to have been types in that period that very often occurred in American families. Dorothy says that her course of action was influenced by a need to "get into some work that interested me, and be freed from having to live with my mother, and do the sort of thing she felt would be likely to make me a good marriage. I loved Talcottville but I had very little in common with my mother, who

59

was most unhappy on account of my brother's behavior, and the wreck of my sister's life, both of which catastrophes she felt responsible for—and as I look back on the earlier years, I judge that she was right. My visits at home were depressing. It was difficult for me to do my part, and I felt as if I could not stay in the atmosphere of living in the past and listening endlessly to unhappy details of what could never be undone. I literally ran away."

In the eighties, medicine was still not considered an appropriate profession for a woman. The men doctors did not want them. The medical professors said that a woman's training was wasted because she would either not be up to finishing or would marry and fail to practice. But Dorothy had enough confidence in her own tenacity and her brains to accept the formidable challenge. She was not at all, however, the much ridiculed type of the women's rights champion. She had become aware, she says, for the first time, when a student at Smith College, that she was genuinely good-looking; but, she adds, she never took to herself any special credit for being so, since one's looks were accidental. Yet one cannot be unaware that it gives one prestige to be handsome, that it predisposes others in one's favor. And this Dorothy certainly showed in the maintenance of her almost queenly bearing and her ability, when she wanted to, to charm. Her attitude toward men alternated between the challenging and the charming: she liked first to put them down, then briskly to win them back. I am a little shocked, though not really surprised, to learn from Dorothy's memoirs that when Dorothy was working in a hospital in New Jersey, where my uncle Reuel, also a doctor, had placed her, his wife, my aunt Caroline, a model, as she thought, of conventional correctitude, wrote to Cousin Grace that she was very sorry that, in view of

Dorothy Reed's then status, she would not be able to see her socially. Aunt Caroline's family, the Knoxes, had come from Knoxboro, not far from Talcottville, and Dorothy was quite as well bred as—though a good deal more outspoken than Caroline. She says that this incident made her feel for the first time what it meant to belong to a minority. Her mother and her Talcottville family had been much upset by her studying medicine. "Aunt Lin, in all the years I was in Baltimore, always alluded to my 'being south for the winter.' Medicine was distinctly not a ladylike occupation."

But she entered Johns Hopkins in the class of 1900. Dr. William Osler was then lecturing there. He became and remained a great hero of hers, and he invited her to his house—she seems to have been one of his favorite students. An incident that, she says, occurred during her second year at Johns Hopkins "nearly sent me out of medicine." A nose and throat specialist gave a lecture "on some disease of the nose. But from the start he dragged in the dirtiest stories I have ever heard, read or imagined [they depended on comparing "the cavernous tissue present in the nasal passages with the corpus spongiosum of the penis"], and when he couldn't say it in English, he quoted Latin from sources not usually open to the public. Unfortunately I had majored in Latin at Smith, and seven years study made most of his quotations understandable to me. Nearly fifty years has passed since this night, but much he said is branded on my mind and still comes up like a decomposing body from the bottom of a pool that is disturbed. Simon Flexner, who had impassively presided, afterwards apologized." The women were also subjected to "unpleasant practical jokes." "I decided after much thought that as long as I was in medicine I would never object to anything that a fellow student or doctor did to me in my presence if he would act

or speak the same way to a man. If he were a boor, he
would act like one . . . but if he discriminated against
me because I was a woman . . . was offensive in a way he
wouldn't be to a man, I would crack down on him myself,
or take it up with the authorities if he proved too much
for me alone. On the whole, this was the right way to
take the position of women in medicine in the nineteenth
century. It made life bearable, allowed me to make
friends with some men who were not very pleasant persons—but knew no better, and earned me the respect and
friendship of many of my associates. It didn't endear me
to one or two I fell foul of, and undoubtedly I developed
an independence, even an arrogance, which was foreign
to my original nature. I was distinctly not such a nice
person, but a stronger one, after Johns Hopkins."

She was a fellow student of Gertrude Stein, who must
have been adept at evading her courses, as she had already been in William James's. She was evidently very
lazy and afterwards succeeded in evading a serious literary career by acquiring a reputation on the accomplishment, after *Three Lives,* of very little at all exacting
work—she substituted an effortless vagueness and interminable repetition. Ernest Hemingway, who knew her,
once told me that she always made a point of spinning
some of this rigmarole every night and thus managed to
keep up the illusion that she was producing literature.
Gertrude Stein at medical school seems to have given the
impression that she was not necessarily going in for practice. When at Radcliffe she had written on an examination paper, as she tells in *The Autobiography of Alice B.
Toklas,* "Dear Professor James, I am so sorry but I really
do not feel a bit like an examination paper in philosophy
today," William James had given her an A and written,
"Dear Miss Stein, I understand how you feel. I often

feel like that myself." But the doctors at Johns Hopkins were not so generous. The professor of obstetrics, says Dorothy, did not want to let her get a degree. "She could do nothing with her hands, was very untidy and careless in her technique and very irritating in her attitude of intellectual superiority, which was marked, even in her youth. At medicine, she worked only in a half-hearted way, and her grades were always poor. When it came to obstetrics in her third year, Professor Whitridge Williams, an aristocrat and a snob, couldn't stand her marked Hebrew looks, her sloppy work, and her intolerance—so he flunked her. Dr. Mall, probably influenced by Florence Sabin [who had succeeded in getting a degree], thought that she should be given another chance. She professed total indifference to practical work and claimed she was preparing for further work in psychology. The faculty decided to give her another chance, so in her fourth year Dr. Mall set her a problem similar to one Dr. Sabin had completed successfully in her fourth year. This was the sectioning of an embryo human brain and its reconstruction, and a study of the development of the centers in the brain and the tracts leading from them. She worked on it for weeks and finally handed her reconstruction to Dr. Mall in the hope that it would be credited to her instead of obstetrics and allow her to graduate. Some days after, Dr. Mall—the greatest living anatomist at the time—came to Dr. Sabin and said, 'Either I am crazy or Miss Stein is. Will you see what you can make out of her work?' Florence worked over it for several nights and came back to Dr. Mall with the answer that Miss Stein must have embedded the cord turned back under the embryo brain, instead of extended from it, and the centers of the outborne cells of the cord she had located in the brain, and other mysterious features of the reconstruction, could be explained only in this way.

She asked Dr. Mall what she should do with the model. As usual, he said nothing, but shied the entire model and explanatory test into a waste basket. Miss Stein was refused her degree. Yet in *Alice B. Toklas* she tells briefly of student days in Baltimore and mentions a model of an embryo brain which she had made and which was of much service to the students." [I cannot find this statement in the book.]

Dorothy, however, was graduated, and then worked in the Baltimore Hospital. Her account of this shows the hazards for a woman of training to be a doctor. She barely escaped rape and murder when the Negro caretaker of the building in which she lodged repeatedly came to her room and asked whether he could do anything for her. She produced a six-shooter, which, however, was not loaded, and locked the door against him. Half an hour later, he had found an unprotected woman and raped and murdered her. Dorothy in Baltimore insisted on taking the colored ward in the hospital, though the doctors warned her against it, and here and elsewhere had some curious adventures with patients for whom her attentions brought her into the underworld. But she says that she got on with her Negro patients better than she did later on with the whites. They were probably more docile. She went in for pathological research, and was assigned the task of investigating what is known as Hodgkin's disease, thought at that time to be a form of tuberculosis. She discovered that its identifying trait was a giant cell not tubercular. This cell was given the name of the "Sternberg-Reed cell" (Sternberg being the name of an Austrian pathologist who identified it independently of the same time), and her work on it laid the foundation of a considerable reputation.

In all this early period, she says that, unlike her sister Bessie, she had never had any interest in sex, that "no man had ever laid a hand on me twice," until in Baltimore she had conceived a real passion for a young man who had also had medical training. Her decision to break with him, she says, caused the greatest emotional upheaval of her life. She came to the definite conclusion, as she was likely to do with men, that he was weak and unreliable, that he only asked her to marry him in order to "have" her, that he would make her unhappy if she married him and that it would end by wrecking her career, with which she had gone too far to be willing to give it up. She married a little later, instead, an old friend, Charles Elwood Mendenhall, whom she had known from earliest childhood. She surprised him when he came back from abroad, and she told him she was ready to marry him. His father was a retired physicist, a stern puritanical man, a Quaker, who had not approved of Dorothy. One gathers that he did not enjoy being challenged. A childhood anecdote about the son indicates the rigor of the family morality, which apparently insisted upon absolute truthfulness. Charles had been invited to a children's party to which he did not want to go, and because he was unwilling to tell an untruth, he refused to write to the hostess that he "regretted" he could not go. His mother insisted that if he would not write regrets, he would have to go to the party—an alternative he was forced to accept; but he would not take part in any games and stood leaning against the fence. His training had been so Spartan that, though, unlike his wife, he loved music and played the violin, he would invariably, if served any food that he liked, refrain from eating very much of it because one had to chasten oneself when tempted by indulgence of the flesh. Although Dorothy says that she was never again to find herself passionately in love as she had been with her former suitor, she had evidently in common with her husband their old-fashioned "high seriousness"

and devotion to public service. Charles Mendenhall, like
his father, was a distinguished physicist, who was summoned to serve on important committees and international
organizations. He was a professor of physics at the University of Wisconsin, and he and Dorothy spent their lives in
Madison. She had apparently made a very sound choice:
he is said to have been perfect at handling her and marvellously patient under the constant pressure that she was
likely to put on other people. Dorothy, after her marriage
and the birth of her four children, the first two of whom
she lost, had an extremely active career as a lecturer and
writer on child welfare and gynecology, partly, she says,
inspired by the need to make up for the loss of these
children. She travelled all over the West, partly under
government auspices, instructing the women on their isolated farms. Her strong medical interests appear in her
descriptions in detail and at length, with a complete lack
of prudery uncommon in her generation, of her own
gynecological troubles, which were serious after her first
deliveries, and of her husband's death of cancer of the
prostate gland. This seizing of hard realities had always
been characteristic of her and she seemed to take a certain pride in it.

In summer, Dorothy Mendenhall and her mother and
the Furbish children lived in the Stone House, while we
stayed in a brick house a few doors away, with Homer
and Minnie Collins, also of the family connection.
Cousin Dorothy would get out from the trunks upstairs
old hoopskirts and embroidered waistcoats, and we would
dress up in them and play charades. A memory that sticks
in my mind is of Dorothy Mendenhall and our cousin
Merwin Hart of Utica sitting on the stone steps and talking about Walter Lippman, who was then a coming man

but of whom I was hearing for the first time. Merwin
Hart was a son of my aunt Lucy in Utica, my grandfather Kimball's half-sister. He ran at one time for Mayor
of Utica and lost. I remember that I was rather excited
to see his name and face on the banners. Merwin had
once been director of a business that manufactured fur-
naces. It failed, and Merwin thereafter was the head of
an organization that called itself the New York Economic
Council, which was nothing more nor less than a lobby
for the New York State industrial interests. They were
trying to repair the damage which had been inflicted on
them by the recent social legislation that prevented them
from employing children and made them pay higher
wages. I came to realize as I grew older that Merwin was
extremely stupid and that he believed in his reactionary
ideas. When, later, in the early thirties, at the time of
the great depression, I was writing leftist articles for the
New Republic, Merwin one day called me up and said
that he would like to talk to me. When we met, he explained that he and I were working toward the same
goals by slightly divergent roads: that we both thought
"the best people" should take a more active part in running things. This was not at all my understanding of
the objects I had in view (though as far as Marxism went,
he may have been more correct than I then would have
cared to admit), and when I asked Merwin what he
thought should be done about the terrible unemployment
of the depression years, he explained that most of the
unemployed were actually "unemployables." I encouraged
him to develop this point of view, and when he presently
began to make the Jews responsible in part for our economic disasters, I asked him how his ideas differed from
those of Hitler. He replied, after a moment's thought,
that the American people would never stand for a leader

with a mustache like Hitler's. It was not very much later
that one of his sons attained a certain notoriety as a
champion of fascism at Harvard.

For me, in my boyhood, my cousin Dorothy Mendenhall was one of my most interesting relatives. I was aware
that she and my mother were not on very good terms.
Dorothy's attitude toward non-professional women was
likely to be rather patronizing: they were merely wives
and mothers, had accepted roles which, with Dorothy,
were necessary but part-time occupations. I was surprised,
however, just now, when reading her autobiography, by
the frankness with which Dorothy expresses this lack of
friendliness. She believed that it was my mother who had
somehow prevented Paul Kimball from marrying her
sister Bessie and calls her "a snake in any grass." This
seems a strange characterization, for, though my mother
on occasion was tactlessly blunt, I certainly should never
have charged her with any sort of malignant duplicity.
These remarks in Dorothy's memoirs are all the more
surprising for her having written me, when my mother
died: "The notice of your mother's death was a shock
to me. She is associated with my youth and is one more
link removed. The worst thing about old age is the
rapidity with which your periphery shrinks." On thinking
about this since, it has seemed to me that these two
women had really a good deal in common. Both were
products of a generation which had still the pioneering
qualities of the time when the women were depended
on to shoulder responsibilities and keep their enterprises
and their families going; both liked to manage other
people's lives, whether the other people wanted to be
managed or not; both were dominating, dynamic, long-
lived. Better than many men, they got through the years
when a diversion of purpose from serving the community
and the new republic to getting rich and achieving "con-

My cousin Dorothy Reed (Mendenhall). (*Portrait by N. Vollet*)

spicuous waste" was demoralizing their husbands and brothers. But my mother, though she married my father, was fundamentally somewhat prejudiced against the intellectual members of the family whom I liked to cultivate. At the time when the Stone House belonged to her, Helen Augur (of whom more later) and Dorothy Mendenhall were never there. It was only in my mother's last years, when I had moved in to Talcottville without her, that she suggested my inviting Dorothy for a visit. It did not seem to occur to her that Dorothy might not care to accept so tardy an invitation conveyed in this oblique way.

In reading Cousin Dorothy's memoirs, I have come to understand better why her family's inability to buy the house should have been such a bitter disappointment. Dorothy had already once written me that she believed it had hastened her mother's death. They had leased it for twenty years and had filled it with their own furniture. And I see that Dorothy's attachment was due to the fact that up to the time when, rather late in life, she and Charles bought a house in Madison, she had grown up without a real home, and that her mother, and the Furbish children, after their parents' death, had never had a real home for any length of time at all. When Uncle Tom, instead of selling Cousin Grace the house, as she had always expected him to do, married the, we thought, very unattractive daughter of a farmer farther down the road—she had a pince-nez and protruding teeth, and we children dreaded her kisses—he no longer wanted to sell the house, and, after his wife's death, it was too late, and my father bought it from him in my mother's name, with the understanding that Uncle Tom should continue to live there as he had before and that my father would provide him with an income. My parents spent part of every summer there, but I paid them only short visits. By way of prep school and college I was then beginning

to see the world, and Talcottville was very dull for me.
It was so still during my years in New York, but in the
period of my radical enthusiasms, in the summer of 1933,
I went up to do the report on the milk strike, which is included in my book *The American Earthquake*. I was
struck by the fact that my mother, in other matters intensely conservative and shy of subversive activities, was,
as a matter of local solidarity, very firmly on the side of
the farmers.

But I am going too far into the future when, in my
chronological story, I have only reached the point where,
emerging from a dimmer past, I can at last see our family
group quite clearly in and about the Collins house:
myself and the other children playing croquet on the
lawn or jumping down from the hayloft in the stifling
barn onto a pile of hay below, tasting raw milk for the
first time or watching butter clotting in the churn, catch-
ing tiny transparent crawfish in the brook that ran
through a nearby field and trying to keep them alive in
kitchen pans, listening to the apples falling and reading
the murder in *Martin Chuzzlewit* in a bedroom that
looked out on the cemetery where the Bakers and Cousin
Bessie were buried—she beside a great boulder to which
had been fastened a plaque; hilarious conversations with
my cousin Sandy after we had gone to bed and were
eating the doughnuts called "fried cakes" which we
secreted and hid behind a steel engraving till the kindly
but severe Mrs. Collins found us out by the grease stains
on the wall; my father, who had put off the formality of a
Red Bank lawyer and public figure, cleaning trout or
trying to teach me to shoot, which I did not in the least
want to learn; the smell of cows and hay and pastures, so
much identified with the place, which every summer had

upon me an exciting effect. I find that Dorothy in her autobiography also speaks of this.

It comes back to me that Homer Collins, my father's devoted companion on his fishing expeditions, who had once been in the navy and had named his dog Funston after the general who had put down the Philippine rebellion and had captured their leader Aguinaldo, used to sing what must have been the most ancient comic song that I have ever heard at firsthand. (I find in *British Music Hall*, by Raymond Mander and Joe Mitchenson, that this song was popularized by "The Great Vance" sometime after 1864.)

There is a school of jolly dogs,
I've lately come across;
They're game for any mortal thing,
From this to pitch and toss.

And they always seem so jolly, oh!
So jolly oh so jolly oh!
They always seem so jolly oh!
Wherever they may be,
They dance, they sing, they laugh ha, ha,
They laugh ha, ha, they dance, they sing,
What jolly dogs are we! . . .

Slap, bang, here we are again, here we are again,
Here we are again,
Slap, bang, here we are again,
What jolly dogs are we!

VII

The following are selections from my diary-notebooks, with occasional interpolations, covering the period 1950-1970, during which, after my mother's death in 1951, I often visited Talcottville and spent a large part of my summers there. There is a good deal here about myself, but I had become, from my childhood associations and from my later settled life there, almost as much a part of the locality as the more deeply rooted residents and my preoccupations belong as much to the story as theirs. It ought to be explained that in 1950, when I first returned after an absence of, I think, seventeen years, I was fifty-five years old; my wife Elena, forty-four; my elder daughter Rosalind, twenty-seven; my stepson Henry Thornton, eighteen; my own son Reuel, twelve; and my younger daughter Helen, two.

It may be well at this point to explain that Talcottville and Boonville lie in a kind of trough between the lower ranges of the Adirondacks, visible from our house, and a large very wild plateau originally known as the Lesser Wilderness and now called simply Tug Hill. This last rises sixteen hundred feet above sea level, and snow con-

tinues to fall here for ten or eleven months of the year.
It sometimes reaches a depth of from eighteen to twenty
feet. At one time, human beings, Irish, German and
Polish, tried to make a living there, but the land does not
lend itself to cultivation or dairy-farming. Mr. H. E.
Krueger, the author of articles in the *Conservationist*,
published by the New York Conservation Department,
in its issues of December-January, 1966-67 and February-
March, 1967, to which I am indebted for a good deal of
my information, makes the statement that this bristling
and unrewarding area "should never have been cleared
at all." Though its spruce was in demand at one time,
the logging in the long run turned out to be unprofitable,
as did the small cheese factories and creameries. Such
almost impassable roads as remain give an impression,
with their abandoned wooden churches, their collapsed
houses which disclose inside a dismal tangle of slatlike
boards, their empty foundations now enclosed by woodland, their rotted ties of a long-ago scrapped railroad, that
it has hardly ever been frequented. Their only identi-
fiable remains are occasional bleak and sparse cemeteries.
To the north, in the neighborhood of the town of Adams,
from the subsiding hills of which the gray waters of Lake
Ontario may be seen, there are a few widely isolated
farms, immense cornfields that feed the fowls of chicken-
raisers. The strong winter winds, with their blizzards, that
blow across this part of the upland make it an almost
unlivable location. Here, according to Indian legend, the
Iroquois sprang out of the ground, and students from
Buffalo, as I write, are cleaning up some ancient skeletons. So many bones of Indians were discovered in 1850
that a battle was thought to have been fought here. There
were reported at this time the finding of giant skeletons and
skulls with double rows of teeth; but of these tales there
was no later corroboration. Tug Hill is inhabited by deer,

wildcats and bear, as well as mink, otters and beavers, and there were formerly wolves and panthers, of which rumors are still sometimes heard. It is dangerous on this account to stray without a gun very far from the roads, and it is easy to get lost in the miles of forest.

Lewis County, in which I live, which includes the greater part of Tug Hill, covers 1,270 square miles and has a population of 23,249. This population had hardly increased or decreased during the last sixty years. The prosperous county seat of Lowville, largely composed of handsome old houses, though with the usual dingy commercial section of upstate New York towns, is inhabited by well-to-do dairymen. Boonville in Oneida County, just across the county line and nearer to Talcottville, has always been our shopping center. Utica, in the Mohawk Valley, about an hour's drive south of us, is now rather a flat-tired industrial center, but it has remained, nevertheless, the big city for our locality, and I still, when I go for a day there, look with eagerness into the shop windows and make a point of visiting the museums, which, through the bounty of old textile families, are well equipped and well kept up.

1950-52

In 1950, I became rather worried about the family house in Talcottville. My mother, to whom it now belonged, had been hoping every year through her late seventies and early eighties, to be able to spend the next summer there, but except for one brief visit of inspection of which I have already spoken, she had never felt strong enough to make the journey—let alone to move and set up her household. Our cousins Otis and Fern Munn, who lived there all the year round, kept the keys of the house and acted as caretakers in her absence. I decided, without telling my mother until after I had got back, to make an expedition myself and check on the condition of the house. Neither I nor any of the members of my family could drive a car at that time, and I had the local taxi driver, with whom we were on very friendly terms, drive me over from Wellfleet on Cape Cod, with my son and my older daughter. The trip took place in June, 1950. It was for me, as it had always been in my youth—and now in a special way, after so long—a rather emotional experience.

June 16-18, 1950. New Hampshire, with its schools and dense trees—ponds, big dark pines, twilight birds and bats, sober old brick buildings, old white houses. Vesper service at St. Paul's School Chapel, quietude upholstered by shrubbery. The school still remains distinguished, kept up to a certain standard but rather uninteresting. There is a St. Paul's type: quiet, well-bred, slightly stooping and tanned—doctors or lawyers, business men, sun-reddened and breathing drinks—they have a deep conviction of superiority, without necessarily much serious substance. Dry vein of the Head Master, Kittredge—Harvard accent superimposed on Barnstable. A boy soprano, a little golden-haired girlish type. Memories of Andover, and, in my youth, Sunapee Lake.

Vermont: green hills crowded close together, furred as densely as caterpillars or chestnut burrs—primitive—insignificant little towns, almost no attempt to make a show for tourists, maple syrup signs, degenerate people up in the hills.

After this, New York State opens out: wide cow pastures with their stone fences, first glimpse of the Adirondacks, quite different from the Green Mountains, more mysterious, grander, more interesting. Then Glens Falls,

appls.

big town full of factories, area of cheap modern houses,
general cheapness and tarnishment; tacky town end of
Lake George, steamboat that is waiting for excursion, big
restaurant-bar, with Italian-looking barmen and Polish-
looking waiters, hard and crass little street of stores.
But after this, the Adirondacks: blue range behind blue *Adir...*
range, with sharp broken ridges, not furred—spaces opening away, non-New England horizons, not cramped; road
through the North Woods, a few camps and places to
stay, but miles through the woods and the lakes without
passing a car or ever seeing a human dwelling: Raquette
Lake, Blue Mountain Lake, the early stage of the Hudson, still a shallow river with gray stones that runs beside
the road for a time (Hudson Falls, Bad Luck Ponds,
Death Creek).

At last, you emerge into the country of Oneida and
Lewis Counties—it was misty, just at sundown, and beautiful, the mist lying along the green silky fields, the
blurred orange light in the sky (the next day, clear, liquid
and bright—white, yellow and orange)—it always gives
rise in me up here to a kind of lofty and purified thoughts:
dignity and beauty of the country which somehow has
ennobled the lives of the people and all that old story of
their immigration and their living, away from New England, among the hills and the fields and the forests, where
they were all alone, but independent—free, flourishing—
their human relationships and labors against the non-
human grandeur of the setting—riding along those up-
and downhill roads, a man behind a horse in a buggy, a
farm wagon or carriage, under the high heavens, with
fluid orange light or dark blue thunder clouds.

Fern Munn had done her best to make the place habit-
able for our visit; but it had badly deteriorated: wallpaper
hanging off the walls, cigarette holes in the horsehair

upholstery—it was evident that the young people had been getting in for parties; the floor had fallen through in the downstairs bathroom of what used to be Uncle Tom's quarters, a peculiarly grisly sight. All the old pictures still there: the two painted landscapes, originally from Utica, in their gold oval frames, which looked as if they were copies of landscapes in Europe rather than of anything in the United States; the engravings of Dickens, Charlotte Corday, Washington and his family; the "Reformers Presenting Their Famous Protest before the Diet of Spires." The black kettle in the dining room fireplace and the brass warming pan beside it. The fireplace in the northern sitting room, where Aunt Lin received us as children and where I used to sit with my mother, reading in front of the fire. My mother's two rows of peonies are still blooming on the side lawn, but they are all that is left of her flower garden; and the currant and gooseberry bushes are now being choked with weeds. The place is a problem now: I don't expect that my mother will be able to do much about it.

Otis Munn (my great-aunt Adeline's grandson): the only relative left who represented for me the original upstate race. He came in from the movies, with open-throated white shirt—broad farmer with big stomach but not fat—brawny; with self-assurance, ease and authority. In his good clothes, he looked well—wearing a brown suit and tie—when we went there to lunch next day. Bare farmer's living room, tidies on backs of chairs, antlered heads in dining room of deer shot by Otis and his father—portraits of two large trout caught by Thad, his father, on successive casts and painted by Doig, the Boonville portraitist of fish, who now has a certain reputation. Fern brought out a picture of a trout caught by her which her father-in-law had had painted for her. He had had some of his animals stuffed. When he died, they had put them in the attic.

There they had lost their luster, and Fern decided to burn
them up; but the wild cat for some reason would not
burn, so the boys put it up on the stone fence. Four or five
neighbors, taking it for real, brought their guns and shot
it. Each time the boys put it back.

The old graveyard on the hill that was not cared for
any longer—the church was gone now, burned down?—
covered with wild roses and devil's paintbrush; a chip-
munk, reddish brown and black-striped, whisking on one
of the tombstones—in the foreground, the Reuel Kimballs
with their Saras and Cleanthes clustering around their
family obelisk—at the back, in a light growth of woodland, Hezekiah Talcott leaning askew, and some members of the Augur family, with whom the Bakers had
intermarried. Not enough people left who are related to
these families to get this graveyard cleaned up. In the
Talcottville graveyard, it was noted that one of the
Munns had been cremated.

Along Sugar River, on the way to Flat Rock, forget-me-
nots, big white anemones, big purple columbine, an almost bearish-looking woodchuck living in a hole among
the stones.

Return from Talcottville: you lose the glamorous country as you come down on Utica. The Mohawk Valley has
its grandeur but is partly industrialized, as by the Beechnut chewing-gum plant at Canajoharie; announcements
of deer crossings and falling rocks. The Berkshires loom:
green clotting or thickening of the large trees and rich
fields. Pittsfield, Lenox—the suburban environs of Boston:
no sense of decoration, lack of taste.

My mother died on February 3, 1951, and had left me
the Talcottville house.

The poor old place badly rundown, grass and leaves

and shrubbery all grown up around it—Joe McGuire had done nothing since Mother's death. Dead branches on the lawn—only the path worn by the neighbors' coming through my place in order to cut off the corner. Moldy-smelling inside—so much of the stuff now seemed cheap and rubbishy. But I have my ambitious ideas about it—shall preserve it, make it something my own. Though I always at first find it smaller and less distinguished than I expected, I soon get into the spirit of it and am conscious that it does make one feel its dignity and amplitude, as I go from room to room and up- and downstairs. It always bucks me up to come back: partly those qualities in the country, partly because it brings me closer to Father, who enjoyed it so much and handled it so well. He liked to go to the meetings of the local Grange, of which he had been made an honorary member; liked to sit around and talk in the blacksmith shop; liked to read in the big bed, with the carving of Columbus's head, in which he and my mother used to sleep at the Collinses'. He would never wear pajamas, nothing but an old-fashioned white nightgown.

The old complicated water system that my father had installed: rainwater in a wooden tank under the roof for washing, and filtered water from Sugar River piped into the house for drinking and supplemented by Vichy from the Boonville drug store. The old well, exploited by Thomas Baker, was now boarded over, and I shouldn't have ventured to use it. I had a new well dug.

June 4, 1952. The house faces eastward, and from about 5 in the morning, I could see from my bedroom window a tree silhouetted on the mist that gave the effect of a photographic negative but with the darks and the lights interchanged. Then the light came and, pouring in from behind on that night-wet world, it seemed to be

drenching everything: big green elms, a field of yellow
clover, and beyond it a field of brown ploughed earth, the
growth of foliage along the little river, the low blue hills
in the distance. Bracing, even exalting—rich and fresh
and brilliant landscape now blazing with light.

How live the little shallow river seemed.

By day the windows in my corner bedroom look like
painted panels. Elena said that the old glass in the panes
—with its fine rippling texture—gave a silky effect to the
landscape.

Trip back to Wellfleet interesting, though it took us—
going fast—six hours. At one end, the fruity fragrance of
the country in the clear bright upstate air; at the other,
the salty smell of the sea in the damp and dimming fog.
The houses of New York are larger—more freedom and
spontaneity. Berkshires intermediate (fine and fancy white
church at Lee)—closed-in and hot, the uncombed mountains hunch their backs, face down. New England older,
solider.

Returned to Talcottville, July 25, 1952. Strange feeling
I had that the old house had slipped into blurredness and
dirtiness—behind the fresh and vital and colorful countryside—and that I must bring it up again to this countryside.

Horrible filthiness of the third floor, which, with its
windows and arched ceiling, used to be attractive and
lived-in. Between the two rooms, there is a dark and unventilated closet, in which I am told two maids were once
put to sleep. In the closet now, bare skeletons of crino-
lines, motheaten underwear, an old embroidered waist-
coat—an enormous floppy white hat; pictures: a volcanic
eruption painted in color of flame on the black of a slab

of slate, perhaps a happy idea; watercolors of flowers and sheep; the "Cathedral Driveway" in the woods at Lakewood, New Jersey, and from Lakewood Pandora opening her box; old magazines rolled and tied up, as if they had been mailed; books caked with thick dry white mold or clotted with spiderwebs. Behind the handsome windowed rooms is an equally unventilated black attic that runs the whole length of the house. Reuel and I cleaned it up pretty thoroughly, laughing at the things we brought out, while Elena sat on the lawn reading in a steamer chair and quietly repelled by all this old rubbish. Almanacs from the eighteen forties; a flat pasteboard box falling apart, with something hairy put away in fern leaves that Reuel and I imagined might be an Indian scalp. Elena said it was a "tippet."

I have eliminated the Franklin stoves that they had in every bedroom, selling them to Mr. Parquet at the Parquet Hotel in Constableville—all different, one designed like a cathedral.

In order to get two of the fireplaces working, which my mother had boarded up, I had to have the chimneys rebuilt. One morning a brood of swallows fell down one of these chimneys: five little ones with the nest they had now outgrown. We put them on the pedestal of the trunk of a tree, where they were seen as five black spots that gradually moved together as one large one. The mother and father were also inside the house, fluttering in the curtains, but we caught them and put them out. They did not find the fledglings but wildly flew away and left the children to die in a day or two. While these were still alive, they made a horrid angry hissing sound whenever one went near them.

I was about to hand over an old "barroom chair"—sometimes called "captain's chair"—to a junk dealer, but the Loomises told me it was worth $20. I found I had a whole set. They are for some reason highly prized now. In the attic, I found a rolled-up painting that I had never seen before. It was one of those peddled portraits produced by an itinerant artist, who carried round with him a male and a female set-up and painted in the customer's face. It was evidently Great-Grandfather Baker's first wife, the mother of my grandmother. I took it to New York and had it restored and framed, and it now hangs in the hallway—Elena does not like it. I was told in New York that these itinerant portraits are now being forged. Many things have been stolen, from the red barn especially—to be sold, I suppose, to antique dealers—that were here when I wrote about the place in 1933.

Fern Munn: "As sure as preachin'"—this is an old expression. Fern has a certain robust and yet sensitive attractiveness—gray eyes, a little bovine but not too much so. By the cowbarn, where she walks with partly high-heeled black shoes, in the mud among the cow and goose manure, wearing a somewhat smeared bright-violet apron, she has decided sex appeal.

The Munns took us for a ride to the St. Lawrence without explaining their intention of treating us to a picnic. At one of those picnic grounds in the woods which are furnished with wooden benches and tables, they unexpectedly produced from the trunk of the car several baskets of sumptuous and varied dishes. When we had eaten, we went by motor boat to Boldt Castle on one of the Thousand Islands. This unfinished monument of a millionaire is the most depressing and grisly of all the attempts at magnificent living characteristic of this part of the world. George C. Boldt was a big hotel man, the manager of the Waldorf-Astoria, and the creator of the luxurious American hotel, who began his St. Lawrence

castle as a romantic tribute to his wife. Boldt came from
the island of Rügen in the Baltic, and this no doubt
accounts for the hideously Germanic design of his dream.
But, according to the official version, before the castle
was finished, the beloved wife died. According to a local
tradition, however, she ran away with some menial. At
any rate, Boldt dropped the project midway, and the
structure has never since been touched. It remains a
curiosity and a horror. One hesitates to mount the great
staircase. The ornate ceiling is sagging. Doorways open
on nothing. It is exploited as a sight for tourists.

By that time, I had persuaded my cousins, the Sharps,
to come back to Talcottville for the summers. Dorothy
Furbish had married Malcolm Sharp, whose father had
been with the Reeds at the pension in Berlin. Malcolm
was then a professor at the Law School of the University
of Chicago. He was a very pleasant companion—I shall
describe him at greater length later—and we joined them
every afternoon for drinks. They stayed in the house of
Aunt Addie Munn, my old friend, the grandmother of
Otis. John Gaus, who was born in Stittville, between Talcottville and Utica, who had taught with Malcolm at
Amherst at the time of the Meiklejohn administration,
and was now in the Department of Government at Harvard, spent his summers not far from us at Prospect and
would come to join us for conversation or to take us on
long drives. He was an authority on the geography and
the local history, which I now came to realize I had never
known much about. He and Malcolm made for me the
nucleus of a new group of associates.

Golden moon in the trees as we sat on the back porch
at night and looked at the shadows on the old stone barn.

Pink and blue-violet lawn seen from the front windows.

Cape Vincent. First visit with the Gauses and Sharps.
It stands at the point where the St. Lawrence River flows
out of Lake Ontario—the Thousand Islands are just beyond. On the way, the trees that get the wind off the
lake, so straight when they are further inland, have been
blown into bent postures. This part of New York was
settled by the French, and there is a town called Chaumont, which they pronounced Shummoo, in honor of the
French Jesuit Joseph-Marie Chaumont, who came here
in the hope of converting the Indians. A house was later
built for Napoleon, with the idea of having him flee here
from France. In the neighborhood is one of those curious
so-called cup-and-saucer houses—the saucer a thin roof
sticking out all around, the inverted cup on top of this.
Everything in Cape Vincent seems so clean, neat and
clear. A big square stone mansion, trimmed with green,
at the same time very upstate New York and characteristically French. It has just now changed hands from the
original family, and they are selling some old things in an
antique shop—none of them very attractive. The people
have probably made some different disposition of anything of any more value. The water—"By Blue Oneida's
shore"—a greenish moiré blue. The old customs house and
the docks. The lake steamers. The distant Canadian side
and the islands so narrow that the spare straggling trees
seem to grow out of the water—almost no habitations.
Thirty families had once lived there but had left; abandoned barns and farm machinery. About a hundred wild
wandering cattle; in the fall, a lot of people turned out to
round them up—they took them to the mainland and
sold them. We explored these islands on later occasions,
when we stayed at the more or less comfortable old
Carleton Hotel on the water, with its especially fine speci-

mens of muskellunge and bass stuffed and mounted in the
lobby, with the fishermen's names on brass plaques. We
fished with Reuel in a hired boat, and he caught a lot
of tasteless lake trout, and one whopping big black bass,
which we had the hotel kitchen cook for us. It was all so
uncongenial to Elena, who, however, did her best for the
children and occasionally went in swimming on the rocky
shore, that I would sometimes have to concentrate on
what I felt was the admirable solidity and balance of my
coming book—*The Shores of Light*—in order to justify
myself and give myself some satisfaction. On the main
street, an "Exhibit of Wild Life" in a fishing tackle store,
run by an old Frenchman who said that his father had
been a soldier of Napoleon: loons, heron, grebes, eagles,
a sparrow hawk, a snow owl and a great horned owl—a
black bear and its cub. At the end of the road is a light-
house, and between there and here, on the other side from
the lake, a row of summer places of well-to-do Syracuse,
Buffalo and Rochester people with big houses and ample
lawns, well-mowed.

I read aloud to Elena and Reuel Hemingway's *The
Old Man and the Sea*. Then when I called up Dos Passos,
who was staying in our Wellfleet house, I remarked that
I thought it very good. "Why shouldn't it be?" he said
rather tartly. It turned out that he rather resented the
publisher's having put it over by sheer power of high-
pressure publicity. "It's like a magician's levitation act,"
he said. "You don't ask whether the girl is beautiful. It's
the operation that counts."

Elena, who is not at all interested in ghosts, says that
when she came down early one morning, she saw a
woman in an old-fashioned pleated dress going into the
smaller living room. Her shoulder was just disappearing

in the doorway. Elena says she saw the dress without being aware of any head above it. When she mentioned this to the Loomises, I thought that she was joking, but almost twenty years later, she repeated it the same way. She said it gave her a queer feeling of an experience she had never had before and that remained vividly with her. Later, we found old photographs of women in such pleated dresses. Dorothy Mendenhall calculated that she knew of fifty people who had died in this house. A murder was once committed on the pathway on the south side. A woman who lived down the hill was running from her drunken Irish husband to take refuge in the Stone House, but he killed her before she could get into the door. The Reed children used to pretend that they could still see the blood on the flagstones. I have had some bad dreams here but have not seen any ghosts.

Another morning when Elena came down early in her nightgown, she saw a little whisky left over in a bottle from the night before, and she drank it up out of the bottle—not at all a characteristic gesture. Then she became aware that an old man was looking in through the vines of the low kitchen window. This is one of the things that have made her uncomfortable.

I, on the contrary, am quite at home here—the only place, perhaps, that I feel I belong. Everybody knows me —and, quite unlike the general attitude in New England, where anyone from two miles away is "a foreigner"— everybody seems good-natured and comfortable; even the dogs are not yappy and snappy, as they are likely to be in Wellfleet. They visit us and make friends with Helen. Reuel plays ball with the village boys in our back lot. It is easy for me to get things done: cleaning, lawn-mowing, carpentry, getting water from the spring. Fern has done a good deal of painting for me—and Elena has done a good deal, too. The general store is right at hand, with a bigger stock than I remember. We get green vegetables from Carrie Trennam across the road and chickens from the Robertses on the hill. I enjoy the informality of being able to go out on the street in my bathrobe, and even having the cemetery so close, where I can look up the family dates.

This little town is at once a point of permanence for me—since we always came back in the summers—and a phase in the flux of American life. You feel both the struggle of the settlers to make themselves a place in the wilderness, the will to found a society, and the spirit of adventure, the thirst for freedom, the need to make new lives for themselves, that carried them farther and farther West. The families were so few that one can see very clearly the strains that were competing to establish the tone and the habits. There was the Calvinism of Great-Great-Grandfather Kimball that aimed at a godly community; the Toryism of the Talcotts that tried to preserve feudal dignity; and the Jacksonian democracy of Thomas Baker, who cared little about either of these ideals, but was out to make what money and what kind of career he could. I once wanted to write a play about it.

The Loomises' anecdotes: Some of the Collinses had lived in the pentagon house at Constableville. When old Mr. Collins died, they had had to take the casket out a window because the doors were too small. Mrs. Collins had been asked whether she wanted a last look at her husband before they nailed up the coffin. "Look at him? Haven't I seen him for fifty years?"

Some relation had said, "Why should I go over to Constableville to see those long-nosed Collins girls when I can find Sally Talcott right here in Talcottville pretty as a pink?" He married her.

My father, Edmund Wilson, at the door of the Stone House

(The Loomis sisters were old friends. I remembered them from my childhood. Even when well past maturity, they were known as "the Loomis girls.")

Last day, September 1, I walked over to Flat Rock across the fields, trying to find Father's slender cane, one of those he had whittled himself, which I had forgotten there. In the rainy weather, the colors of the wildflowers seemed to come out much more brightly than they do in the sun: purple asters, orange and red devil's paintbrush, blue bugloss—they seemed to burn in the grass.

VIII

1953

April 23-24. I went up alone to attend to repairs. I had
never been there before at this time of year. The weather
was warmer and pleasanter than I had expected it to be.
There is a new little train to Boonville—they call it the
Bee Line—put on, I suppose, for the ski trade, a great
improvement on the old milk train. Whenever a door
was opened, one heard a chorus of frogs of a loudness that
at first seemed incredible. Driving in to Talcottville,
it seemed to me that the landscape toward the Adirondacks had a pinkish look—though this was due to some
trick of the light on the dun and buff fields as seen framed
in the light woodwork of the window of the car. After
finding things at the house so moldy when I had come
back here before, I was surprised to find them now so
neat and clean. But inside it was as if the whole winter
cold had been concentrated and kept in the house, and
I had to go out of doors from time to time in order to
get tolerably warm. Richly yellow double daffodils I
had never seen before blooming where the bushes grow
behind the house, the survivors from Aunt Lin's garden;
the old stone bowls and the square stone container on

the porch full of dark dead leaves like the front steps;
branches that had been blown down strewn all over the
lawn.

I stayed overnight with the Munns, had never been
upstairs in their house before. I had never seen another
house that gave me the same impression. In spite of the
unpainted exterior, everything inside was clean and in
good condition; but it represented a family which, fond
though they were of one another, did not seem to have
any home-life at all. No exercise of taste, hardly any
pictures—two heads of deer in the dining room and the
Doig portraits of trout caught by Thad, two small bookcases, a small phonograph, piles of newspapers, and
among them, when I first came in, Otis was asleep on a
big red couch. Upstairs there was a large bathroom, but
no tub and no hot water, and the toilet did not work.
They said that the pressure wasn't strong enough to keep
a heater running. Seven bedrooms that opened out of a
hallway—with old Talcottville-type beds in them—like an
architectural fan. Tube-contained lights on the walls that
flicker when they are first turned on. Big kitchen with
deep-freeze still containing some winter venison; little
restaurant-type table and chairs. Their meals were most
irregular. They get up at six and milk the cows. They
have the largest dairy farm in the county. Otis asked me
whether he was "stunk up" from the cow barn—they got
used to it and didn't notice it. Then they come back
about eight and get breakfast. Then Fern went to Boonville to the Coöp (the Dairymen's Coöperative), where
she made out the milk checks—that winter she had really
run the whole thing. Otis got himself some lunch—
opened a can of soup or made himself some bread and
milk. They eat mostly in the kitchen. I imagine they
rarely use the dining room, though they once gave us
dinner there. The family came and went, without wast-

ing conversation, but I have never heard any of them say a disagreeable or even a sulky word.

Otis Junior, who resembles his mother—same solid build and rather handsome gray eyes—married the daughter of a man in the logging business and made $5800 this year. He begins the first of January and, during the weeks when the logging is going on, he makes about $500 a week, of which, however, he gets only about $300 clear, on account of current expenses and eventual deterioration of his truck. This occupation rather galls his father, because the land they are logging on once belonged to the Munns. Otis Junior has travelled a good deal by car, but has been in a train only once, when he rode from Boonville to Lyons Falls, just to find out what it was like. The trucks sometimes overturn—it's quite a strain carrying a load of logs—"but you don't get hurt because it turns over slow."

That evening Fern had to go to preside at a square dance given to raise money—the third—by the man whose barn had burned down last summer. I was sorry to have to miss it, but felt too ill with my cold and went to bed right after dinner. Fern told me the next morning that there were a hundred people there, including many Poles, who did Polish dances. I was reading the Civil War stories of Harold Frederic, the Utica novelist, and the life of that country is so well described and it has changed so relatively little that the stories and the present reality easily merged in my mind. In the story called *The Copperhead,* you are told that when old Abner's barn is burned, he cannot expect the neighbors to raise money for him, as was and is still the custom—by giving a husking bee—on account of his unpopularity for opposing the Civil War. In most of these stories, Frederic is interested in showing how American democracy—neighborliness, belonging to a common community—in the long run asserts

itself over the rather superficial class differences, created
by more money and superior education, and over differences of opinion. Only the story called *Marsena* is cynical
in the vein of *The Damnation of Theron Ware*—the
girls in both these stories are snobbish and insufferable
flirts, a type at the hands of whom Frederic himself must
have sustained some wounds. The class line-up also
appears in *In the Valley* in its more acute pre-Revolution-
ary form, and here, of course democracy triumphs. These
stories, the contemporary ones, are excellent in the accuracy of their picture of the local life and their feeling
for historical significance. He makes one feel the trauma
of the Civil War, and how it at once stimulated antago-
nisms—among the people of the North itself—and brought
them closer together. Old Abner is the type of indomitable
independent who had stood up to the British in the early
days and who, in spite of his non-conformity, eventually
commands the respect of his neighbors, so that, after the
war is over, they do get together to rebuild his barn. His
kindness and his sense of justice are unexpectedly made
to emerge when his barn has been burned and we are
prepared to have him swear vengeance. When Frederic
has good feeling prevail, we feel that he is not entirely
trying to meet the demands of the comfortable feminine
audience of the nineties but making a serious point about
the American society of the time—in *My Aunt Susan*, for
example, since certain of his stories, such as *Marsena*,
do admit the possibility, in other cases, of heartlessness
unmitigated by any humanity. How would these stories
appear to someone who did not know the country?
They seem to me in more or less the same category as
the neglected stories of Henry Fuller—such as *Waldo
Trench and Others*—too sober and unobtrusive, too instinct with fundamental irony, too dependent on social
criticism for their point, to have interested the public at

the period when America was supposed to be booming.
But in the case of Harold Frederic's upstate New York,
as in the case of Fuller's Chicago, the cultural poverty of
the upstate milieu that produced him may have had something to do—except in the case of *Theron Ware*, which
raised religious problems—with the little attention they
attracted. You feel the limitations of that life and its relatively meager history, limitations one is still aware of.
People in Frederic's period loved to read about New 1890s
England—which was richer in history and better established. We had had fed to us in school in the early nineteen-hundreds Longfellow, *Thanatopsis* and Oliver Wendell Holmes. People in my mother's generation liked to
read Mary E. Wilkins Freeman. I had had to find Walt
Whitman for myself, my curiosity aroused by the many
parodies.

July 17—September 2. The house had been painted
and the balcony and porch repaired. The chimneys had
been reconstructed. Helen Augur, who had gone up there
before I arrived, had given the place a good cleaning and
planted flowers in the stone things in front of the house.
The grass had been well taken care of, and in the bare
patches was growing again. Elena had painted the bathroom white last summer, and the red linoleum had been
laid after we went. It delighted me to see the place looking so well again.

Paolo Milano, the Italian writer and teacher at Queens
College, had just finished a stay at Yaddo, and I met him
there on my way up here and brought him to Talcottville.
We had very pleasant conversations. He is calmer and
more serious away from New York. We would walk up
the hill in the afternoons or sit in the evenings in the
front room, with the door opening out on the lawn. He

read me Belli and Dante, and I read him Swift and Yeats.
It is so quiet, only occasionally a dog barks; at night the
Lincks' cow sometimes moans. I like the feeling that I
am occupying the largest and most distinguished house in
the town—though the population of Talcottville is now
hardly more than eighty people, that everybody knows
me and takes me for granted—that I can say or do whatever I please, with the town at my door and all about me.
At night we can sit on the porch and talk while the village people pass.

Helen Augur is a true Baker woman, more than she
realizes, not having seen very much of the Bakers: warm
and vital voice, bustlingly capable and energetic, ambitious in a worldly way and instinctively tending to dominate a household. What is pathetic is that she has no household and has neurotically doomed herself not to have one.
In this house, she has become like that female beaver in
a book I once read about beavers who, when taken into
the beaver-fancier's house as a pet, was one day possessed
by her beaver instincts, and began madly building a dam
with mud against the front door. She eventually became
so tyrannical, undoing everything I did and thwarting
whatever I tried to do, putting away things that I needed
and snatching other things out of my hands, that I
began having acrimonious scenes with her. And her
nervousness, which takes the form in all this of ostensible
efforts to help which are actually efforts to interfere,
eventually become intolerable. Nevertheless—though she
was never here much as a child—one feels she belongs in
this house. It has been a satisfaction to me to have her
here: the other members of the family seem not to have
approved of the Augur connection, so behaved to them
rather unfairly. But Helen's passion for managing affects
me rather like my mother's, and though I like to have her

around as a sort of substitute sister, I very soon begin to
react against her. The ambitious Baker qualities here are
complicated by something that derives from the academic
tradition of her father, who was the head of a girls' school
in Minnesota, and her grandfather Adams, who was head
of Lowville Academy, at that time an important institution of learning, to which students came from all over
northern New York. She is really an intellectual but not
quite enough of one: the vigorous practical side (except
perhaps when she was a foreign correspondent) has never
been effectively integrated with the moony and cerebral
one. She seems to live a good deal of the time in some
self-centered adolescent fantasy, which she cannot exploit
as fiction—all her books have been reportorial or biograph-
ical—but which keeps her from grasping clearly what is
going on around her. Her sudden sorties out of this
among the situations of the outside world turn out to be
at crosspurposes with what other people are actually up to
and so become merely annoying. She is always trying to
fill in my sentences before I have been able to finish
them, and I don't remember one occasion on which she
has got it right. Helen's combined self-indulgence in her
dreams and something like a certain lack of self-respect,
due, I think, to her failure as a woman, now appear in her
slumping figure, the cigarette always hanging out of her
mouth and her yellow upper lip—though sometimes the
pretty Baker woman comes back and reminds me of how
well she looked when I first got to know her, then married to Warren Vinton: blond, plump, pinkcheeked,
smiling, *pimpante* in her bright clean clothes. Today her
nice smile seems usually a mask for the dig of some catty
remark. At times, as when I talked to her the other night
in Aunt Addie's house, she surprises you by being quite
lucid and capable of self-criticism; but most of the time
she gives the impression of not wanting to face herself

and her problems, of resorting to all kinds of expedients
—the source of her annoying mannerisms—to direct people's attention from her weaknesses (her aggressive manners that spoil her cleverness), to protect herself against the
world at the same time that she wants to challenge it. She
has a different idea every day about what she is going
to do to give herself a satisfactory life: get a job with
children, get a job up here, get a job with flowers and
plants. She has had no experience of gardening; but she
has enjoyed her pulling up of weeds at Aunt Addie's and
believes that, on account of her grandmother and mother,
she ought to "have a green thumb." She is one of several
women I have known—Louise Bogan, for example—who,
when married, have tied themselves into knots as to
whether they should leave husbands by whom they have
had no children. I always think they would be foolish to
do so; but then, when they are actually divorced, they
seem to get on better alone. Helen, though she used to
weep horribly and apparently be tearing herself to pieces
when still married and living in affluence in her duplex
penthouse in Stuyvesant Square and although she told
me once this summer that she sometimes thought of
suicide, does not seem to be quite so tormented as she was.

I am writing this on the third floor in the room that
looks out on the old stone barn and commands a view of
the general store. I first saw Helen cross the lawn at her
morning slumpingest and yellowest; then, a little while
after, Fern Munn got out of her car in order to go to the
store. She walked, in spite of a figure which is now getting rather ample, with a firm step and upright carriage,
looking very handsome. (She tells me that she is a mixture of Irish, New York State German and Pennsylvania
Dutch.) She accomplished her errand, then walked back
to her car in the same unhurried but purposive way, and

drove off with her trailer full of milk cans. This summer
she suddenly bobbed her hair (going to a beauty parlor
in Constableville), and they left it a little frizzy. I don't
like this nearly so well as the great thick old-fashioned
bun that she used to wear behind—she says that her hair
reaches down to her waist. She is the best-dressed woman
around here—Elena says that Fern must spend more on
her clothes than *she* does. Her big gray eyes look at you
with an innocence that is all the more winning for seeming to contrast with her executive ability and, I think, a
certain amount of shrewdness. But this animal innocence
is associated, perhaps, with a slight touch of Irish co-
quetry. It is as if she were aware of her attractiveness, of
her sound and erect physique, of her mastery of whatever
she is doing, even in the barn at milking time, in her
dirty old overalls and boots, walking in the cow manure,
clamping on the milking machine and shooing away the
bull. She sometimes seems a little shy, but has never
Helen's bad self-consciousness of the kind that can only
come with cleverness. At haying time, driving the tractor
with the baling machine attached, she seems a figure
almost symbolic—bare-headed, her solid round behind on
the seat, with her legs in their farmer's pants apart and,
at her back, the piston of the pounder working steadily
with a movement that is powerfully phallic; the wire-
bound square bales of hay were excreted in close succes-
sion from the aperture behind, and Otis Junior, her
broad-shouldered son, with the help of a hired boy, piled
them up on the platform there. Round and round the
field she drove. To impose the baler on those big hay-
grown fields, mastering all their produce, packing it away
in the barn, between the soaking downpours with their
dangerous thunderstorms, was a serious and challenging
labor. There was something august about it.—Yet she had
fainted in the heat from the sun the afternoon of the day

when she came to get me in Utica. She and the children
have had several dreadful accidents, and so have the
other farmers. Their work involves continual pushing
and lifting, covering large areas, disposing of copious
products, marshalling large animals, maneuvering un-
gainly machines, all of which lets you in for making
heavy blunders, blunting miscalculations; you are handling bulky materials by main force of machines and
muscles, and there are moments when you will fall off
something, not see that something is coming, have a
finger or a toe caught in one of the machines, get at cross-
purposes with the cattle.

Helen does not like the Munns' bad grammar, and
they don't, or I think that she thinks that they don't,
understand her kind of literary work. She said to Paolo
Milano that Otis's father had married a "peasant" and
that Otis had married "another peasant." She has no respect for the fact that Otis and Fern between them have
rescued the family from a tragic decline. They themselves, in reaction from the bad example of their fathers,
never touch alcohol and they have four vigorous children.
Helen first gave Fern the impression that she had to do
serious work and did not care to see people, then made
it a grievance that Fern had never asked her to her house
or called on her. When Fern was painting the bedroom
here, she complained that it kept her from writing and
that she slopped the paint around.

On the second of August, Elena arrived from Wellfleet.
Rosalind had driven her and Helen [not Helen Augur,
our little daughter], with Bambi, our spaniel, and Pussinka, Elena's Abyssinian cat. Elena cannot make herself
at home here, and she has a most dismal time. She says
that the climate is all right for *me,* because on the Cape I
am too keyed up and Talcottville tones me down, whereas

the sea-bathing at Wellfleet keeps her toned up and Talcottville lets her down, so that she never has any energy
and can hardly get breakfast in the morning. It is true
that the high altitude puts everybody to sleep at first. This
summer the first weeks of her stay were full of uncomfortable accidents. There was immediately a thunderstorm, in which a big elm by the stone barn was struck,
and a huge limb that overhung the street came down on
the electric wires and cut off all the current as well as
obstructing the road so that early-morning motorists could
not get past. The little girl woke up and began to cry;
Rosalind says that a sheet of flame seemed to be flowing
up that side of the house. I saw a shower of sparks crackling out of the wires on the corner. A day or so later,
Elena and Rosalind and Helen started out for a picnic
at Flat Rock. Elena was wearing a red dress and Rosalind
had on red pants; and, whether by this or by the baskets
they were carrying, which the cattle took for salt, they
attracted the attention of the cows, the whole herd of
which came after them, not merely walking but running,
plunged down the steep bank of Sugar River after them
and even crossed the river. The ladies dropped their
lunch and their bathing suits on a stone at the edge of
the river, scrambled across, slipping in the water, and got
under the fence on the other side. Later, when Elena
and Helen and I were walking on Leyden Hill, Helen,
not looking ahead, started to cross the road to see some
cows, and if we had not been able to stop her, would
have been hit by a speeding car—which scared us and
heightened the general feeling of lack of coördination.
Elena cannot find any field here, as she has been able to
do at Wellfleet, for her capacity for home-making and
charming. Her spirits sink; she tends to sulk. She imagines that the water is polluted and does not want to
swim in it. Helen, however, seems to love it, as our chil-

dren have always done, and has made friends with the
children of the village—including a little girl, pretty and
very dirty, with whom the other children have not been
allowed to play. The ostracism of this little girl has, however, aroused very strongly Elena's Russian democratic
instincts, and she has explained to Helen that it isn't
right that this little girl should be excluded, so now they
all play together. Rosalind, too, likes being here; she says
—I suppose, rightly—that it is too absolutely American
for Elena to make connections with. When we would
talk about going on a picnic or spending an afternoon at
the County Fair or taking a trip to some point of interest
—a kind of project that she would elsewhere have welcomed—she would mutter or simply be silent. When
Rosalind and I would exclaim over the landscape, she
would say that it reminded her of Germany, to whose
scenery, though she is herself half-German and has lived
a good deal in Germany, she seems to feel a certain
aversion. On a beautiful evening when we were driving
back from dinner at Constableville, she remarked she
didn't think she liked cows. Helen Augur came to their
defense and said that she liked to smell them. Elena said
she did not like their smell—you expected to breathe
fresh air and what you got was the smell of cows. As
she says, she has been moved around so much in her life,
from country to country and place to place—France, Germany, Switzerland, Canada, the United States—that,
having dug herself in at Wellfleet, she does not want to
have to adapt herself to any other locality. It makes me
feel rather guilty at having to impose on her this part of
the world, where she is bound to be uncomfortable.

She thinks wrongly that the people are not friendly.
It is mainly, I believe, that most of them have never seen
anybody like her and do not quite know how to deal with
her. Certain of them, I learn, are saying I have married

a model. She has, however, charmed Lillian Burnham, an old friend of the family, to whom my mother through all her later life, continued to send magazines. She lives on Leyden Hill, with her large herd of cows in the pastures below, and has managed her farm, with a boy to help, all the years since her husband's death. As a special mark of favor to Elena, whom she had invited to tea, she confided a family recipe, which was not to be divulged even to me. She gave Elena chocolate cake with a particularly thick rich icing which had been made by a special method supposed to be known only to Lillian's deceased sister-in-law. The sister-in-law had always promised to pass it on to Lillian before she died; but on her deathbed, after bringing up the subject, she announced that she had changed her mind: "No, I'm not going to tell ye!"—and died. After her death, Mrs. Burnham had somehow found out for herself. The Loomises had tried to get her to tell them the secret, but she had always refused. "Don't make it here," she admonished Elena. "Just make it in Massachusetts." Eventually Elena betrayed the secret to me. It was simply that Lillian's sister-in-law had used condensed milk—the very last thing, in that dairy country, that any housewife would ever have been able to guess.

I feel this summer, as I did not last year, that I have really moved into this house, that I have to some degree taken possession of it. I fill it with myself and my family. My own work and my own mind now occupy the big room where Aunt Lin used so grandly to receive and where first Cousin Grace Reed, then my mother used to sit in front of the fire. I remember reading Michelet there in one of the not very comfortable chairs in the tightening end of summer; and I now throne it there in the corner, with a window on either side, in the over-stuffed armchair from Red Bank, with the Hebrew Bible

propped up on a card table. On another are my notebooks
and typewriter; I handle my correspondence at the desk
and pass comfortably from one chair to the other. I have
partly dispelled the past; the house has now entered on a
distinctly new phase since the Talcotts, the Bakers, the
Reeds, Uncle Tom and Aunt Nelly, my parents. Though
the southwest bedroom has been done over in yellow and
does not look as gruesome as it did last year, I still have
to struggle, when I sleep there—as Reuel says he did, too,
Elena says it gives her the creeps—against a certain oppression: it is the room where Cousin Bessie died and in
which my father slept when he had already developed
pneumonia before he came home to Red Bank and died
there. I had a very bad dream here after reading Barrett
Wendell's book on Cotton Mather in an effort to make
connections with that end of the family. This bed, with
the carving of Columbus on the headboard, does not come
from a good period: ill-proportioned and of a too light,
not well-seasoned wood. I much prefer, I feel perfectly
at home in, the mahogany four-posters of the earlier
times. The bed in which Huldah Kimball died, in which
Huldah Loomis now sleeps, seems admirable today and
quite practical for modern life, when these later pieces
look antiquated, suggest visions of sprawling sleepers
in nineteenth-century nightgowns.

Helen at Talcottville: "Little girls like lemon-drops,
and fathers understand because they like lemon-drops,
too. But mothers resist lemon-drops."

At Flat Rock, paddling and sitting around in the shallow water: "Oh, this is so enjoyable!"

Elena Mumm Wilson, at twenty-five

IX

July 7-13. I arrived July 7. Though at the time I left Wellfleet, both Elena and I had been in bad states of mind about my going away, and though I had done a good deal of drinking at Zoltán Haraszti's the night before I left Boston—as soon as I started out with Bill Peck driving to Talcottville, my head became thronged with ideas for books. The summer visitors to Wellfleet are at once frustrating and tempting. In coming over here I shake off a kind of entanglement.

This year in Talcottville I have hardly been aware of the past, which used to come down on me so, so surround me as soon as I arrived in the house. It was probably that I was so much preoccupied with the second of my Hebraic articles, which I finished here, writing steadily morning, afternoon and night, Mrs. McGuire bringing me meals, which I ate on the same table. But it is also that I now feel I fill the house, that it has little relation to anyone but me. Last summer and the summer before, I had my cousins—Helen Augur and the Sharps—here, and felt that the place belonged partly to them. Also, getting the new screens put in and the obsolete wiring removed makes the place look fresher and cleaner, and it is possible thoroughly to air it. For the first time, nothing smells musty. And having the good-natured Mrs. McGuire to get meals and sweep the floors, the Linck boy to mow the grass and the Rice boy to get rid of the rubbish and bring the water from the spring [I had not had the well dug yet] makes living a good deal easier.

I went to New York for four days and met Elena. We stayed in her uncle's apartment. It has an erotic bachelor atmosphere: old prints of the Rhine and of horses and innumerable pictures of women, photographs of his old girlfriends and pictures he has clipped from magazines. In the bathroom is a full-page drawing clipped from *La Vie Parisienne*. The heading is *Ça Fond*. A naked woman and a man in pajamas are sitting on a bed. Near the bed is an Alpine picture, in which the snows are melting and trickling out of the frame. The caption says, *"Il va falloir nous modérer."* In this setting, I felt almost as if Elena and I were having a clandestine love affair. At the end of our stay, I went back to Talcottville and Elena went back to Wellfleet.

Fern met me at the Utica station. I am always impressed by the change from her appearance in the cow barn with her great rubber boots to her attractiveness when she is well dressed. She was looking very smart in a dress she told me she had just bought—a gray upper part over a white lightly flowered skirt. She has been wearing glasses this summer, and she now told me that she had had a blood-clot last winter and had temporarily lost the sight of one eye. She had felt stunned at first as if somebody had hit her over the head, and had then had such a headache for nine weeks that she had only kept going with codeine, but she had never for a moment stopped working. The doctor had thought that this blood-clot must be a belated result of her fall when, two or three years ago, the winter wind had blown her off the rampart to the barn. She has also had a length of her intestine removed. It is wonderful how she remains so vigorous and able to do so much.

Breakfast in the kitchen at the Munns' is a little like sitting in a bus terminal. Fern gives orders to all her boys either directly or on the telephone—where they are to go and what they are to do. Even her daughter calls her up. They are all very dependent on her.

She loves these children, always knows where they are, feels that she must always look after them. On the way to The Antlers, where they took me for dinner, she and Otis were saying that they would soon meet the boys coming back from the woods, and in the midst of a conversation in the restaurant, she was at once aware of it when they passed, one behind the other, in their trucks. Driving into Utica one morning, she said that we should soon meet her daughter Ann going in to work in Boon-ville from Stittville. If Fern is going somewhere and sees her little grandson, she picks him up in her gruff way and takes him along. She says that Otis Junior loses patience with the cows: if they won't let themselves be milked, he will smack them and shove them, and you can't do anything with them that way. She herself, in spite of her brusqueness, has a sound basis for good relations both with animals and with people. Coming to our house just after I had arrived with the kittens for Helen, she went straight to the kitchen to see them—"the tunnin' little things!" She held one during our conversation. So different from poor Helen Augur, who seems to have no real relations with anybody, and is always attempting to establish them or substitute for them by importuning people with *petits soins* or complaints to make them pay

attention to her. Yet she is better, I think, than last summer. California has done her good, and she is pleased by
the reviews of her book.

I brought back two Persian kittens for Helen, and have
now become fonder of them than I have ever been of any
cats, including Elena's rather peculiar supposedly Abyssinian cat, who has died since she was last up here with
us. The kittens were six weeks old when I bought them
—are supposed to be male and female, but I haven't yet
been able to tell which is which. They seem fine and
rather fragile, as if they were butterflies or moths. They
have short little kitten tails. Their color is a café au lait,
which verges, however, on orange, and their eyes, which
seem rather weak, are now pale and bluish, but will no
doubt turn green. Their profiles seem flatter than most
cats'. I was surprised that they were able to get up the
stairs, bouncing lightly from step to step. When they
first arrived, a mouse—the first I remember to have seen
here—came out from under the hatrack, sized the situation up and went back again. Unless I shut the door
when I am working, they come in and crawl all over me
and chew the things on my table. Sometimes one of them
will go to sleep on the back of my chair and the other
on the windowsill beside me. Yesterday morning as I was
reclining in the two-piece chair I just bought in Boonville, one of them lay on my chest purring. Sometimes
they scamper madly or roll one another around on the
floor. Now that I come to think of it, I have never had
kittens in the house before. In general, I don't really like
cats, but I wanted to fill the place of Pussinka for Elena,
and Helen has been yearning for a kitten. It is also a bait
to bring them to Talcottville.

I feel at moments, when I'm living alone here, that it's
all myself and nothing else—house, village and Lewis

County. I might get tired of the view from the door if I didn't feel that it was also mine, a part of my habitat, imagination, thought, personality. Of course, one can tire of these, but one cannot want to detach oneself from them any more than I want to do from the view.

X

1955

Dinner at the Sharps'. Fascinating to see Cousin Dorothy Mendenhall again. She has come to stay with the
Sharps. I had seen her only once since my childhood, in
the summer of '39, when I had been lecturing at the
University of Chicago and had gone up to Madison to
call on her. She is now eighty-one. She still wears her hair,
which still remains dark—I do not believe that she dyes
it—in her old kind of Phrygian cap coiffure that always
seemed to present a challenge. She is now somewhat
dumpy, has lost something of her magisterial dignity of
carriage. She had a bad accident in Madison, fell downstairs and broke both her arms and had to have her little
finger amputated. She says that her knees are giving out,
are like water. I complimented her on her fine eyes,
which now, however, have pouches under them—and she
said that that was the Kimballs. I thought that she was a
little shy, ashamed of having grown old. Her old shining
presence, which exerted such a spell, is gone. You only
feel that rare dimension occasionally in what she says or
in her handsome humorous smile. I was aware now that
her accent and her turns of phrase were more upstate

than I had noticed before but still retained certain New Englandisms—*lahst, bahth* and the way of pronouncing *it* so distinctly at the end of a sentence—mannerisms that the people up here now don't have. She also, I imagine from her period in Germany, pronounces words such as *finger* like *junger,* and has old English pronunciations like *neview.* When I mentioned this, she told me that her father came from Lexington, Massachusetts. But otherwise she reminds me of my mother—and I have something of that way of talking: "That looks like the postmen t'me"; "I'll have a lot of money 'fore-uh go," when Malcolm had given her $50; "Well, we got our face washed ennaway," when the garage boy had cleaned the windshield. She likes to wear purple; and when we went out one day to a restaurant, she wore white gloves, explaining when she took them off, that she couldn't eat with dirty hands. I told her I couldn't write without washing my hands.

We took her out for rides, and she recognized everything. When I told her that Hezekiah Talcott's tombstone was falling over, she had it set up again. The fields are full of flowers. The long green grass is stained with the white of daisies and the yellow of buttercups, marvellously sprinkled here and there with the pink and white meadow mallow—fringes of blue bugloss, pools of blue iris—great glowing fields of yellow mustard that overpower the green of the grass—enormous brown dandelion tops. Red-winged blackbirds bringing color to the air. Cousin Dorothy at one point spotted among trees at the edge of the road the red tops of Deadly Ammonita mushrooms and had us stop to examine them. She pushed one with her foot, with something of the conscious lack of feminine squeamishness of one who had dissected corpses and diagnosed disgusting and dangerous maladies.

Cousin Dorothy's way of always taking charge and giving orders. Dorothy Sharp says that she thinks that her aunt is having a very good time but that she is wearing to have in the house. She insists on providing the food and buying more than they need. Everything has to be done on the dot. At 5:30 every afternoon she has one stiff drink of bourbon on the rocks, and she likes to have everybody there to drink with her. But when this ceremony has taken place, she tries to act as a brake on Malcolm's further pouring of drinks. She rather resented it one day when I had refused to come in at all, just as she had rebuked me the day I first came for appearing at 6 instead of 5:30. The fact that I had asked Fern to come to the Stone House at 5:30 did not interest her in the least. Her attitude toward men is alternately challenging and charming. After snubbing them and telling them what's what she compliments and sweetly smiles at them as she teased me about the Bakers when we were looking through a box of old photographs, then when I left gave me a bunch of forget-me-nots. Contrast between the two Dorothys on our frustrated trip to Highmarket. Dorothy Sharp has always been terrified of thunderstorms and didn't want to drive toward a looming black cloud; Dorothy M. said, "It's not going to do anything—it knows we're afraid of it." I think she thought it followed her own technique. She teased Dorothy but not unkindly, and then aquiesced in going back. It is impossible for Dorothy S. in her shyness to ask questions as to how to reach somewhere; but Dorothy M., like me, doesn't even understand such an inhibition. She says that she enjoys getting into conversation with people. When we had driven to a restaurant, Dorothy M. insisted on giving Huldah Loomis, who was driving, directions as to how to park and when to get more gas. "Don't let her do those things to you!" Dorothy Sharp cried; but Huldah

always succumbed, and it was curious to see this obedi-
ence, because Huldah among her sisters was always the
dominant personality.

I had said to Dorothy M. that I wanted to ask her some
fundamental questions. She said, "All right, but I'll warn
you that if I don't know the answers, I'll make them up."
I was shy about inviting her to the house. She is ambiva-
lent about the family feud; she adores the memory of the
Baker women. Her mother had been considered a rene-
gade for having sided with the Bakers, because, she said,
she "liked them better," and Dorothy had been ostracized
by her Talcottville relatives, who would not speak to her
on the street. Yet she still believes that the Talcotts had
the right to keep the estate intact and not have it split up
into lots and sold. The Talcotts had Tory ideas and
wanted to practice primogeniture. One day I saw her out
the window walking by along Water Street and invited
her to come in. She explained that she had been married
in 1906 between the two front windows of the big north
room: "You couldn't see a fencepost the snow was so
thick. It was nip and tuck whether we could get married
that day, because we couldn't be sure that we could get
a minister there." When they came back from their three
years in Germany, they found that the energetic Aunt
Lan had, along with other alterations, had the old ballroom torn down. I went through the house with Cousin
Dorothy, and she would dismiss quite handsome things
as "Baker" as if, on this account, they could not be interesting. Among the objects she recognized were the cane-
bottomed dining-room chairs, the red Bohemian-glass
bottles on the mantelpiece, the fingerprint goblets and
tall celery glasses, the copper grain measures which I had
taken for beer-mugs, a spit for roasting corn which I had
supposed was intended for marshmallows, a blue lamp-

base, which they had brought from Germany, and a small bust of Dante with a broken nose, which, since it was damaged, they had left behind though they had taken its companion, a Beethoven, with them. The sense of belongings in that part of the world is very highly developed. In the early days, everything had to be brought from a distance, and every woman knew about every object of use and decoration, every piece of furniture, in every other woman's house. My mother left me an inventory of all the furniture in Red Bank—whether it came from my own or my father's family, etc.

Cousin Dorothy deplored my having given away the old broken-winded melodeon made of rosewood, which had been played by Aunt Lin. She told me that I ought to have cleared away, because they obscured the view, the small trees and bushes that had grown up in front of the house. When any of her end of the family told me that I ought to restore the big dining room to its original state as they remembered it, I would say that I would if Dorothy would give back the big sideboard which they had taken away when they left and which Dorothy now had in Madison. When Dorothy saw that I had there the bust of herself she so hated, she told me that she was going to wait till she knew I was not in the house and have it thrown into the pond again.

I enjoy "galvanizing" this old house into life, as I feel I have at last been doing, making it express at last my own personality and interests, filling it with my own imagination, yet feeling a continuity with everybody who has lived here, basing myself in some sense on them—the older I grow, the more I appreciate them. Intellectually and geographically I travel further from them, yet also now more fall back on them, probably become more like them; feel more comfortable and myself here probably than anywhere else in the world.

Dreamlike quality again: like the fairy tales—*Beauty and the Beast*—in which somebody lost in a forest comes upon a well-appointed castle, in which he is waited on by bodiless hands. Mrs. McGuire gets me meals and sweeps; Albert Grubel drives me; Jimmy Linck cuts the grass; Mrs. Failing does the laundry; Chet Rice attends to the electrical arrangements, and his boy Eddie brings water, burns the rubbish and buries the garbage. They come and go, in and out of the house—I take them for granted and hardly think of them. Fred Reber from Boonville—an old Swiss in his late eighties, who has been there as long as I can remember—mends the furniture, paints the hearths and neatly reframes the pictures. The mail is brought to the box without my being bothered to pay extra postage then and there; a boy brings the Sunday papers. Mrs. McGuire gets groceries from the village store or supplies them from her own house.

Another illusion of the time sense: the first day that the former Jean Sharp, Dorothy's young married daughter, was there, we all went to Flat Rock, but without her mother, and it seemed to me perfectly natural—as if she were her mother at that age and as if I were that age again, too. Actually she is older than her mother when I used to see Dorothy Furbish here in my childhood. She looks very much like her, and seems to be a little bored by people telling her so. She is perhaps even prettier than Dorothy was.

Elena, Helen and, later, Reuel have arrived. I was very glad when they came. [I had been so constantly reading and writing about Israel and the Dead Sea scrolls that I had virtually, with no outside exercise and with only the kittens for companions, been living in Palestine, and there was nothing here—there's so much at Wellfleet—to interrupt or impede it. I had become hardly conscious of the countryside, and the very fine views from the windows had come to be like pictures hung on the walls. What was going on in my mind could expand in comfort and freedom, could take up as much room as it pleased. But, at the end of three weeks of this, I had begun to feel a little dotty.

4th of July: our champagne punch party, I think, a success. There was a wonderful full moon: coppery at first, then brightest white. After the guests had gone, I finished the punch, sitting out on the back porch and watching it set steadily behind the big trees. I realized that Elena did not have much sense of the nobility and mystery of this country. She says that when she first comes here from Wellfleet, she feels as if she didn't exist. I reflected that the champagne which her Mumm family made was a part of her essential personality—she has a natural affinity with anything that at all resembles champagne: the Cape with its dry, mild, exhilarating air—she is able to *champagnieren* at Wellfleet. She likes to make things delightful, not sharp, not full-bodied, not emphatic, not dionysiac. The loneliness of this country, its grandeur, the effort and ordeal of the past that life up here implies, scares her a little and puts her off. She cannot imagine herself what she pronounces "a peeoneer woman," and is somewhat dismayed, I believe, by my interest in someone like Harriet Beecher Stowe. It is silly because perfectly futile to demand her appreciation of something so alien to her. The punch she made tonight was a masterpiece—so perfect in flavor, so cool, so smooth, so well tuned to promote the amenities, to put people pleasantly out of range of the commonplaces of life. In coolness and smoothness and color, it resembled this coppery phase of the moon, seemed in its way as perfect. But the moon moving through the trees brings out a romantic wilderness that I have never felt in America anywhere else but here, and that I am always somewhat astonished still to find that I do feel.

Strange that the family, in its upstate connections, should now include mainly farmers, the Munns, who have largely lost their education; and rather "advanced" writers and academic figures such as the Sharps, the Mendenhalls, Helen Augur and myself. The financial industrial element has disappeared: Jimmy Pitcher, the president of the Boonville bank; the manufacturing Harts of Utica. The Loomises and Lillian Burnham, though farmers, with tenants to run their farms, all went to college and sometimes taught school.

August 14.
    —At morning and at evening, those golden elms,
    those golden fields
    The blue Adirondack hills, still seeming
    unexplored
    —Gray-silver above rain-sated green hay
    —The leaves on the maple in front of the house
    already turning orange-pink
    —The crescent moon like jewel-weed drooping
    in the sky

Elena told me that Helen, walking on the beach at Wellfleet, had come out with the following rhyme:

> Boys can have their bosoms bare,
> But little girls they wouldn't dare.

Later she announced the following:

> Triumphant pages
> Escort me through the ages.

I think she made these up herself.

Elena has been getting on somewhat better. She has installed an electric stove instead of the old iron one that had to be stoked with coal, and she has done over the dining room and the smaller sitting room. I had sent some furniture to be re-covered, and the "mohair" of the samples I chose turned out to be simply red plush. She was horrified by it at first, but then discovered that the darker pieces, which had a gooseflesh-making sheen in the light of the living room, looked all right in the duller dining room. It has proved to be a good thing to eliminate my mother's figured wallpaper, which completely kills the pictures. To our surprise, the old oval landscapes looked for the first time quite handsome. The blue skies came out attractively against the new gray of the walls. Elena, also, likes the Sharps, and we have seen something of the Edmondses. They arranged to have us meet at their house Constance Robertson, the granddaughter of John Humphrey Noyes, and the Edward Roots of Hamilton College. He is the son of Elihu Root.

When Cousin Dorothy walked Elena home from the Sharps' one night, she said, "It's hard to live with a genius, isn't it?" Elena thought she meant me, then realized she meant herself, and was thinking of her cousin and companion who was staying with her at the Sharps'.

Contrast between rough river stones of pavements,

scratched and pitted from prehistoric times, and the well-knit house with its gratuitous elegance of front door and fireplaces—human art in the selection of view and the designing of windows to frame it. My tendency is to feel that the view is a series of pictures and panels, that it is actually due to the intention of the builder.

This kind of life, in the long run, does, however, get rather unhealthy. One evening (August 13, Saturday) I drank a whole bottle of champagne and what was left of a bottle of Old Grand-Dad and started on a bottle of red wine—I was eating Limburger cheese and gingersnaps. This began about five in the afternoon—I fell asleep in my chair, but woke up when Beverly came, thinking it was the next morning. I decided to skip supper and felt queasy for the next twenty-four hours. Otis told me the next day that a brother of his mother's had died the next morning from a combination of homebrew and Limburger at night.

August 17.

> I saw the orange-spangled pane;
> The orange filagree shows white;
> Chairs, bedposts, pictures now appear.
> The daytime room grows real from night.
> —The vines on the stone barn door make a wreath of shadows in the moonlight.
> —This house the old backlog of all our family.
> —Those old half-opened doors—standing ajar with their doorknob eyes

These last two notes were made on whisky. After going to bed early on several whiskies, I woke up to see the white carved fireplace, one of the simplest of them, shining in the moonlit room. I had dreamed so many times for so many years of coming back to this house and entering into possession; but in these dreams I seemed to be coming here only on a visit, had to go away again— always found things, in the dream, in disappointingly bad condition, sometimes had to drive away local people who had come in and were sitting around. But this summer, when we have got things in better shape and I do not feel that the people who have lived here are still present and crowding me out, I have had, at this moment of waking up and looking at the fireplace, the feeling— I think unique in my life—of a dream having literally come true, and so being now satisfactory as a real dream could not be. I felt such joy that I could not help getting up, drinking more whisky and walking around the house, delighted with everything about it. Of course I was the worse for it the following morning, but I did not really regret it.

August 31. We made an expedition to Kenwood and Clinton: had lunch with the Roots at Hamilton and visited the Oneida Community with Mrs. Robertson, who with her husband had had lunch with us.

The Roots are real Henry James characters—not the timid Americans abroad of the New England Prufrock type, but, like the Jameses, New Yorkers from the better upstate towns—he from Clinton, she from Albany. I was reminded by one of the guests that "the American" had come from Utica and Daisy Miller from Schenectady. The Roots had originally kept a tavern, the old house they are living in; the grandfather, Oren Root, had with difficulty got himself an education. Mrs. Root is the daughter of a Presbyterian minister in Albany, and she has the special kind of distinction that I have always attributed to Albanians. They are more worldly and more flexible than Bostonians, intellectually very able, a little bleak perhaps,

This seems so dated now '96. I wonder if these regional differences and characteristics still exist. (They probably do)

rather old-fashionedly snobbish with a highly developed
social technique. As my second wife's Albanian uncle
said, "You either belonged or you didn't." Mrs. Root
has great dignity and good manners—a rather masculine
face. She takes a conscientious interest in her husband's
collection of paintings and his activities in connection
with the Utica gallery. He is deaf, wears a hearing aid,
talks in a very low voice. They had an old-fashioned but-
ler in a dinner-jacket, rather stooping and not very effi-
cient. Mrs. Root got up to carve the roast on a side table
against the wall. After lunch, she put on a long cape,
which made her a magistral figure, and took us out to a
studio to look at her husband's pictures. He does not,
I think, have very much real taste, and has obviously been
sold, says Elena, a certain amount of junk by the New
York galleries: Prendergast, George Luks, Arthur B.
Davies (who came from Utica), Everett Shinn. The
abstract paintings seem ridiculous. One feels that he
bought them simply because they are having a vogue.
Back of the house, a great myrtle bank, winding garden
paths and a background of woodland—round the house,
all the old-fashioned flowers. Next door lives the grandson of Grant, who has married Edward Root's sister.

At the college, they had looked up the records on my
grandfather Walter Scott Kimball. I found that he had
missed only his Senior year, when, as my mother had
told me, he was robbed of his wallet, so could not pay
his tuition. Later, when he was practising medicine in
Eatontown, New Jersey, the college made him an honorary M.A. He was in the class of 1851, and I found on
the lists of those years the names of Knoxes, Wetmores
and Clevelands. Charles Dudley Warner, the writer, col-
laborator with Mark Twain on *The Gilded Age,* was a
classmate of my grandfather's. A Martin Luther Kimball
of Leyden, who was one of my grandfather's uncles, had

also been to college at Hamilton. There is a portrait of John Jay Knox, whose daughter, my aunt Caroline, married my uncle Reuel Kimball, Walter Kimball's son. He was a banker and trustee of Hamilton, who became Comptroller of the Currency during the Republican administrations of Hayes and Arthur, but resigned with the advent of Cleveland in 1884. He had put the country on the gold standard in 1873. The Knoxes are all listed as from Augusta, Oneida County, which is now a little town near Knoxboro, not very far from Hamilton, which became the seat of the family. The Knoxes and my grandfather spent their summers next door to one another at Monmouth Beach, New Jersey, and it was natural that they should intermarry.

Hamilton is a good little isolated specimen of the traditional "liberal arts" learning. There is a "Languages" building and a "Philosophy" building. The college, like Dartmouth, was originally intended for the education of the Indians. There is an Indian chief, a friend of the founder's, buried in the college graveyard; but the last Indian student went to Hamilton in 1803. The reddish local stone—as the President pointed out to me, taking me around the campus—gives the various buildings their unity. There is also a purplish red shale that the Roots and other old inhabitants have for generations had on their drives, but which the President seemed to disapprove of on the ground that it was messy when it was tracked indoors. Compact and self-sufficing, still maintaining a pretty high standard, Hamilton made me understand more solidly the Kimballs and the Knoxes and the rest. I could imagine them going to their classes in the old rectangular stone buildings, narrow-windowed, ugly yet not unimpressive, that look like those old halls at Princeton which they seem to be gradually getting rid of. There

is a rather good white near-Colonial chapel that is peculiar in having three storeys, the top one simply an attic.

Mrs. Robertson, whose husband at present is the director of the Oneida Community, which now makes Community Plate, drove me over to the "Mansion House."
She told me on the way that, on account of the professor
at Hamilton who had led a crusade against the Community and had played a part in inducing them to drop
their planned breeding system, it had only been very
recently that the people belonging to the original group
would allow themselves, as she had done that day, to
accept invitations to the college. The Mansion House,
with its ancient trees and its very well kept-up lawns,
something like a big hotel, something, Elena says, like a
Swiss sanitarium: outside woodwork sometimes ugly,
sometimes not so bad; high-ceilinged narrow corridors;
braided tapestries under glass—a kind of thing invented
by one of the group—now faded and, though curious, a
little dismal; auditorium with paintings on the ceiling of
figures that we couldn't identify; old photographs of various festivities, presided over by the bearded John Humphrey Noyes, much like other upstate gatherings of rural
people. Library, very serious in its period: old sets of
standard authors, old bound periodicals, old globes. The
librarian, one of Mrs. Robertson's innumerable cousins,
has a very pronounced form of the local accent: "Car-
loile," "surproise." Visitors inevitably try to imagine the
situations produced by directed breeding, and Mrs. Robertson is understandably a little shy about this aspect of
the Community. She told me that she had never, as a
child, known any children who were not her cousins, and
when someone had brought into the Mansion House a
reproduction of the Sistine Madonna and she was asked
who the baby in the painting was, she had answered,

"Why, that's little Cousin Jesus." She is forthright, friendly and humorous.

My father had usually, at sometime in the summer, taken us for a visit to Canada, and, being here again, so close to the border, I decided to go up there to get some idea of what it was like at the present time. I had had some correspondence with Robert Weaver of the C.B.C., the founder and editor of a literary magazine, *The Tamarack Review*, and asked if he could arrange for me to meet some of the literary people there. I took Elena and Helen to Toronto, where I had never been before.

We were invited by Weaver to a party, where for the first time I met Morley Callaghan, the novelist and short story writer, who had been a friend of Hemingway and Scott Fitzgerald. I took the opportunity to ask him the truth about the once widely circulated story of his boxing match with Hemingway. He said that he had never before told what had really happened (he afterwards partly published it in his book of memoirs *That Summer in Paris*). He had been a student at the University of Toronto when Hemingway was working on the Toronto *Star*. He had first known him then. Callaghan had been writing short stories which he had shown to Hemingway. I believe, since reading Callaghan's stories, written before Hemingway's, that since the subjects are of a quite different kind, the striking resemblance in style must have been due on Hemingway's part to the influence of Callaghan. In any case, Morley told me that Hemingway had first criticized his work sympathetically; then, at a certain point, when Callaghan had sent him some stories, he had never written him about them, and when Callaghan had seen him again and mentioned not having heard from him, had said, "I thought you were going good—there was no need to write you about them"—

*how typical
an H. sentence.*

though he afterwards spoke contemptuously about Callaghan's work to others. Later, they met in Paris. The story I had heard already was that, after the first dinner in Hemingway's flat, he said to Callaghan, "Shall we go to a show or shall we put on the gloves?" He did not know that Callaghan in Toronto had done a good deal of boxing. After that, they used to go to a gymnasium. "We had some rather distinguished referees. Miro used to referee us. He is a dapper little guy, and when we were walking together, Miro carrying equipment, people used to think he was Hemingway's servant. Hemingway didn't know who he was and was taken aback when I told him. He always prided himself on being in the know about everything. One day Scott Fitzgerald refereed us." Scott at that time, Callaghan said, had been completely infatuated with Hemingway, had told Callaghan that Hemingway was as good as young Stribling. Callaghan had undertaken to enlighten him, had said, "Scott, you need to understand that he is not as good as young Stribling—compared to the professional people, he and I are just clowns." Hemingway, he found, had very little science, he improvised his play. Once when Callaghan hit him in the mouth and made it bleed, Hemingway stood there and glared at him, then spat out the blood in his face. Callaghan had not known quite how to take this, whether he ought to get angry and retaliate. He asked Hemingway why he had done it. "That's what the matadors do," said Hemingway, "to show their contempt for the bull." On this occasion, Callaghan knocked him down twice. The first time he stumbled over something behind him. The second time Hemingway said bitterly, "Well, at least you didn't push me over a [something or other]!" but Scott Fitzgerald was so dumbfounded at seeing his hero knocked down that, sitting crosslegged on the floor, with his watch in his hand, he forgot to keep

time on the round and let it go on and on, with Hemingway getting the worst of it. When the contestants
realized what was happening and stopped, Hemingway
said to Scott, "OK, if you want to see me getting the shit
knocked out of me, don't do it in this way." He was furious, and they couldn't pacify him; but fortunately a
young man who had been looking on came up and said
to Hemingway, "I've been watching you and if you don't
mind, I'd like to say that the idea in boxing is to defend
yourself." Hemingway said, "Oh, is that so?" "Yes," said
the young man. "The object is to hit the other man without getting hit yourself." "Oh, that's very interesting,"
said Hemingway. "Would you like to show us your
method? Demonstrate it with *him*," nodding to Callaghan.
Callaghan and Hemingway, of course, could not be sure
what they were up against. The young man did not look
strong or tough, but Callaghan thought about Jimmy
Wilde, thin and wiry but a formidable fighter. So he
approached the young man in a gingerly way, and it was
a little time before he realized that the boy knew nothing
about boxing. When Callaghan had grasped this, he
drove the boy into a corner. Hemingway now offered to
take the boy on, and triumphed in a very spectacular way.
Much taller and with a much longer reach, he simply
stood with his left arm held out, and when the boy tried
moving around him, Hemingway would turn around with
him, still holding out his arm. The young man now admitted with candor that it was possible to look on at a
sport and think that you understood it, and it was easier
to think you knew about it than it was to try to practise
it. This incident put Hemingway in such a good humor
that he forgot about his earlier misadventures. But this
story got around in New York, and a literary columnist
ran an incorrect version of it, in which it was asserted
that Callaghan had knocked Hemingway out. Callaghan

says that he had already written to the paper to explain
that this was not the case, but he received a telegram
from Hemingway which said something like, "I learn
from the *Herald Tribune* that you knocked me out. Please
wire when and where this occurred." Hemingway also
brought pressure on Scott and bullied him into making
a statement that went so far as to falsify the incident, and
Max Perkins, I think it was, told me that, when later
Scott had somewhat got over his abject devotion to Hemingway, he confessed he was ashamed of this.

(It is so easy to discredit the pretensions of Hemingway
and to tell comic stories about him that, since his suicide,
one has to restrain oneself from overdoing this. I have just
read four stories of the war in Spain that have been published with the reprint of *The Fifth Column,* and they
are well up to the standard of his earlier stories. Hemingway was preoccupied with questions of honor, and the
fact that he was so often guilty of violating his own code
and was afterwards uncomfortable about it made him a
sort of expert on the subject. His best work will always
be read.)

August 20. Went with Otis and Fern to the Lowville
Fair in the evening. I was somehow touched and impressed. Fern, the day before, had been kicked by a cow
in the back, and she found it uncomfortable to get
around. When she had come to see me after work in the
afternoon, she had at first thought she wasn't up to going
at all, then decided she might as well. Her face looks so
heavy and plain at times, so full of warmth and charm
at others. They examined the farm machines, admiring
the biggest ones. We threw away some nickels on the
glassware table, where the coins skim right out of the
dishes, so that there is no chance of winning anything

except, as I once did, a tumbler, out of which they are not so likely to bounce. In the cattle tent, Fern patted all the cattle she liked. She gently prodded a Brown Swiss with her foot and made her get up, in order to admire her straight back and square build. At the end of the tent was an enormous black bull, for which the owner had paid $5000. She patted him on the haunch. We stopped to have hot dogs and iced tea, and then went into the grandstand to see the drum corps competition. First there was a corps from Mexico, New York, who were rather overanxious and strained; they would force themselves and hit false notes. Then a Canadian corps from Kingston—very military in khaki—no drum-majorette but a male leader with a long staff, who marched with a strong and true beat but was soldierly to the point of burlesque, jerkily sawing the air with his arms, from time to time standing his men at attention and exhibitionistically saluting to an officer, whom he proceeded to the front to meet. These were much applauded. Fern, on a narrow seat in the bleachers, had no back to lean against, so I thought we had better go. As we left, I saw the big swing that turns you upside down, slowly whirling its blunt-ended bright-lighted spokes against the dark upstate sky, and there seemed to me something grand and wild about even this transient amusement park: The fun that the people were having beneath this immense somber heaven in the mountain-horizoned countryside, a gaiety which, though hearty, was lonely, but contrasted with their rural lives. Some, they told me, went every night. Just before leaving, Fern bought some taffy—which they were making hot in the booth and which had a delicious smell—to take home to her grandchildren.

I had gone into a show of wild animals in cages. A fine horned owl—it must have been a young one, since Walter

Edmonds tells me that they may reach a wingspread of
six feet and this one was nowhere near that size: great
yellow eyes that looked as if they were made of glass. It
ruffled up, put its head down and glared when a dog
came near the cage, and when you got on one side of it,
it would turn round its head, and if you kept on around
it, it would snap its head back and keep following you
in the way that has sometimes made boys believe that it
could actually revolve its head and led them to keep on
walking around it, expecting to see it wring its own neck.
Walter told me that his guinea-fowl had begun disappearing one by one. He would find some feathers and a piece
of the windpipe. They had seen a flock of crows which
behaved as if they were after an owl. Presently he found
a nest from which a great horned owl peered down at
him. He shot it, and the mate disappeared. It kills its prey
by attacking the windpipe. He told me about another
owl, wounded, I think, in the wing, which tried to attack
the hunter, running down the snow-slope with outstretched
wings, brave as an eagle. There is something impressive
about the horned owl.—There was also a wildcat in a cage
at the fair: large paws, black hairs at the tips of its ears.
I scrutinized it for several minutes, and this seemed to
make it uneasy. Its short tail writhed—I hadn't known
how flexible and mobile this was. At last it faced me and
made as if to snarl; then, apparently realizing it was
helpless, it walked to the other end of the cage. "And you
felt embarrassed," said Walter, when I told him about
this. He was right. Rosalind, my older daughter, refused,
in a later summer, to go in with me to one of these
animal shows. There was also a red fox, curled up but
attentive to everything. I find foxes, in their sharpness and
slyness, attractive. It reminded me of the fox cub that I
tried to buy, at the end of the first war, from a Negro
soldier at Brest. He agreed at first but when I came back

to get it, he said that he had changed his mind and couldn't bring himself to part with it.

I come to feel, when I have been here for any length of time, the *limited* character of upstate New York. It does not go back very far into the past and it does not come very far forward into the present. A phase of American life is preserved here and is still flourishing; and yet there is still about the better-class life a sort of cold-storage quality. The people have been nice here and decent, more amiable and outgoing than they are in New England, serious-minded and moderately cultivated; but there is no great liveliness of interchange, no density of the "spiritual" life. Religion now hardly exists.

Walter Edmonds's pretty blue-eyed wife comes from Bangor, Maine, and says that her upstate New-York-ness is merely a kind of veneer, that she cannot remain unaware of the fact that there are other beautiful parts of the world. Walter says that he is completely unreliable about it—as, indeed, am I.—Elena still obstinately refuses to admit that it is a nice day or that the landscape or the sky is fine. One day, coming out of the Loomises', she said to me, "You see what I mean?" It turned out that she was referring to her having already said to me that you expected to breathe fresh air, and then you got the smell of cows—a novel point of view for anyone up here, for whom the smell of cows is fragrant. The children cannot help be affected by her negative attitude. Reuel looked in on a couple of square dances, went on a bicycle trip to Canada, in the course of which he had what he thought was rather a sinister encounter with an Indian on a reservation, then decided that he wanted to go back to Wellfleet. Helen, dictating a letter, wanted to say it was "very dull here"; when I remonstrated with her a little, she said, "Well, make it *dullish*."

It is true that the altitude and the breathlessness and heaviness of the mid-summer days do let Elena down and make her languid. She complains that she feels as if she could not breathe. Such weather merely makes me sleepy. She thinks, perhaps rightly, that in Wellfleet, with its sea air, I am overstimulated and that Talcottville keys me down to a point where I am steady and comfortable. She depends very much on having people like her, and now she feels that they do. The first summers that we came up here, we had given a couple of over-all parties, to which I invited everyone I knew, including all my Munn cousins. I wanted to take stock of my family and connections. On one occasion, Elena flew up from Wellfleet carrying a huge cooked salmon; on another, she made with chicken a big Russian *kulebyaka*.

This summer we had a small party to which, among others, we invited the Sharps and their daughter and her husband, the old Munns, the Loomises and Lillian Burnham, and we thought it was quite a success. These, "the family," stayed after the others had gone and sat around in the big north room. Otis and Mrs. Burnham talked about farming with feeling and expressed themselves very well. Otis quoted the rhyme:

Some folks say there ain't no Hell
They've never been farmers—how can they tell?

But then they went on to advantages that offset the hard work and constant hazards: independence, freedom from office routine. Mrs. Burnham declared that the idea of producing food gave her gratification. Even the Loomises, one feels, though they talk about selling their farm, are actually reluctant to do so. I can understand the satisfac-

Lillian Burnham, Dorothy Sharp, Huldah Loomis, Helen and Rosalind, with kittens; EW and John Gaus; Fern and Otis Munn and Jane Gaus

tion they must derive from dealing directly, in such a magnificent setting, with the animals and fields that belong to them. Otis must lie awake nights—he so often returns to the subject—thinking about the fifty thousand acres that once belonged to the Munns. He wishes he could find some defect in the titles of the present owners. He mentioned also that they had had ten thousand acres in Texas before it became a state.

Otis, when Helen Augur had asked him how he had liked my novel, *Memoirs of Hecate County,* had answered, "*When Knighthood Was in Flower* is more my style."

Elena and Helen went back September 3, and I am staying on till the 9th or 10th. I find it for awhile delightful living here by myself. I understand that it is dull for the children. At Reuel's age, although as a younger child I had been so happy here, I did not want any more to come to Talcottville at all: like him, I was meeting new people, visiting in livelier places. But now, at my present age, when my principal aim is to write, it is an ideal place to retire to. I have been sitting out on the lawn in the afternoons, giving the kittens an outing, reading a little, looking out on the country, watching the repairs on the house and enjoying the changes in the weather—some days soft, warm and dry, others on the verge of rain. I never get over feeling how curious and piquant it is to find a house so commodious and comfortable, designed with so much taste, even elegance, in the midst of what was once a wilderness and where now one looks out on a farmland that—with the blue Adirondacks in the distance—still merges with wild forests and hills. I also like having the life of the village going on around me—even when last May I was working on the front porch—though

sometimes I wish the road still ran as it originally is said
to have done just over the slope in front of the house,
where a line of trees still marks it.

A few days ago, from my bed, I looked out into a kind
of great grotto of green made by the two high elms and
watched the yellow leaves falling into it at intervals one
by one. Today (September 8th) the trees have become
so thinned that the cavern hardly exists, and in front of
the house the maple has been coming out in patches of
orange-pink that first flared and are now fading. The
lawn, which a few days ago, was cleared up by Jim
Linck, is now covered with leaves again. I should like to
stay another week, but must go back on account of Reuel,
who has to return to school on the 18th.

September 8. Last night Dorothy Sharp was showing me
Minnie Collins's collection of photographs. She passed me
a picture of the Stone House, with their furniture that is
not here any longer and the plates that I now remember
hanging on the wall, as the fashion was then, above the
big doorway in the double room. I said that I was going
to put it in my pocket. She said sharply, "I'm going to
take it myself. I have much more right to it than you." I
said that I was making a collection of pictures of the
house, and she answered, "So am I." This seemed to me
rather unlike her, but her dignity at once reasserted itself:
"Take it if you want it," she said. We put it back in the
box.—Not only did she lose her mother here at seven, but
she undoubtedly had come to feel, from her grandmother's
chagrin at not being able to buy the place and Dorothy
Mendenhall's love for it, that her family have been dis-
possessed. I am shy about talking to her of her childhood
and all that. I asked her to write me a memorandum about
her memoirs of Talcottville, and she told me the next day

that, after thinking it over, she couldn't bring herself to do it. Some of her memories were too harrowing: the night her father had come up for the 4th of July and had set off all the fireworks for his children over Sugar River. I couldn't bring myself to ask why this was harrowing, but knew that it must have been because the rest of the family had more or less ostracized him.

I have read this summer at Talcottville: the Book of Ruth in Hebrew (which sounds somewhat different than in English—the famous "whither thou goest, I will go" passage plainer and less eloquent than it does in the King James version, because the Hebrew was the language that was spoken at the time it was written whereas the language of the English translation has the poetic character of the seventeenth century); Barrett Wendell's biography of Cotton Mather (which gave me nightmares); Harriet Beecher Stowe's *Lady Byron Vindicated;* Aldous Huxley's *The Genius and the Goddess;* Peyrefitte's *Les Clés de Saint-Pierre* (which the Gallican church, I understand, paid him to write against the Roman Church as fundamentally an Italian institution—it is a snide performance, like all his books, and you can't tell how much is reliably informative and how much is malicious fiction); M. L. Clarke's *Richard Porson;* Faith Compton Mackenzie's *As Much as I Dare;* Siegfried Trebitch's *Chronicle of a Life* (mainly the parts about Shaw); Chapman-Huston's *Bavarian Fantasy* (skimmed—about Mad Ludwig); Turgenev's *Nest of Gentlefolk;* Gorky's *Lower Depths;* went through *Brokenburn* and *Heroines of Dixie* for my chapter on the Southern ladies; went through new books and papers on the Dead Sea scrolls; read *The Abominable Snowman,* by Ralph Izzard; *The Loved and the Lost,* by Morley Callaghan (he had given us this when we saw him in

Toronto—Elena read it first and thought that I ought to read it: this was my first discovery of Callaghan); Maxim Litvinov's *Notes for a Journal*; Zhitova's *The Turgenev Family* (one didn't know then that she was actually Turgenev's half-sister, the illegitimate daughter of Turgenev's mother and the Dr. Behrs who was Tolstoy's father-in-law).

I read Helen *Juan and Juanita,* an old serial in *St. Nicholas* of 1887, which I had loved to have read to me at the Collinses'. Helen greatly enjoyed it, too. We have read to her, also, the volume of Andersen's Fairy Tales, which Aunt Laura used to read to me under the big tree in the field opposite the Collins house.

XI

1956.

May 21. Strange to see the landscape so denuded. The view clear to Sugar River and even to the barns on the other side; the feather-duster elms only broomsticks beginning to fledge yellowish leaves. I found a little green and brown bird, not yet quite able to fly, hopping across the pavement; and a humming bird who came to the bushes in front must have got very slim pickings. It was so cold in my big room this morning that I took my card table out on the porch, where it was comfortably warm in the sun, and wrote on *A Piece of My Mind* with the birds and the village people going about their business around me—we say hello and comment on the weather—and the meadow in front of the house and the newly ploughed patch for a garden giving me the piquant sensation—which I always enjoy so much up here—of living elegantly on a moderate eminence among the fields and the forests. Orioles and red-wing blackbirds. Then, about noon, it clouded over, grew chill, and I came back in, built a fire and, simultaneously, made myself some soup; and went on writing all afternoon. Then it grew warm again, as I found when I went outside. It excites me to see this country—I have never before been here at this time of year—in transition from its long naked coldness of winter to the rich and bright foliage of summer. The few buildings—Carrie Trennam's house and mine—seem more solitary, sprinkled on the hills. How the snow and winter winds must sweep them!

The house seems all mine now—I know it well and simply come in and find everything in its place. In this big room, when I sat yesterday in front of the fire, the memory of how, in the evenings, I used to sit here with my mother, seems already of something very far in the past. I no longer have any sad or gloomy feeling about the room in which Cousin Bessie died and in which my father slept just before he went back to Red Bank to die. I do, however, seem to myself here a little more than elsewhere like Great-Grandfather Baker—which, in some way, I rather enjoy. Everybody so much more good-natured, and I feel so much more at home with them, than with those closed-in New Englanders of Wellfleet. A square bed of daffodils and narcissi—somewhat clogged with dead leaves—behind the house, that I had never seen blooming before. Very quiet now, no traffic, children all at school. Also, easier to get people to do things before they begin their haying. Laurence Kraeger—whose brown-and-white bitch is terribly jealous of the tractor and won't let anybody go near it—is clearing out the lot across the road—which will please Dorothy Mendenhall—she was complaining that the view was obscured—and Carrie Trennam on account of the snakes there (she calls them adders and insists on killing them, though I afterwards learned that the snakes here are harmless except for a very rare rattler). She is planting her own showy garden and has kindly put flowers in the stone bowls and boxes that line my stone porch. Billy Crofoot, after school and on holidays, comes to pick up and mow my lawn. I like to feel this activity around me, to visit the people from time to time. I also like the companionship of the birds: since the trees are so leafless now, one can see exactly what they are doing. There is an oriole's gray baglike nest hanging on one of the branches just in front of the porch. The male has real style and a smart way of flying—very sure twinkling movements of the wings. He will sit on a twig making a chirring sound; then he will visit the nest and give cooing noises that sound full of affection. But there is also a much less attractive bird—I don't know whether a starling or a grackle, who has a nest in a hole in the wall of the house. I see him bringing large bugs to his brood. He makes a harsh buzzing noise, and his way of flying is vulgar compared to the orioles.

Torrential rains with thunder at night. A night and day, with wind, rain and cold, seemed almost exactly like autumn.—One feature of the climate up here is the rapidity with which it changes: it may go through several phases in a day.

Albert Grubel from across the street, a retired German farmer who drives me to town, said "I guess there'll be quite a few killed tomorrow!" Tomorrow was Memorial Day. He often talks about people's accidents, and they do have some very bad ones up here.

June 7. I have never before seen the deep-purple lilac bush blooming at the northeast corner. It reaches to my bedroom window.

Reading this summer:

Turgenev—*The Inn*

Jean Genet—*Pompes Funèbres,* a work of genius, much better than Sartre; but though Genet makes homosexuality more attractive than either Proust or Gide, to read

about it at length gives an impression of futility and silli-
ness—which, as in this case, they try to offset by deliberate
brutality and dirtiness.

Mirsky—*A History of Russia* (77 pages)

Norman Douglas—*Alone*. This is the least attractive of
those of his travel books I have read. He is usually agreeable enough to read, but I don't think there is much in
him. His science is that of a dilettante; and he does not
have any idea of what is going on in the modern world.
Too much of this book is complaint about not being able
to get good wine or the right kind of macaroni. He doesn't
even care much about literature—was not, I should say,
very widely read. How could he have spent some time in
the Embassy in Russia and learned Russian as well as he
apparently did without, so far as one can tell, having read
Russian literature? I have yet to find a single reference
to any Russian writer. As for his learning, he has many
odds and ends of out-of-the-way information. The problems of archaeology that he investigates are mainly trivial.
Nor does he ever make his personal life interesting. Except in one instance in his book about his accumulation
of calling cards, any incident concerned with his personal
relations is made to take place offstage. He was obviously
very narcissistic, adored himself as a boy—see the picture
of him looking at his youthful bust—and it must have
been himself as a youth that made him admire his boy
friends. He had had money and no parents to advise him
or pull him up, and he was totally independent. His
books are full of petty sadisms, especially in regard to
animals. He has tried to offset this tendency occasionally
by making a show of kindness, as in the pamphlet in
which he explained how much more than D. H. Lawrence he had been humane in his dealings with Maurice
Magnus. Though Douglas's admirers and sometimes himself like to emphasize his masculinity, there is something

about him rather old womanish. He is always fussing about something. He is always accusing people of being disagreeable, yet he does not give the impression of being particularly agreeable himself. What is most admirable about him is that he is not afraid to be himself.

Donald Elder's biography of Ring Lardner. It is depressing to read about Lardner—so unsatisfied as a writer and actually so inadequately equipped. It is the satirical and fantastic side that is original and diverting; but even his queer imagination is rather two-dimensional, as his physical appearance seemed incomplete, as if his half Indianlike profile had been cut out of cardboard. A good deal of life he didn't understand—politics, etc. Was he really interested in anything? Not baseball or any other sport. He had begun by writing about baseball, but the baseball players in his stories are either neurotics or idiots. I remember one day at his house—I had gone to visit the Fitzgeralds—when he read out to us the rules of the golf club in such a way as to make them, in their formal solemnity, seem absolutely ridiculous. Yet part of him was perfectly banal. He made a determined effort to live up to his suburban obligations to his family and the life he had chosen, or rather perhaps half fallen into. But this bored him, and he had no real aspiration to do anything different from this. When Scott persuaded Ring to let him get together a book of short stories, he turned out to have no copies of these, and Scott had to look them up in magazines.

Charles Angoff—*H. L. Mencken.* It gives you all that was coarsest and most brutal in Mencken. Angoff at one time worked with him in the *American Mercury* office, and Mencken, conscious no doubt of the young man's disapproval, tried to shock him and pull his leg. Though Angoff does write about Mencken with a certain amount of admiration, the effect is very much like J.-J. Brousson's memoirs of Anatole France. Such older men have a way of playing up to their young secretaries by horrifying them and boasting of their sexual exploits. On the other hand, it is not much to the credit of either Brousson or Angoff that he elicited from the Master only such low-grade observations. Anatole France sounds entirely different when he is talking to Ségur, for example; and Ruth Jencks, who saw Mencken often—her father, Raymond Pearl of Johns Hopkins, was a close friend of his—found Angoff's book quite objectionable. She had never seen that side of Mencken. You had quite a different impression of him, she says, if you ever saw him playing Beethoven at their Sunday evening concerts. He would shout with exultation when they had finished a symphony. So Angoff does admit that he was moved when Mencken talked about Schubert.

I felt, after reading this book and Don Elder's book about Lardner, that the twenties had been a squalid period. Ruth Jencks agreed with me about this. She said that she had reacted against her parents—both from New England—with their newly liberated ideas, had felt that these had no longer any real moral basis. At the parties in Baltimore then, she said, that she used to find herself, after the first few minutes, talking most of the time to Mencken's wife. They would be the only people who were still making sense.

Cabell—*There Were Two Pirates* and *The Devil's Own Dear Son*. Not bad, but not of his best. The too familiar Cabell themes: the bad man who accepts conformity, settles down to a comfortable unexciting marriage; the recurring phenomenon of the split personality, with the real half leading a commonplace life while the other half lives in a dream.

Went through *The Meaning of the Dead Sea Scrolls*,

by A. Powell Davies (the Unitarians are thoroughly enjoying this controversy), and *The Qumrân Community*,
by Charles T. Fritsch, under whom I studied beginner's
Hebrew at Princeton; *Dublin's Joyce, by Hugh Kenner*,
and *Joyce*, by Marvin Magalaner and Richard M. Kain,
on which I did *New Yorker* notes.

George Scott—*Time and Place*. Read a good deal of
this without expecting to when I picked it up—the point
of view of a lower middle-class Englishman, very young
at the time of the war, given a taste of Oxford, where he
was partly made to feel himself an outsider but got something from David Cecil; now regards himself as a rebel
but tried to go along with the Tories till he found they
were doing nothing more serious than attempting to perpetuate the old order. He corresponds in some ways to
Kingsley Amis, whose horseplay, however, he rather
deplores.

Angus Wilson—*Anglo-Saxon Attitudes*. His best book
up to date; but I don't quite believe in his middle-aged
heroes who get themselves muddled up and then make a
moral effort to straighten themselves out. The characters
seem more plausibly human and more subtly imagined
psychologically in the first part of this book than in
Hemlock and After; but later—when the Dance of Death
begins—the catastrophes and the nasty scenes slip back
into his purely satirical vein, which tends to be somewhat
fantastic, and the characters no longer seem real. (He
later wrote much better books. *The Middle Age of Mrs.
Eliot* is too long and a bore, but *The Old Men at the
Zoo, Late Call* and *No Laughing Matter* are excellent.)

Anthony Powell—*A Question of Upbringing, A Buyer's
Market* and *The Acceptance World*. The series which
he calls *The Music of Time* is a kind of watered-down
British Proust. The Proustian observations on human life

anthony Powell

are largely unsuccessful: the Latin of Proust's style in French sounds rather pompous in English, and Powell is not profound or poetic. These books are full of bad writing, with instances of even bad grammar. What is good in them is the lightweight comedy that one finds in his earlier novels. One is astonished by the statements on one jacket—by Betjeman, Pritchett and Elizabeth Bowen—which talk about the "beauty" of these books and the excellence of Powell's writing. (I nevertheless keep on reading this series—though I am usually unable to remember the characters, with the exception of Widmerpool, from one volume to another.)

Compton Mackenzie—*Thin Ice*, a curious and rather unsuccessful book. He has attacked the subject of the pederast more seriously than in *Vestal Fires*; but it is hard to know what his intention is. Is this a parable of the collapse of imperialism or a tract against the homosexuality laws? I imagine that the idea is that imperialism, like buggery, is a sterile assertion of power, uncomfortable for the object. The friend who is telling the story, adoring and apprehensive—though he believes himself to be a liberal—is the passive obverse of the pederast.

I have been reading a few too many more or less light British novels lately—a holiday after finishing *A Piece of My Mind*. They are beginning to blur in my memory: elderly pederasts in difficulties, careerists who ring false, nobility and gentry who are losing their grip, discontented and rather fast or bitchy wives, lower class pansies and impudent spivs.

H.L. Mencken—*Minority Report*. I have been trying to read this posthumous book of notes, but I doubt whether I'll ever get through it. Some of the paragraphs are effective: characteristically clear and crackling; but his ideas, stated baldly, are very often quite stupid. It is only when he embroiders them, sets them to music, that, as Cabell says, one no more thinks to ask whether what he says is true than one asks whether a symphony is true.

I read Kingsley's *Water Babies* to Helen. It made upon me very much the same impression that it did when it was read to me in my childhood. The satire on the professor—which is both Rabelaisian and preachy—is as unassimilable to grown-ups as to children. The moralistic fairies that represent virtue, with their obvious priggish names, are very annoying, too. The escape of the chimney-sweep and his adventures with the water creatures are charming. These parts are a pleasure to read aloud, on account of the sound English rhythm and the vocabulary made up almost exclusively of Anglo-Saxon words— no Latin derivatives except such simple words as *interest*. Kingsley's Victorian moralizing prevents the book from belonging to the same class as Carroll and Lear.

John Allegro—*The Dead Sea Scrolls*. So far the best book on the subject in English. I am going to review it for the B.B.C. He needs to be defended against what he calls the Establishment. (I afterwards had doubts about him, and the Establishment in connection with him was not always wrong.)

Jean Genet—*Querelle de Brest*. Perhaps the best of his books that I have read. Masterly picture of Brest: sailors, doctors, shipyard workers. An elderly woman, as in *Pompes Funèbres*, whom he likes to make more or less ridiculous. In *Notre Dame des Fleurs*, you have the feminine homos, *les tantes*; here Querelle is supposed to be ultra-masculine: well-muscled, audacious and hard; he has committed a series of murders. The people he kills are invariably weaklings—the young sailor, the Armenian pansy—they seem to represent his own passive nature that comes out, in spite of himself, in the episodes with the policeman and the brothel keeper. As usual, the theme of betrayal—the point of this evidently is that it makes the heroes feel more alone, it is only in stripped solitude that they feel their strength. This is one of the aspects of Genet that make it possible to compare him, as Sartre does, to certain of the Christian saints: one has to denude oneself of all attachments. The episode of Gil being hidden away in the abandoned *bagne* is very well done. It has a curious resemblance to the final episode of *Huckleberry Finn*—Tom Sawyer and Huck hiding and rescuing Nigger Jim. But Querelle, after going to a lot of trouble to enable Gil to escape, becomes enamored of the policeman and betrays him to the law. This side of Genet is rather hard to stomach.

Turgenev—*Two Friends*. I find curious the distaste of a Russian friend of ours for what she calls Turgenev's stories of "provincial boys and girls in white organdie." This one at the beginning is perhaps a little dull when you have read a good many others; but I do not think that our friend has very much real literary sense. I have been reading Turgenev straight through and, though I break off from time to time, have never lost my appetite for him. She evidently does not taste his quality, and she says that his criticisms of Russia are an old story to her. The truth is that people like her and like some other of our old-regime friends, not much enjoying literature for itself, do not want to read about old Russia. They seem hardly to have read Turgenev or Chekhov. I think they feel that Chekhov is too lower class, and sometimes they do not know that he was anything but the popular humorist who wrote *A Horsy Name*—which, on account of the difficulty of translating its collection of possible horsy names for the doctor whose name cannot be remembered, is entirely unknown in English. What they like best is *War and Peace*, realistically heroic and aristocratic.

They rarely read *Resurrection,* which gives such a depressing picture of the Russia of the Tsar in Tolstoy's era.

We sailed on July 20 for Europe, and I left Talcottville on the 17th.

Before Elena left, her old German uncle Walther called her up to say that Light Ginger (one of the kittens) had little ulcers all over her belly. When she got back to Wellfleet, she learned that he had taken her to a vet, who explained that the ulcers were simply her teats.

The day before I leave: the morning is simply marvelous, with its light and its cool live air. Walking out on the road was to find oneself in an element almost like water flowing over the trees and the hills. Little clouds are drifting with it above the distant mountains.

Sorry to leave the old house after this satisfying period of reading and writing—when I have got it at last into such good shape after its having been shut up for so long a time.

XII

1957

Arrived here May 17 after my usual stopovers in Boston and Northampton. Bill Peck from Wellfleet drove me up. The first day the new state highway had been opened, and we had the first accident on it. Our right front tire blew out, and Bill steered the car to the side of the road, where, fortunately, it stuck in the soft shoulder and did not go into the ditch. Three trucks stopped, one after the other: the first pulled us out with a chain, and the men from one of the others stepped in and energetically changed the tire, addressing Bill Peck as "Pop." He and I both tried to give them money, but none of them would take it. They said that we might help *them* out some day. I told Dan Aaron at Northampton about this, and he made the same sort of comment that I was about to make: that that was the kind of thing that made one feel better about America. I have been so depressed lately about the country that I forget that such friendliness exists.

It was a little less exciting than usual to come back to Talcottville this year. Every year the place is more familiar, and the arrangements I have made are more comfortable. It reminds me less of the past—I am not

at all haunted as I was before. Only when I saw the
narcissus and the little white bells in the bed by the front
door did I feel it was touching and queer that these
flowers of Aunt Lin's should persist, should have gone
on blooming among the weeds and the seedlings from the
trees—which I thoroughly cleared out last year—for years
when there was no one here, and I had a little twinge of
sadness when I found that nothing had come of the
bittersweet that—in order to replace Aunt Lin's—I had
planted by the front porch. But I now have everything
I need; I simply move in and start functioning. Everything is ready to my hand, and I fall into my old routine.

The first two days were cold and rainy. It poured more
or less steadily for twenty-four hours. I burned quantities
of wood in the fireplace. Then the morning of the 21st,
I was wakened by the burst of white radiance beyond my
bedroom window, somewhat milky in the moist air. Still
cold in the house, but beautiful outside. In the afternoon,
I had Albert Grubel, of whom I have spoken, one of the
old German inhabitants of Talcottville, drive me to the
edge of the woods, where the road goes in along Dry
Sugar River, the great picnic ground of our childhood,
where the river disappears between the tablelike gray
blocks of its bed. I remember my father, on one of these
occasions, unexpectedly saying to me—it was uncharacter-
istic of him—"I'm glad to see you children so happy." I
found it far from dry where we usually go in to this bed
from the dirt road that is still passable through the wood.
There is a torrent so deep when it comes down from the
rocks that I could not touch the bottom with my stick. I
had to cross at a lower point. Beer cans and other remnants, which show that the young people from Boonville still sometimes picnic there. No very interesting
flowers: yellow violets and the first forget-me-nots, some

wild phlox, less purple than blue and with bigger freeer
flowers than the garden kind; most showy were the coarse
marsh marigolds. The most brilliant thing I saw was a
bright red bird with a black tail and black wings, aware
of its beauty, I thought, and so little fearful of men that
it allowed me to come quite close to it. I find that this
must have been a scarlet tanager.

May 22 not so cold, but cloudy—in the afternoon, it
rained again. When the night before I was going with the
Munns to the movies, Fern had said that there were
"mare's tails" in the sky.

May 24. I was interrupted in writing this, the day before yesterday, by the arrival of Gertrude Loomis. She
had just been to the funeral of Tharett Best's mother,
who was ninety-one when she died, one of those old-
fashioned New York ladies, who lived in state in the
family house, crowded with nineteenth-century furniture,
bric-à-brac, cut glass and the memorials of Tharett's years
at Princeton: class photographs and one of those huge
framed Princeton tigers that they used to sell to fresh-
men; it hangs now in their dining room. I said to Gertrude, "Huldah isn't with you?," and she explained that
she would have to go back right away and release Huldah
from her looking after Florence. They take turns with
their failing sister. Huldah is the master mind of the
family, and Gertrude is so used to depending on her and
having her take the initiative and do all the talking
to people that one rarely sees her alone. I made her come
in for a drink. They have had a hard winter with Florence, who is the oldest of them, seventy-four. She has
hardening of the arteries of the brain and has gradually
been becoming more deranged. They have to dress her

and feed her, and sometimes she tears off her clothes. She likes to have Huldah read to her and is likely to recite German rhymes—they are the children of a German-Swiss doctor, who used to live in Constableville. They don't want to send her to a state hospital, but she is wearing them down at home.

The trees, when I first arrived, had little feathery stitchings of leaves, like the backgrounds of Chagall's etchings. Since the rains they have been rapidly enriched, and the ferns in front of the house have grown from little fringes to large fronds. The orioles seem to be building somewhere in back of the house instead of in the tree in front. I watch them while lying in the bathtub. The grackle, thank goodness, is baffled. I had the crack on the balcony filled up with concrete, so it is now impossible for him to make a mess on the porch.

Albert Grubel continues to regale me, on almost every trip to town, with his usual gruesome stories. A barn burned down in Constableville, and all the cattle were burned to death. They didn't get them out because they didn't know the fire had started. "There they was layin' there. I didn't go up to see 'em." A boy had been drowned in one of the lakes. A doctor in the Osceola hospital had gone out on a fishing trip—some place he had often fished—and never came back. They'd sent out bloodhounds to find him.

Moments when the taste of cold air and water brings me back to the Collinses' in my childhood. It was pleasant lying in bed last night under that old distinguished pink-and-white checkerboard quilt. The weather is not unlike autumn and reminds me of lying in bed in my youth and

reading Thomas Hardy's novels and the old oil-lamps at
the Collinses', in which the fat moths would get burned.

All the Currier and Ives prints I have collected in
Helen's room, together with Aunt Laura's Pandora,
which I used to see in Lakewood, and my mother's childhood picture, to which she was much attached, of the
shaggy mother dog teaching her puppies to catch rats.

Elena gave me a diamond-point pencil for Christmas,
something I have long wanted, and I have been having
my poet friends write verses with it on the panes of glass,
sometimes directly on the windows here, sometimes on
panes that I carry around. Those on the third floor, which
look out on the sky and the tops of the trees, all deal with
lofty missions or mythologies or the elements: by Saint-
John Perse (Aléxis Léger) some lines from his *Vents*—

> C'étaient de très grands vents
> Sur toutes faces de ce monde

—his script is bold, clear and elegant, perfect for writing
on glass; by Charley Walker, the well-known lines from
Prometheus—in Greek and in his translation—about the
winds and the waves and the innumerable laughter of
the sea; a poem by Phito Thoby-Marcelin about a Haitian
goddess:

> Où est Caonabo?
> Caonabo n'est plus
> Qu'au sein d'une pensée . . .

a passage from Isaiah in Hebrew (6.8.) by Isaiah Berlin:
"And I heard the voice of the Lord, saying, Whom shall
I send, and who will go for us? Then said I, Here am I;
send me." (When he wrote this, he insisted that it was

not at all his idea about himself; but I believe that it has been, a little.) On the second floor, passages about dreaming and sleep: John Wain, who came to see us here, in the bathroom, on the window, so I can read it from the tub, though it occurred to me afterwards that I should have had him inscribe it on the mirror:

> It tells you what you do but never why,
> Your image in the glass that watches you:
> You cannot catch it napping if you try. . . .

Edwin Muir, in the little bedroom, though too high so that it is hidden by the shade, a translation from Hölderlin about a stag with agate eyes; Stephen Spender, on the window at the top of the stairs, where it comes out beautifully, shining, in the late afternoon light—I won't allow curtains to be hung over it: "I think continually of those who were truly great". . . ; Louise Bogan in Helen's bedroom: "The landscape where I lie". . . ; Wystan Auden in the back bedroom:

> Make this night loveable
> Moon, with eye single
> Looking down from up there
> Bless me, One especial
> And friends everywhere. . . .

On the door to the balcony Vladimir Nabokov's:

> бывают ночи только лягу
> в Россию поплывет кровать....

all in the old spelling. I have not worked out for the first floor a satisfactory principle of selection, and there are not so many inscriptions as elsewhere. Alfred Bellinger and Stephen Spender composed for it special quatrains;

Dorothy Parker, so far advanced in her afternoon drinking that I was surprised she was willing to do it at all,
inscribed a rather undulant version of what she says is
the only poem of hers she cares for:

> Whose love is given overwell
> Shall look on Helen's face in hell,
> Whilst they whose love is thin and wise
> May view John Knox in paradise.

Driving me to Utica, George Munn told me about the
pet fox they had had. One of his brothers had seen a fox
in the pasture and had thrown a rock at it. The fox had
dropped something from her jaws, which turned out to
be a baby cub, with its eyes not yet open. He took it
home, and they fed it with a medicine dropper. It grew
up as tame as a dog—would sleep curled up in a box
or jump into their laps and curl up. It wandered about
freely but would always come back to the house to be
fed. Their dogs paid no special attention to it. It proved
to be very playful. They taught it to sit up and beg, to
retrieve a ball that they threw on the lawn and to pull up
a handkerchief they had buried. It would seize a hand in
its teeth and pretend to bite, like a puppy. It differed
from wild foxes in two respects: it did not have a rank
smell because it did not live in a den, and it did not bark,
no doubt because it had never heard a fox bark—the only
sound it ever made was a little growl. It sometimes went
out fox-hunting with them, as if it had been a dog. It
stayed with them three years, but eventually went away
and never came back. It must have met another fox.

I had not realized how serious Fern's accident had been.
A man had come out of a driveway without blowing his
horn, and to avoid a collision she had swerved aside and

run into the railing along the road. She had been thrown right through the windshield and landed about twelve feet away from the car. She was horribly cut below the knee, and her back was also cut. She was in the hospital a week. The man had driven quickly away, and the State Troopers had not been able to find him.

Nostalgic since last summer for London and Paris. The point is that—except for Talcottville—it is only in London and Paris that I can find, more or less unchanged, the things that I knew in my youth. In New York, there is hardly a single house left that I went to in my college days, and in those days I did not know Boston. Of course, what is happening now in Paris and London is quite different from what was happening when I first used to go to Europe; but the streets and the buildings and the old institutions are for the most part still in their places, and I haven't stayed long enough lately to be bothered by the social changes, the political atmosphere, etc. I revisited the scenes of my boyhood in England, of the war years in the army in France. I am beginning to feel again about Paris the truth of all the clichés that, since my Francophile phase, have annoyed me: "gracious living," "respect for literature," etc. Today it still seems to me quite wonderful that there should be a rue Huysmans— he is an old favorite of mine—and I reflect that the effort to get Washington Place renamed for Henry James, who was born there, met with no success whatever. The places in which I feel most at home—since I am always somewhat at odds with Princeton—are thus Talcottville, London and Paris.

Visit to Ithaca, May 25-28. George Munn, Otis's son, drove me. He did not bring a coat and came to dinner at the Nabokovs' in one of those floating fancy shirts he

wears, which caused Volodya to tell him that he looked
like a tropical fish. He does not know what to say, so
doesn't speak until spoken to, but has dignity and is not
embarrassed, runs true to the old tradition. I thought that
George would be bored by the literary and learned conversations, but he always appeared to be interested, and
afterwards told his mother that the thing he got the most
kick out of was an animated argument between Volodya
and me—which had something of the rhythm of a tennis
match (Volodya is apparently good at tennis) and almost
became heated—about Russian and English versification.
We have been having this out for years. Volodya's in-
sistent idea that Russian and English verse are basically
the same is, actually, I have become convinced, a part of
his inheritance from his father, a leader of the Kadets in
the Duma and a champion of a constitutional monarchy
for Russia after the British model, a belief that these two
so dissimilar countries are, or ought to be, closely associated. In the middle of the seventeenth century, the
Russians wrote syllabic verse—that is: a line had a certain
number of syllables; but by the middle of the eighteenth
century, they were writing accentual verse—that is, verse
in which the formal unit was not the syllable but the foot,
the iambus or trochee or whatever being constituted of
alternating stressed and unstressed syllables. But the
spoken language of Russia did not lend itself to the system
of stresses of German and English poetry. It was made up of
swooping and slithering runs punctuated by emphasized
main stresses. Thus an attempt to impose on it the western
rhythms results in, on the one hand, keeping to regular
iambics or whatever in a way that English poetry, with
its many substitutions of trochees for iambs, etc., avoids
the monotony of doing, and, on the other hand, achieving
its variety by juggling these main stresses. There is, in
this versification, a great variety of effect in Pushkin but

when one comes to look at the line, one sees that he hardly ever resorts to substituting one kind of foot for another. Volodya attempts to reject the whole idea of the metrical substitution which is so important in Shakespeare and Milton, and so denies that the "Never, never, never, never, never" of *King Lear* is a line in iambic pentameter entirely made up of trochees and asserts that these obvious trochees should somehow be pronounced as iambs, or else that it is a line of prose. He seems to think it is meant as a reproach to Pushkin to say that, from the point of view of English metrics, his verse is less flexible than Shakespeare's, and even declares that it is more so. George Munn was also very much interested in Nabokov's stories about the animals he had seen in the West. In Montana, he had looked down from above on some kind of long creature with claws that he thought could not be a bear, and he says that when he asked the zoölogists about it, they immediately changed the subject. He came to the conclusion that it was something that they had actually been made aware of but that they did not want to talk about yet. His idea is that it may have been such a giant sloth as has left its prehistoric remains in, for example, the caves of Las Vegas. George said that there are still some black bears, a species quite different from the brown kind, back in the wooded region of Highmarket. There are, he said, lots of porcupines, which are hard to kill—I didn't know we had them there. Also, lately, timber wolves. The state zoölogists have coined the word *coydogs;* these are supposed to be the hybrids produced by the mixing of wild dogs with a load of coyotes intended for an eastern zoo which had escaped from a railroad train; but this does not seem to me plausible. A large skin exhibited in a Boonville shop window, at the time of the Boonville centennial, was labelled "Timber Wolf."

At Monday evening supper, George appeared in a good

heavy brown shirt. Jason Epstein was there, having come
to negotiate about publishing *Lolita,* and a German professor who teaches French and is going from Cornell to
Princeton. I hope I did not freeze his blood, which had
apparently already been a little chilled, by telling him
what to expect in the way of provincial gentility at
Princeton. Volodya was playing the host with a good
humor, even joviality, which I had never seen him
display before and which I believe is rather alien to him.
The success of *Pnin* and the acclaim of *Lolita,* with the
fuss about its suppression in Paris, have had upon him a
stimulating effect. With no necktie and his hair *ébouriffé,*
consuming his little glasses of "faculty" port and sherry
(as Frohock at Harvard calls them), he was genial with
everybody and seemed full of high spirits. But when I
saw him the next day after supervising his two-hour
examination—at which Vera, of course, had helped him,
he was fatigued, rather depressed and irritable. He said
that Roman Jacobson, the philologist, who had just visited
Russia, had been trying to induce him to go back and
lecture; but that he would never go back to Russia, that
his disgust at what had been happening there had become
for him an obsession. He is undoubtedly overworked here,
with his academic duties and writing his books. Just now
he has a hundred and fifty papers to correct. That night
his nerves were still on edge but he exhilarated himself
with drinks—in which, in spite of my gout, I joined him—
and was at first amusing and charming, then relapsed into
his semi-humorous, semi-disagreeable mood, when he is
always contradicting and always trying to score, though
his statements may be quite absurd—as when he asserts,
on no evidence whatever and contrary to the well-known
facts, that Mérimée knew no Russian and that Turgenev
knew only enough English to enable him to read a newspaper. He denies that Russians deserve their reputation of

being remarkably good linguists and says of every Russian who speaks good English that he or she had had the advantage of a governess or a tutor—though I met in the Soviet Union a number of young Russians who had learned to speak excellent English without ever having been out of Russia. These false ideas, of course, are prompted by his compulsion to think of himself as the only writer in history who has been equally proficient in Russian, English and French, and he is always hopping people, with accents of outrage, for the pettiest kind of mistakes such as Steegmuller's *verre à vin* translated as if it were *verre de vin*—when he himself occasionally makes mistakes in English and French and is even in error about Russian. He and Vera would not believe me two summers ago, when I told them that *fastidieux* in French meant *tiresome* and not *fastidious,* and Volodya declared with emphasis—contrary to the authority of Dahl, the great Russian lexicographer—that *samodur* had anything in common with the root of *durak.* He tried to tell me just now that *nihilist* in English was pronounced *neehilist.* It is, of course, very difficult for him to function as resourcefully as he does between two such different languages, and the task is made even more difficult by the differences between English and American English.

Vera always sides with Volodya, and one seems to feel her bristling with hostility if, in her presence, one argues with him. She had revived our discussion of metrics by inquiring, with a certain deadliness, whether it wasn't true that I had said that *Evgeni Onegin* was written in syllabic verse, and when I answered that this was absurd, she seemed to intimate that they had letters of mine which could prove the untruth of this disclaimer. When I attacked the subject of controversy from some angle—such as Greek and Latin—about which Volodya knows nothing, he assumes an ironical expression. They had put me up at a kind of club. I had brought Volodya *Histoire d'O,* that highly sophisticated and amusing pornographic work, and in return he sent me in my quarters a collection of French and Italian poems of a more or less licentious character, which I think he had been consulting in connection with his translation of Pushkin. I had a very bad attack of gout and had to sit with my foot up, and even during meals had to eat away from the table. I think it irked Vera a little to have to serve me thus. She so concentrates on Volodya that she grudges special attention to anyone else, and she does not like my bringing him pornographic books and, as I once did, a magnum of champagne, which we merrily consumed on the porch. The next morning after the gout-harried dinner, when I was leaving and he came out to say goodby, I congratulated him on his appearance after his bath. He leaned into the car and murmured, burlesquing a feature of *Histoire d'O,* *"Je mettais du rouge sur les lèvres de mon ventre."* Vera had just asked me, "Did he give you back that little horror?" She had evidently looked into it. When she had found us talking about it, she said with disgust that we had been giggling like schoolboys. In the book, there is inserted a more or less realistic picture of a Russian family in exile living in Paris which reminded me of Elena's relatives. I asked Volodya whether it seemed to him that there was something a little queer about the French, and suggested that the book might have been written by a Russian. He answered, "A Pole, perhaps."

I always enjoy seeing them—what we have are really intellectual romps, sometimes accompanied by mauling—but I am always afterwards left with a somewhat uncomfortable impression. The element in his work that I find repellent is his addiction to *Schadenfreude.* Everybody

is always being humiliated. He himself, since he left
Russia and as a result of the assassination of his father,
must have suffered a good deal of humiliation and
suffered it more acutely because there is something in
him of the arrogance of the rich young man. As the son
of a liberal who defied the Tsar, he has not really been
accepted by the old-line and strictly illiberal nobility.
He has now at least his characters at his mercy and at
the same time subjects them to torments and identifies
himself with them. And yet he is in many ways an admirable person, a strong character, a terrific worker, unwaver-
ing in his devotion to his family, with a rigor in his devotion to his art which has something in common with
Joyce's—Joyce is one of his few genuine admirations. The
miseries, horrors and handicaps that he has had to con-
front in his exile would have degraded or broken many,
but these have been overcome by his fortitude and his
talent.

Morris Bishop of the French Department here, who, I
suppose, discovered Nabokov through his contributions
to the *New Yorker,* for which they both write, and arranged to have him come to Cornell, tells me that the
pressure to publish at Harvard is at the present time
overwhelming. That is the reason why the people there
are plugging their books so hard, and I suppose that I
was unconsciously responding to this pressure when I
would shut myself up in the Widener library and work,
almost with no pause, for six or seven hours. Since I
have been up here, I have done nothing but write this
journal, correct proof on the Turgenev essay and write a
letter to the Boonville *Herald* protesting against the dis-
continuance, proposed by the local merchants, who do not
want to have their shoppers diverted, of the band concerts
on Saturday nights. And I believe I have been let down

this spring by not being able to afford to make any more improvements in the Stone House.

Visit to Mrs. Burnham on June 22, when I got back after an absence. She was all alone in the house and lying on her back in a little bed in the dining room. She had had a bad fall when she went out one day to feed robins, and then had had another when she tried to walk around the house before she was ready to. She could hardly move her left arm. We spoke of the Sharps' accident, Dorothy Mendenhall's fall and the Loomises. "Well, Edmund," she said, with a sweet humorous look, "I guess all our good times"—and paused. I asked her what she had been going to say. "I guess all our good times together are spoiled."

Beverly turned up looking rather badly and more nervous, I thought, than ever. (She was the young niece of Mabel Hutchins. Both worked for us.) She couldn't get married, she said, before she had paid for her car. She only saw her fiancé once a week at weekends. Her teeth were in bad shape, one of them ached terribly. She would do as much work as she could for me so that she could make some money to pay the dentist, though most evenings she was tied up at the grocery store where she has a regular job. The second time that she came, I saw that her jaw was swollen and urged her to go to the dentist right away; but the next day, when I asked her about it, she said she had to go to the beauty shop in preparation for the 4th of July. It seems that her father deserted her mother about six months ago and has gone to live in Utica with a woman—the wife of a fellow factory worker—who has deserted a wife and eight children. Elena and I had been struck by the appearance they had given of a happy family: they played various musical instruments together and seemed fond of one another. The parents had been married twenty-three years. The other woman was not attractive but she had run away with men before, and Beverly had been hoping that she might go back to her family; but her husband now said he had divorced her. One of the children he had sent to a grandmother or aunt, and he had a niece come in to live with him to look after the youngest children, but this niece was out on the town a lot. All this had shocked and saddened Beverly. Her mother had decided, she said, that they could not go on living in their house; Beverly's father now sent them only twenty-five dollars a week. The grown-up children who were not married would marry the people they were engaged to, and Beverly's mother would take the little boy, who was twelve, and go to live somewhere in rooms. The next time Beverly came here, she said that her father, very drunk and accompanied by his girlfriend, had come to the house and made them a scene. He told his wife that he had never loved her and that he "hated all of us," but he tried to take the little boy away with him. They didn't know what to make of him—the mother thought he'd gone crazy. Beverly is getting worn out and bored with her work in the veneer factory, for which she has to get up at 5:30—though last year she was enthusiastic about it.

Margaret De Silver and Dawn Powell came up to see me—June 28-July 1. They, too, were rather the worse for wear; had been having particularly trying ordeals with their respective not quite normal children. Margaret said it did her good to get away. Dawn's mechanical jokes, always followed by her own "Ha-ha-ha" and the infantile remarks of Margaret seemed to have reached an extremely low level. Still we managed to have a moderately jolly time. I took them for dinner to Constableville and the restaurant near Snow Ridge: at the latter we played the jukebox all through dinner, I selecting familiar old numbers such as *Yes, sir, she's my baby,* and Dawn instructing me in the new stuff—Belafonte.

This is a bad year for everybody. If the world goes on as it is doing—with ridiculous impotent governments in the U.S., England and France, and the government of oafs in the Soviet Union, with gigantic taxes here for atomic weapons and foreign occupations, and a foreign policy consisting of the ineptitudes and lies of Dulles, who assures us from time to time that he has it from reliable sources that the Soviet government is about to fall, I feel that there may be a catastrophe which will result in some kind of revolution. It will not be a Marxist revolution, and there are no signs at present of any new political philosophy. In the *Times* of July 3, one reads that the Senate has defeated an attempt to cut the President's appropriation bill demanding $34,534,229,000, that the Air Force has just granted a contract for "an undisclosed number" of guided missiles which will travel five thousand miles and cost $73,000,000, and that Dulles, in a press interview, has elaborated on his recent speech in which he declared that there had been no change in the administration's policy of not having any dealings with Communist China: "The Chinese Communist Party . . . came to power by violence," and we must not "betray" Chiang Kai-shek—who also came to power by violence, as did for that matter the U. S. government. I sit here brooding on writing a pamphlet or article in which I should make an overall protest, explaining that I had not paid my income tax and had no intention of doing so, and that the government was free to send me to jail or to wipe me out financially. But I am too old, at sixty-two, for the struggle I should let myself in for, and I must not ruin the family, and, with my unpaid tax, in the past, since I do not on principle disapprove of taxation, my case would appear too weak.

Huldah Loomis invited me for dinner the evening of the 4th of July. She thought that we ought to do *something* to celebrate. We drank a bottle of New York State champagne. Florence greeted me naturally enough, but dropped her eyes, being conscious that I knew about her. She came to the table, but hardly ate—they have to feed her, it seems. Her hands do not coördinate, and she cannot see the things in front of her. Her eyes have become dull and gray. She would manage to take part in the conversation by always saying, "Oh, that's it!" when anybody explained anything, and *"Wundershayne und wunderbar!"* when anybody expressed enthusiasm. She upset Huldah and Gertrude by knocking over her champagne glass, which fell to the floor and broke: "One of Aunt Martha's goblets." "They'll cry over that all night," she said to me when her sisters had gone to the kitchen. Through dinner she would unbutton her blouse, then when they had buttoned it up, she would begin unbuttoning it again. She was "very naughty," they told me—would go into the bathroom and soak all the towels without turning the water off. They don't leave her alone in the house. She said pathetically that she wanted to go to bed, but they got her into the car and off for a short ride after dinner. They drove me through Collinsville, where Homer Collins's family had lived. Houses of the Collinses and Deweys, some of them well kept up, some deteriorated: big dark square Victorian house, in which old Mrs. Dewey had lived, that I should like to see the inside of.

This afternoon, July 6, I sat out between two trees on the lawn, reading and watching, from my deck chair,

the sky and the tops of the trees. Everything was so beautiful and interesting that I stayed out till 8:15. There
were chipmunks or small squirrels chasing one another
across the back roof, and through the trees swallows and
other birds, a butterfly as high as the top of the elm,
which looked a bright red when the sinking sun shone
through its wings. I had never felt so much before that
I had the freedom of that realm of treetop, roof and sky;
and I could look away toward the river, where the shadows were falling on the pastures. Later, when I was
getting dinner, I looked again at this view through the
open front door: deep blue and very dark green.

Only cheerful event, the wedding of Elena's son,
Henry Thornton, for which I went to New York.

Albert Grubel's tales of horror: A man somewhere
near Utica had been leading a dog on a chain. The chain
had got into contact with an electric wire that was down,
and the dog had been electrocuted. The man tried to
get him off the wire, but when the man touched him,
the man was electrocuted, too. The man's wife tried to
come to the rescue but also got a shock and was now in
the hospital. She had six children between two and eight.
Near Silver Lake, he told me, two cars had had a collision
head on, and both burst into flames. Six people were
killed, and the only survivor was a nineteen-year-old girl.
He told me the whole story twice, first on the way to
Boonville, then again on the way back. He believes that
it ought to be against the law to go more than fifty miles
an hour.

Beverly's aunt, Mrs. Hutchins, drove me to Boonville
one day. It turns out that her grandfather was a Zimmer,
some relative of the Zimmer to whom Great-Grandfather

Baker sold the Talcott farm across the road. She tells me that he and her grandmother were married in the Stone House. She is worried about Beverly and her fiancé. The explanation of the $3000 car is that Beverly and the boyfriend agreed to buy it together, but, lately at any rate, Beverly has been making all the payments. Her family think that, when the car has been paid for, the boy will simply drop her, and she is terribly afraid of losing him. At one time he stayed with Beverly and her mother; paid them $10 a week and demanded pork chops and steak. The car is bright red, and Beverly likes to wear a bright red dress. She came to clean today (July 30). She is having her vacation from the factory now, and she tells me she is trying to get a job at the state insane asylum.

The pale stone creeper-spangled barn, shadow-mottled by night.

The family are with me now. Helen has made friends with the Coes, who live in an old stone farmhouse, built about a hundred years ago and now in rundown condition. They have the compass that belonged to a man named Topping who was the first settler in this part of the country. I find that the Talcotts intermarried with the Coes at the end of the eighteenth century. The Coes are very nice and goodnatured. Helen's friend Frances, twelve, has beautiful red hair, and eyelashes and eyebrows so pale that they are almost invisible. Helen goes over every day to ride the Coes' pony. She practices riding bareback around the alfalfa meadow. Sometimes she and Frances ride together.

Dorothy Sharp has perhaps aged, but her accident has given her a rest, and I somehow found her this summer more distinguished and more sympathetic. A moment comes with many women when they have resigned themselves to being elderly. It is partly that she and Malcolm are relieved that his Rosenberg book is out. He is a professor at the Chicago Law School, and has taken a certain risk in bringing in a brief as *amicus curiae* and in defending the Rosenbergs, who were condemned to death as Communists for having given away official secrets. Elena says she has noticed that they have been rather anxious about the book. But having it published and taken seriously and reviewed by Bertrand Russell has strengthened Malcolm's self-confidence. I feel sometimes that his apologia for the American business man and his support of capitalism is to some extent a kind of precaution against getting too far on the wrong side of the academic authorities. Yet he is scrupulous—perhaps a little morbidly—in making sure that no one can impugn his honesty.

I append here a sketch of Malcolm that I wrote, at the request of the *University of Chicago Law Review,* on his retirement as a teacher:

I had met Malcolm Sharp a few times, first in New York, then in Chicago, but I never got to know him well till I inherited a family house in Talcottville and began going there for the summer again, while the Sharps came to spend their summers in another family house. We saw a good deal of one another then, and were in the habit, at the end of the day, of meeting for conversation and drinks at either their house or mine. We enjoyed a pleasant leisure and peace, a freedom from the immediate pressures with which we elsewhere had to contend, as we sat in my ancient living room, with its Boston and Salem rockers and its old-fashioned paintings and engravings, or looked out from the Sharps' back lawn, on a green and unmowed meadow, now soaked in the golden light of an orange and silver declining sun.

I thus had ample opportunity gradually to become acquainted with Malcolm's complex and sensitive and acutely conscientious character, which seemed to me unlike that of anyone else I had ever known. The conflicts involved in this character encouraged a tendency to paradox which sometimes took the form of perversity. I found that he was especially fond of startling with the unexpected. When I first began to know him, he would attempt to disconcert me by expressing opinions with which I guessed he had been in the habit of teasing his university colleagues; but I was not an academic and did not think along the lines with which he must have been familiar, so this gambit was entirely futile. It took Malcolm some little time to discover what my prejudices and principles were and to develop a technique for needling them. It was not that this procedure was entirely mischievous, though mischief did play some part in it. It is rather that his flexible mind, in connection with any problem, always makes him see that several different attitudes are possible, and that his instinct is likely to spur him to give preference to the one which will enable him to contradict the opinion expressed by his companion. This must make him, I should think, an admirable teacher of a semi-Socratic kind: he would compel his students to think about commonly accepted assumptions and thus lead them to become aware of the fundamental problems. For, in spite of Malcolm's love of paradox, he is never superficial, and his paradoxes actually spring from the paradox inherent in his whole point of view—a point of view which I have never encountered on the part of anyone else. Malcolm Sharp is not assignable to any familiar category and does not lend himself to any known label. He cannot be called a radical or a

8/4/96: amazing! & By chance I'm reading
this five days after visiting Alcatraz.

1957   171

liberal or a conservative or a middle-of-the-roader. The
paradox of his position is that he wants to combine un-
compromising vigilance for American civil rights with an
almost unshakable confidence in the workings of American business. Both these tendencies have carried him to
lengths which must appear outrageous or fantastic to the
people who, in dealing with political, social and economic
matters, insist upon two mutually hostile camps, to one
or other of which everybody must belong.

In defense of the first principle mentioned above,
Malcolm Sharp has shown imperturbable courage by
joining in a motion for a new trial of the Rosenberg
couple, by helping, after their execution, to have the
future of the Rosenberg children kept out of the hands
of the state and entrusted to the guardianship of their
grandmother, and by publishing, despite many discour-
agements, a book in which he tries to show that the case
against the Rosenbergs was dubious and that the case
against Morton Sobell, on the strength of which he was
sent to Alcatraz, had no plausibility at all. Though completely unsympathetic to Communism, he has never
allowed himself to be prejudiced against groups including Communist members or against persons who have at
some time been attracted to it, and has always made a
point of espousing, if he thought their civil rights were
threatened, groups and persons against whom this cry had
been raised. He loves nothing, in fact, so much as a legal
case for which nothing or little can be hoped. He always
has several files full of these, which he will nurse along,
like pets, for years, for he will never abandon a stand
once he thinks he has been justified in making it. On
the other side, the pro-business side, he is also unyield-
ingly logical. Though he worked for a time with the
administration in the days of the New Deal, he now dis-
approves of social security and, so far as I can see, of any

of the government subsidies by means of which Franklin
Roosevelt oiled the stalled machinery of the great Depression and thus, for his successors in the presidency,
set a precedent for further measures of the same kind.
Malcolm is impervious, in this connection, to humani-
tarian arguments because he is able to produce counter-
arguments to demonstrate that these measures do not
really help. His sympathy with the sufferings of human
beings has made him a hater of war, but here, too, his
line is quite unorthodox, and, it seems even to me, rather
eccentric. In trying to detach his judgments from the
beneficent professions of political claptrap, liberal as well
as partisan, to estimate strictly from the point of view
of its actual or probable results any step of our foreign
policy, he was led to the conclusion that Eisenhower had
exercised sound statesmanship in this department whereas
Kennedy had been rather dangerous.

I have no doubt that Malcolm, when he reads this,
will deny every statement I have made. I have sometimes
had the experience of picking up from him some idea
that I thought was particularly illuminating and introducing it into something I was writing, only to be told
by the sage himself that this had not been at all what he
meant, that he had, in fact, meant the opposite. And if
his own writing on nonlegal subjects is not always so
effective as I imagine his teaching to be, I believe this
is due to the fact that the paradoxical character, the
ambivalence, of his thinking prevents him, when he is
making an effort to grapple with fundamentals, from
expressing himself with lucidity, from arriving at clear-
cut conclusions. But this does not at all prevent him
from being one of the most stimulating, as well as one
of the most delightful, of companions. When I have
been working on some special topic of journalistic-his-

Malcolm Sharp

torical interest, I have found in Malcolm's conversation an invaluable corrective or caution to whatever line I was taking, because he would invariably suggest objections. One of the only occasions I remember when we found ourselves immediately in full agreement was on a visit to the St. Lawrence Seaway, when, looking down on the mighty river which this feat of engineering was supposed to control, we independently came to the conclusion that it was flowing in the wrong direction and wondered whether—consistently with our usual procedure —we ought not point this out to the authorities. With his subtle and skeptical mind, he combines, without the practical decisiveness, some of the other superior qualities which have made the great American jurists: subtle intellect, philosophic and literary interests, a long view of human history—extended by the far-ranging studies of his brother, the anthropologist—and a combination of moral anxieties with an ironic sense of humor. Very much an old-fashioned American, a native of the Middle West, there is nothing provincial about him. In our discussions on the back lawn at Talcottville, in the little trough of rural civilization that lies between the foothills of the Adirondacks and the wilderness of the Tug Hill plateau, we have covered, in our conversations, many aspects of that disturbed and disturbing world that was invisible from where we were sitting.

John Gaus, who was born in Stittville and now lives in the summer in Prospect, not far away from Talcottville, was a colleague of Malcolm Sharp's under Meiklejohn at Amherst, and through Malcolm I got to know him here. He is now in the Government Department at Harvard, and we occasionally see him in Cambridge, too. He is extremely loyal to upstate New York and enormously well informed about the countryside in this region.

He took Malcolm and me on an all-day drive to the just-opened Adirondack Museum at Blue Mountain Lake. It was strange, among the objects exhibited, for me to find so many things, carefully preserved and ticketed, from what is to me the recent past: old stoves not nearly so interesting as the ones from the Stone House that I sold to Mr. Parquet; foot-baths less distinguished than our own, which, like its pitcher is gaily painted with green birds; old spring wagons and surreys such as those in which we used to go on our family expeditions; drawings scratched on fan-shaped tree lichens such as we used to make in our childhood. In a big hall looking out on the lake through a window of polarized glass that made the landscape give the impression of a colored picture postcard so that it seemed less attractive than it really is, there is a series of scenes behind glass which exhibit the early life of logging and maplesugaring, a beaver dam with the beavers and the old Adirondack summer hotels, with their registers and other relics, dating back no further than the eighties and nineties. You paid a quarter to listen to a little recorded lecture on these scenes that now seem to the young remote. They have procured a real old-fashioned train, which rings a bell, and a little old-fashioned railroad station. A restoration of the shack of a mountain hermit.

Yet the town where the Gauses live, though considerably bigger than Talcottville, is not so much more modern than these buildings and machines that have already become curiosities: two little hotels, one called Toper; children riding horses in the dirt streets; another child sitting in some kind of old wagon driving a white horse; a church or two, a few square and solid residences. The

Gauses' pretty white house, with its narrow doors, extends into a shadowed room with John's books and a comfortable fireplace. Around this and a small lawn are a
few plantings of garden flowers that merge with a wild
field of goldenrod. This rather narrow strip of a place
is not divided from its neighbors even by any kind of
fencing. On one side of it is a garden full of brilliant
gladiolas; on the other, an old carriage with red and black
wheels. I suppose that Prospect owes its existence—as
its name perhaps suggests—to its nearness to what was
formerly Trenton Falls, that great beauty spot once visited
by tourists, now destroyed by a power company; but today
it is a hidden little inland town among mild and rounded
hills. It seems to give Elena claustrophobia, but to me it
offers attractions which make me wonder whether I
should prefer it to Talcottville. I saw no house as interesting as ours, but then no road humming with trucks runs
through it.

Malcolm's story, which he says is Spanish: Somebody
asks Khrushchyov for a definition of capitalism—"Capitalism is the exploitation of man by men."—"What is Communism?"—"Why, Communism is just the opposite."

I've heard this

I have had to have three elms cut down, one across
the road, the other at the corner of the Stone House. It
seemed to me a pity, but now it proves to be an advantage, because the house gets more light and no longer
has that moldy smell.

Pleasant effect of vegetation creeping up to the house
yet keeping to its limits: goldenrod, bluebells and purple
asters all growing close against the stone.
The maple in front of the house first showed, in the

center of its leafage, one spot of salmon pink, and now has a great pink streak with the color somewhat faded.

One morning when I was up at 6, the pane with the Nabokov poem on the upstairs door to the balcony came out in a beautiful way against the pink background at dawn, looking like a pattern of frost. I called up Volodya and told him this, and he came back with one of his inescapable puns: "There's an English word for that, *rime*."

Rosalind and I went on August 22 to Independence River, and I explored it for the first time beyond the bend that is seen from the top of the first falls. It runs level for quite a stretch. There is a path through the woods, but it does not go far; the path stops, and then it becomes quite wild, except that on either side of the river there are single lines of barbed wire, rusty and mostly on the ground. What could these have been for? The forest is too thick, one would think, for this part of the land ever to have been used for cattle. This must be part of the property that discouraged John Brown and his inheritors. Many flowers at the edge of the water: purple closed gentian and blue asters, white grotesque turtle-head, red cardinal flowers and a little white daisy-like thing.

Albert Grubel said just before Labor Day, "Well, they expect that four hundred people will be killed." Labor Day morning he said, "Several people have been killed already." The day after Labor Day, four hundred and forty people had been killed. He has never driven far from Talcottville, refuses to take me to Utica.

Beverly turned up again, looking better and quite pretty in her red dress. She hadn't been able to come to see us in the week she was not working because she had no car. The fiancé had taken the new car as soon as it had been paid for, and she had had to buy an old secondhand car, of which she had not then had the use, because dents were being taken out of it. She now has a job as attendant at the state insane asylum in Rome. The hours are easier than at the factory, but the lunatics get on her nerves and she doesn't know whether she can stand it. Her father went to the hospital for an operation and seems to have come out rather sobered. To their surprise, he appeared at her sister's wedding and gave the bride away. He told them he was sorry for what he had done, he didn't know what had got into him; but he didn't want to come back to the family because he was so ashamed of himself. They told him to forget about it, that he wasn't the only person who had ever done anything like that; but he said it wasn't only the family, it was the neighbors he couldn't face.

The Sharps and I, with young John Sharp and little Malcolm, had supper at Mrs. Burnham's. Afterwards, I went out of the house and looked at the view from the hill. The gray clouded sky had grandeur, with the beginnings below it of the orange sunset, and I realized that all this in itself was something that kept Mrs. Burnham going and gave her her invincible dignity through her accidents, losses and disasters. Dorothy said that she thought it was the view that made her continue to run the farm. She had installed a big plate-glass window at the time when, after the fire, they had to build a new house. Her earphone went wrong at the supper table, which somewhat threw out the conversation—she likes to take an active part, even to hold the floor, and we were rather at crosspurposes with one another; but she afterwards got it straightened out.

Looking out from my window on the third floor, I saw
the change made here by autumn in the landscape and
the atmosphere: they become distinctly more serious,
Nature begins to warn us, reassuming her august authority; the luxury of summer is being withdrawn.

I am leaving by car with George Munn and Lou early
tomorrow morning, September 4. With gout, non-produc-
tion and worries, I was really in the doldrums the first
part of the summer, but later recovered my energies and
got six chapters of the Civil War in shape to be typed—
also did the chapter on Cable as an article for the *New
Yorker* àpropos of Arlin Turner's biography. Also wrote
the mushroom article in connection with the Wasson
book.

Elena had called my attention, in the middle of August,
to a story in the *Times* about a band of Mohawk Indians
who had moved in on some land on Schoharie Creek
near Amsterdam, which they claimed had been assigned
to them by the United States in the Treaty of Fort Stanwix of 1784. I came up here in the middle of October
to investigate this, and so became interested in what
turned out to be an Iroquois nationalist movement of
resistance against the encroachment of the white man
on land that had been acknowledged as the exclusive
property of the Indians. For two years I was visiting
reservations in order to find out the situation, and in
1960 I published a book called *Apologies to the Iroquois.*

XIII

Reuel and I arrived June 7. It is cold, but I am not so depressed as last year. My gout is nearly gone, and my new teeth make life easier. Having Reuel with me is very pleasant. He sometimes has moods, if I make him do things that he does not want to do—when he withdraws into a rather sullen silence; but he is almost always helpful and amiable, and we have long conversations. I am surprised at how much Russian he has learned at Harvard in a year. Last night (June 14) he plodded through a few pages of Chekhov's *Spat' Khochitsya*. He has spaded most of the garden, unearthing large tree roots and stones which hadn't been removed before.

It is likely to seem rather empty when I first get back to Talcottville, but then the world soon fills in around me, and it comes to seem more real than Wellfleet. A little bit sad this year: Florence Loomis's death has rather upset Huldah and Gertrude; Lou Munn has gone home to her father in North Carolina but it is more difficult for her now because he has married again—she couldn't take a job on account of the baby—and she has now come back to the Munns', where I suppose she is as hard-worked as ever. Fern has had another blood clot but does not seem any less energetic. Carrie Trennam is so tied up with arthritis that she can't even cross the street or visit her neighbors the McGuires. Carrie and the Mc-Guires both have field glasses now in order to keep tabs on the town. Watching people in this way through the windows has come to be their chief amusement. Poor Beverly has suffered exactly the fate that her aunt predicted to me last fall and tried to warn her against. She paid all the instalments on the car that had been registered in the name of her fiancé, and when he began to go out with other girls, she asked him to let her put it in her own name; but he refused, assuring her that it made no difference, since they were going to get married soon. Then when the car was all paid for, he took it away and sold it. She is out $2000. When he sees her, he will not speak to her—though, as she says, it ought to be her who refuses to speak to him. She is now already paying for another and cheaper car, but she has had her teeth attended to. She works in a Boonville grocery store, then comes over here after 6 and gets dinner and eats it with us.

Reuel drives me on my Indian expeditions: St. Regis, Onchiota, Quaker Bridge, Salamanca, Onondaga, Lewiston. On the way back to Talcottville, I stopped off outside Rochester to look up my old Hill schoolfriend Ed Mulligan. His father had been a doctor, but I found him a country squire, who, as he said, works at it—a very typical example of the comfortable New York State landowner, who lives independently on his ample estate and isn't bothered by the rest of the world.

Reuel left the day we got back, the 23rd, and I left for New York the next day; returned on July 2.

The 4th of July was rainy so one quite forgot the holi-day. I took the Loomises to dinner at Constableville, and they told me all the gossip.

Lillian Burnham is now eighty-eight or eighty-nine, too infirm and deaf to keep on running her farm in the way that she has so far been able to do. The Sullivan boy who has been helping her has either been married or is about to be and has proposed to her that she let them move in and live in the back of the house, but Mrs. Burnham, understandably, won't have this. Huldah says that Lillian nowadays "gets in her hair," so she tries to avoid seeing her. At the time of Florence's death, the Loomises had wanted to buy a plot in the Talcottville cemetery—Mrs. Burnham is president of the association that manages it. They examined a blueprint map, and Mrs. Burnham was antagonized by the idea that Huldah wanted to take the map away. A scene seems to have taken place. The only plot available was one under a large tree, which the Loomises didn't want—I suppose because it was too much hidden away. Huldah pointed out that in most well-kept cemeteries the large trees were always trimmed. It was this that precipitated the scene. Since then Mrs. Burnham has had the cemetery kept locked, and Huldah has had her notified that, according to the law, the cemeteries must be left open. They finally buried Florence in a little graveyard off one of the side roads, where some other Loomises had been buried. Yet yesterday when Huldah told me all this she had just left a basket of strawberries—Lillian not being visible—at Mrs. Burnham's house.

Dorothy Mendenhall is getting bored with her nursing home and wants to come up here and stay with the Loomises, but they say that they can't have her. Huldah

explains that she spent a good deal of her life looking
after old ladies—she was for years a companion to Mrs.
Henry Stimson—and is not going to do it any more.
Dorothy, in her present state, she says, would need two
or three attendants and somebody to cook for them all.

When the Sharps, just before coming here, had gone
to see Dorothy in the nursing home, she had said to
Malcolm, "Well, *you're* the head of the family now"—
and they had realized that she had always up to then
regarded herself as the head—that is, of the families of
her two sons, of Dorothy Sharp's family and of Dorothy's
brothers. Malcolm was now the senior male. A little later
in the conversation, Dorothy Sharp remarked, in connection with his having done or having offered to do, something for someone, that he was always so good-natured.
"*Weakness,* I call it!" said Aunt Dorothy.

Visit of the Van Wyck Brookses, Friday to Sunday,
August 1-3. Gladys Brooks has certainly been softened
since she has been married to Brooks—though she still
said some characteristic things. Her first remark when she
arrived was, "This house is so much better than I thought
it was going to be!"; later on, in her quiet way, "Wouldn't
it be possible to do something to keep the whole place
from collapsing?" Van Wyck, too, it seems, though he
was born in Plainfield, New Jersey, had had a family
home in New York that had belonged to the Platts of
Plattsburg. He seemed to enjoy himself with us. He is
very much interested in everything, likes to tell you about
the artists and writers he knows and loves to discover
the unpublicized interconnections between well-known
literary figures. He was delighted that, through the Meads
of Vermont, he should be related, or connected by marriage, both with William Dean Howells and with the
Noyeses of the Oneida Community. I took him over to

the Mansion House, and he discussed these relationships
with old Pierrepont Noyes, the son of John Humphrey,
who in a few days will be eighty-eight. He gave us mar-
tinis, which he still drinks himself. Van Wyck and I,
having heard about the escapes through the transoms of
boys who did not want to go to bed with the mates to
whom they had been assigned and with whom, I believe,
they had been locked in, made a point of examining
these and noted that they were very large and would be
easy for an agile young man to climb through. I suppose
it was one of those loopholes that always have to be left
to mitigate the rigors of the various religions: the indul-
gences of the Roman Catholic Church, the evasions of
the Talmudic rabbis of the observance of the Mosaic
prescriptions, the modifications of Calvinism smuggled in
by the more humane ministers, the excuses of Christian
Science for resorting, on occasion, to the doctor or the
dentist. The younger Oneidans, I am told, also had a code
according to which, if the girl put out her shoes, it meant
that the man could come in; if she didn't, she didn't want
him. Van Wyck was thrilled, I think, with Oneida.

He resents the treatment that he is now being given
on the part of the academic world. While he was here,
the London *Sunday Times* arrived with an article by
Anthony West on my article in the *New Yorker* on Eliot.
When I told Van Wyck that it contained an attack on
me, he said that he'd like to see it: I'd been "getting all
the laurels lately." But he underrates his reputation. He
likes to talk literary shop, about which he is rather naïf;
pays attention to all the reviews and knows who got
every prize. He told me that he and I were "the only
men of letters left." He has been doing a book about
Howells, his growing admiration for whom I find rather
depressing, and says he is going on to do a book about
American writers in Italy. He alarmed me by saying he

was thinking of a study of Marion Crawford, who was really, he claimed, a pretty good writer. I have a feeling that these books, with their subsidence into a kind of cult of mediocrities, are sedatives, as the series of *Makers and Finders* was something itself of a sedative to the deep agitation, the near despair, of his breakdown. The lack of discrimination in his later work among the innumerable writers he deals with—who sometimes all seem to exist for him on the same highly satisfactory level—gives the effect, as Waldo Frank once said, of a kind of self-inflicted "lobotomy," after the strained and somewhat nagging anxieties of his previous strictures on American writing. The night before he left, I urged him to put into his present work a little more of the psychological insight of his *Ordeal of Mark Twain* period. He evidently does not want nowadays to go much below the surface. He is at the same time very opinionated. He still cannot see much in Henry James, against whom he confesses a special animus—though he once told Molly Colum that he had had a bad dream in which James bitterly reproached him. His actual hatred of Eliot, though he has tried to do him justice, is extravagant. Jack Wheelock told me that when he had once said to Brooks that Eliot was very ill, Brooks had startled him by snapping, "I hope he dies in agony!" They were at Harvard at the same time, Brooks of the class of 1908, Eliot of 1910, and both, as was natural then, went, after college, to England. Eliot took root there, but Brooks said that, during the months he spent in England, he found himself preoccupied with American subjects. This difference marks the watershed in the early nineteen hundreds in American literary life. Eliot stays in England, which is for him still the motherland of literature in English, and becomes a European; Brooks returns to the United States and devotes himself to American writing, at the expense of what has been written in Europe. Eliot represents the growth of an American international- ism; Brooks, as a spokesman of the twenties, the be- ginnings of the sometimes all too conscious American literary self-glorification which is a part of our American imperialism.

The trouble about Brooks as a critic as well as a literary historian is that he does not understand great literature; he does not really know what to do with it. His concep- tion of it seems to be based almost exclusively on the writers he admired at college such as H. G. Wells and Tolstoy. He blamed Mark Twain for not being such a writer, but one feels that he does not quite appreciate in what the greatness of great writers consists. In en- deavoring to acquaint himself with the whole of Amer- ican literature, he had no time to catch up with the classics. Somewhere he refers to "the classics," meaning the Greeks and Latin writers, as if they all embodied the same ideals instead of representing a great variety of personalities and schools and periods; as if they stood as a solid refutation to the achievements of our own times. And, in the chapter on "Literature Today" in his *Opin- ions of Oliver Allston,* he talks as if the greatest writers were invariably "voices of the people" and gives a list that begins with Tennyson and Hugo and ends with Manzoni and Björnson. Brooks is childish about "form" and "content." He said to me once angrily at Wellfleet, when I questioned his theory of Eliot's evil influence, that Eliot was the person directly responsible for empha- sizing form rather than content and thus misleading the young. Here in Talcottville I kept off modern literature, but he gave Malcolm Sharp his usual line: Proust and Joyce were "haters of life," etc. Malcolm denied this, and he considerably bewildered Brooks by expressing his, as usual, unexpected opinions. I told Malcolm, after the Brookses left, that Van Wyck had thought that Malcolm was pulling his leg. "I was just telling him," said Malcolm, "a few simple truths." It is curious that a man who writes so well, who is very much himself an artist, should not understand style and form in other writers. It must be due to his lack of a classical education and his imperfect education in French. What, I wonder, does he make of Dante, who can hardly be regarded as a "voice of the people?"

Elena says Brooks impressed her as a kind of "good little gardener," with a minute knowledge of plant life. But, not having read his books, she is unable to understand his importance to American culture, his heroism in pulling himself together and carrying out his great achievement of reading the whole of American literature and giving a new description of it. During the years he spent at Bloomingdale, I used to get him to review books for the *New Republic* and when he sent me little notices that simply summarized the books and never expressed any judgment, I tried to encourage him to do something more interesting, but he never replied to these urgings. When he had later emerged, however, and had had a success with *The Flowering of New England*, I met him at a party at Westport and was surprised to find that the man I had known as a pale, neat and shy little figure had expanded to a personage quite florid and portly and apparently quite heartily self-confident. I complimented him on the *Flowering* and asked him whether it hadn't been true that the academic writers of the histories of American literature had simply followed each other and said the same things about the authors. "They've none of 'em read the books!" he exclaimed with a certain jauntiness.

I had a very good time with the Brookses, and I felt
let down when they left. I exchanged a few letters with
him, but I never saw him again.

Dinner at the Edmondses'. For several years now there
have been supposed to be timber wolves around, though
the state department of zoölogy insists on calling them
"coydogs." The Edmonds place is now infested with
them. We heard somebody firing at one, and they have
lately been coming so close to the house—one of them
had just walked calmly past—that Walter was afraid to
have Helen and Marcia Roch play out of sight or go
swimming alone. I told Dan Aaron about this when we
were out on our Indian trip, and he is so absortive of
everything that he took it with all the Indian lore and
immediately, he said, had a dream in which he thought
he saw Indian dogs who were holding a "bow-wow."

On a walk to the Coes along the road to the east,
Elena and I saw a large red fox, the only one I have
ever seen wild. He would let us get fairly close to him,
then run on a little way, moving his long graceful tail,
as Elena said, like the rudder of a ship. It was delightful
to watch him running, springing so lightly over the
ground, made me think how depressing caged animals
are. Elena can't bear to see anything caged (hence her
resistance to restraining our dog). When we got to a
certain point, the fox went into a field and watched us
from the top of a boulder. At the point of the road with
which he had evidently been occupied, there was the leg
of a woodchuck's carcass.

I learned afterwards that there were foxes here with
rabies, and that you ought to avoid them if they are
coming toward you. A Negro, who lives in a cabin, shut

himself in when one of them made for him, and shot it
through the window. He sent it to Albany, for examination, and they found that it was indeed rabid.

Indian trip with Dan Aaron, August 15-18. Elena and
Helen left Friday. Niagara Falls, where I talked to Stan-
ley Grossman, the Tuscaroras' lawyer in their struggle
with the Power Authority, which wants to take part of
the Indians' reservation in order to start work on a hydro-
·electric project for utilizing the power of Niagara Falls.
We went out of town to see Mad Bear, the leader of the
Indians in this struggle. Mad Bear said afterwards that he
had been astonished by Dan's intrepidity in smoking a
huge Indian pipe, which he told him contained marijuana.

[Dan, who was writing a book on the radical activity
of the twenties and thirties, took the occasion of our trip
to ask me about them. The whole thing seems to me so
stale that I can't imagine anybody's now wanting to write
about it, but we ran over the personalities, and I told him
a lot of stories. It seemed to me like that grisly museum
of the early nineteen-hundreds that I had had him visit at
Niagara Falls: old stuffed two-headed calves, motheaten
panthers attacking a stag, dried-up corpses from Indian
graves, big bags made of rubber tires in which people
had tried to shoot the falls—and around it all-powerful
industrial life that no show of resistance could stop, which
had ruined the landscape of the river and was crowding
out everything else.

Lou Munn admitted that she couldn't be in favor of
desegregation because she had grown up in South Carolina, where a Negro was not allowed to come to the front

door. Her father had beaten one up because he had approached them in this way—"I got a big kick out of that."

Good days now at the end of August, after all the days of rain—mornings when everything is painted in the good strong New York State colors. Wonderful calm sweep of the great green countryside, blue in the mountainous distance and tinged in the foreground with yellow fields.

September 1, Labor Day. Albert Grubel, on the way to Boonville, as usual commented on the traffic accidents, which he had been reading about in the paper: "Twenty-six people killed, and others drownded and other things."

6:45 p.m. Receding storm-clouds, beautiful, deep darkish blue, with a whitening lower row; green foreground with its yellow strip, evenly and brightly lighted. The big trees that give the country its unsuppressible strength. Now the bright light has faded, and the top edge of the white cloud-ridge is lighter.—I find that I still tend to write in a vein of old-fashioned landscape description—everything seen from the earth and in relation to the earth. The aviators already see entirely different cloud landscapes. We may lose the old view of things altogether. I have now become almost incapable of writing poetry that involves the "pathetic fallacy"—though the country here still thrills and uplifts me.—Later, all the thick gray was thinned out and it left behind a tender light color drifting away to the east. Close relation of people to the weather here—not romantic, but romanticism partly derives from the relatively primitive relation of people to the environment they live in. Nobler country

here, which, I think, has made nobler people. It is a part
of the whole moral foundation of my life.]

Reuel arrived September 12th and drove back to Wellfleet the 16th. Later on, October 16-22, I came up here
to see my lawyer, Francis Penberthy in Utica, to go to
the Iroquois Little Water Ceremony at Tonawanda,
which I had been told was to be on the 18th, and to
close up Talcottville. But on the morning of the 18th
I got a wire from one of the Senecas saying that the ceremony had taken place the Saturday before. I imagine
that they were giving me the runaround.

Rosalind drove me to Onondaga, however, where I
talked to Henry Rockwell, a ninety-year-old Oneida, who
had come there on a visit to his son. He is almost the
only Oneida left in what was once the Oneida country
and boasts of having a "one-man reservation." The Oneidas in 1842 were mostly induced under false pretenses to
remove to Green Bay, Wisconsin; and such of the nation
as remained were later driven off their land on the pretext of a mortgage's being foreclosed. But Rockwell, the
son of a white man well known locally—there is a Rockwell Street in Syracuse—had the courage to go to law
about it; Indian lands are not supposed to be "encumb-
ered"; and he succeeded in getting reinstated. He is
vigorous for his age, talks emphatically and will go on
any length of time. He has repeatedly refused to approve
a document on rent in which the Iroquois have drawn
up their claims, and they have finally replaced him with
a younger man to represent the Oneidas. I could see,
from his ignorance of the situations in the more remote
communities, that he was out of touch with the present
movement. He has the bitter and declamatory old-fashioned Indian attitude, always asking rhetorical questions,
which he alternates with humor and charm. Educated

at the Negro college, Hampton Institute, he makes out a very good case for the hypocrisy of the whites in calling the Indians barbarians. "Do Indians put on shows like television?: 'You leave town in twenty-four hours!' Stick a revolver at somebody: 'Bang bang'? Do Indian boys kill their fathers and mothers?" When he had come to Oneida from Hampton, he had been asked by a local woman schoolteacher to meet a group of people and tell them about his experiences there. He had at first acted a part for the benefit of the people of Hampton, who thought he was a real redskin savage. He had climbed up a tree and refused to come down, but had then been prevailed upon to sit in a chair, and had pulled three Iroquois feathers out of the back of his neck. They had asked to see his scars. He thought that this was a great joke, that people who were supposed to be educated should be so gullible about the Indians.

On the way back, we stopped off at the Oneida Community to call on Constance Robertson. The more I see of the Community people, the more I realize how still very special they are. It must be embarrassing for Constance so often to have to deal with people who are under the impression that the old Community was some sort of "free love" group. She is likely to explain to visitors that they were under the strictest kind of discipline. "My grandfather," she once said to me, "would probably have thrown me out on my ear." They are dignified, straight-backed, well-educated, intelligent—a high grade of New England intellectuals, but a little at an angle to the rest of the world, and rather inbred among themselves, all showing a family resemblance and talking with the same accent. They reminded me a little of the Samaritan community on Mount Gerizim, who have been intermarrying for centuries. Constance says that they are given to "ancestor worship." I see that this is another case of the curious phenomenon (for America) characteristic of that part of the country: the anachronism which is still going strong. Community Plate is successful, the Community is still solvent. The Mansion House and its grounds are still as well kept up as they could have been in the early days and as Walter Edmond's place still is; and that is yet a kind of dream from which one does not want to escape. I talked about this with Constance Robertson, and I said I thought that Walter had written his books mostly out of his boyhood imaginings and that now that he was getting too old for such fantasies he didn't know what to do. She said that she was making a desperate attempt to get away from her own historical novels—she has done one about a nineteenth-century community—and write about modern life. Her publishers, she was afraid, wouldn't like it, because they were expecting her to go on producing reliable historical fiction. I spoke of my own feeling for the country and said that it was impossible for me to see it objectively, from an outsider's point of view. She said that she couldn't see Oneida objectively, and ended, "All right then—we're a lot of Brontës!" I get to like her more and more. When other people are around, she is likely to stiffen on account of her Community consciousness, in the role of official explainer and guide; but when I drive with her alone in her car, she always loosens up and laughs and becomes amusing. I think it is significant that she and her husband—though he is now the head of the enterprise—do not live in the Mansion House, but on a hill some distance away.

So cold in the Stone House that we spent a night with the Loomises. Jannett Talcott's old album, with her sister Sophronia's verses. When she wrote them, she can't have been intellectually incompetent, as the Talcott side always claim.

Sister, I know you will little expect
From one whom the muses and science neglect;
But wishing and praying in your best behalf,
I leave in your Album my own autograph.
        Leyden, May 8th, 1833. Sophronia B. Talcott

Rosalind and I, when we came back late from our
trip and found all the other restaurants closed, took the
Loomises out for dinner to a place we had just discovered.
They were excited, had heard about it but had never
been inside. Huldah said that it was "a place where girls
meet men illicitly"—and it is true that, under its previous
management, it had apparently been something of a
brothel. When I talked to Fern about it, wondering
where they had got the girls, she said, "Oh, local girls,"
and this somewhat surprised and shocked me because I
couldn't imagine any girl actually practising prostitution
in that part of the world. I had known it when I myself
was innocent, and I hadn't yet come to realize how far
from innocent it is at the present time. Huldah gaily
drank two vodkas—she had never had any before. I
warned her, but she held them very well. She wouldn't,
however, let Gertrude have one, but made her stick to
her usual Daiquiri. There seem to be signs that Gertrude
is going the way of Florence—she gets names mixed up,
etc. A depressing prospect for Huldah.

My father put in a furnace in the Stone House, but
it now was no longer working. It was not till a later year
that I had an oil furnace installed. On account of the
stone walls, the plumber said he couldn't put in modern
radiators, so we still with the oil heating have nothing
but the old hot-air radiators, and there are only two of
these on the second floor, which get only the heat that
comes up from below. The house is full of dead and

dying bees, which came in, I suppose, to get some warmth. These cold bees and crickets have never known that there were families living here, who have called themselves Talcott, Baker, Reed, Wilson.

XIV

1959

April 19. I came up this early to get some improvements done; but the weather makes this impossible. They
have had the worst winter in forty-one years, snow on
the ground since Thanksgiving, and even now I find part
of a dirty drift against the big kitchen window. The
steps of the Stone House are covered with an unpleasant
and unfamiliar crumbly mud that looks as if it had been
digested by earthworms. And the whole countryside has
the appearance of having had the life smothered out of it
by the winterlong oppression of the snow—no color, no
relief, everything neutral; the very grand old elms like
gray broomstraws. Even the Adirondacks seem dim and
flat. Carrie Trennam's house is a blank, all the shades
drawn—she is in a nursing home. Our house in good
shape except the ceiling of my upstairs workroom, from
which the paint, put on last September, has peeled in
patches. The mice, as usual, have eaten the soap and left
their little ricegrain turds in the bathtub and the kitchen
sink.—Beverly looks rather badly, sallow, has to work till
10 tonight. She had had a boring winter, wrote us at one
time a nostalgic letter. What did they do in Boonville

in winter? "Just work, eat and sleep, that's all." If it was snowing, they were afraid to go to a dance: they might not be able to get back. A novelty has been strip-bowling, but this was thought indecent and has been stopped.

I went back to Talcottville at the end of May.

Memorial Day. The feathery filagree of an elm against the gray-blue of the sky and the flat dark blue-gray of the hill behind, on which loomed the darker silhouette of another more distant elm. I thought that the old race of New Yorkers had been more worthy of the landscape than the present ones.

Albert Grubel the day before Memorial Day said that the papers predicted about two hundred and sixty car accidents for the holiday. The next day he asked me whether I knew how many there had been—from the paper he gathered that they had been runnin' double. Then he told me that in April two women had gone out in a car and disappeared, and then they found them at the bottom of a lake under two feet of water.

Drive with Otis and Fern to St. Regis, June 1. Fern, whose father was a cheese manufacturer, couldn't resist stopping off at a big cheese factory on the way. She bought a great paperbag of cheesecurds, which she and Otis ate on the way like popcorn. Fern said to Otis, "It squeaks good," and Otis said, "It squeaks good." They were talking about the sound you can feel it making when you bite it. This means that it is of the right consistency.

Later bulletin from Albert Grubel: two hundred and eighty people had been killed in car accidents on Memorial Day, well over the newspaper prediction, and forty-one had been "drownded,"—three hundred and twenty-eight in all. A party had gone out to pick flowers, and one of the girls had strayed away, and they hadn't found her yet, and bloodhounds had been sent after her. A little boy had also strayed, and bloodhounds had been sent after him, too.

This morning, June 3, Albert told me about a man who had "committed suicide the hard way." He had filled his mouth with gunpowder and lighted it. This reminded him that once he had killed some skunks and skinned them and hung them up; but there was some of the stuff left in one of them, and it smelled so bad near the place where they were making maple sugar that he burned some gunpowder around them, and it took all the smell away.

June 4. I sit at my little card table on which I write, in my mother's old heavily upholstered chair, and look up, after work—6:30—at the old framed map on the opposite wall. The glass reflects and just contains the window behind me now—the white curtains, the June green of the lilac bushes, with myself, head and shoulders, at the bottom, dim but rather darkly ruddy, the line of the mat going through my chest.

Beverly, as her aunt says, is a good girl. I tried to kiss her one night, when freed from work and elated with drink, and she very determinedly squirmed away. I said I was sorry that I had got to the age when I wanted to kiss young girls, but that she certainly knew how to resist. She evidently thought that, on her side, she owed me some kind of apology and told me that it was just that she was "so nervous."

Bill Fenton succeeded this year in getting Corbett Sundown to let him take me to the Little Water Ceremony at the Tonawanda reservation—a most extraordinary performance, which I have written about elsewhere.

Fern and Beverly both have only one way of responding to anything astonishing you tell them—as when, while we were waiting at the Boston airport for the Provincetown plane, I described the Little Water Ceremony to Beverly: by simply shaking the head (though I believe that Fern sometimes makes a sound). The sign for hearing something outlandish is the same as for disapproval. On hearing an unusual or difficult opinion, Fern will say, "It makes you think."

Beverly came to work for us at Wellfleet, looked very pretty on the beach, with her dark skin and slim figure. She complained that she missed cows around her, and we showed her two or three up the Cape, but this, it seemed, wasn't enough.

Elena and I have now arrived at an arrangement about her coming to Talcottville. She spends most of the summer at Wellfleet and comes on for a short time. At Wellfleet, she wants to do everything and is upset if I try to intervene. The result is that I become dependent on her and tend to take no responsibility. Here I attend to everything and am free to make my own routine. I drink less and get more work done. When Elena and Helen are here, it makes me uncomfortable that, at my age and with my self-preoccupation, I don't seem to have quite enough energy, after I have finished work, to do all I think I should for Helen. If I drink after work, I am likely to slump and become disagreeable. Here alone, there is nobody to quarrel with, and I don't have to do anything for anybody—though it gives me a pang to look into Helen's room, with its little things that belong to her, and know that she isn't here.

Tension with Elena now relieved. She is going to meet me at Pittsfield—with her new car, which evidently thrills her—and we will go to some music at Tanglewood, then pay some visits in Connecticut. When we discussed it over the telephone, she said, "This is where we came in." We had gone to the Tanglewood Festival together years ago before we were married.

Albert Grubel, on one of our rides to Boonville, seemed about to run over a boy on a bicycle. He didn't turn aside till I yelled to him. Then he said, "They're supposed to stay on the side of the road."

He made his usual prediction of accidents the day before the 4th of July, but I don't remember his mentioning it afterwards—I suppose because there were fewer accidents than the newspapers had prophesied.

Conversation with Beverly after the Fentons left. She had said last summer that Bill was "real common," and now said the same thing about Olive. I asked her what she meant by this, and she found it hard to explain: the best she could do was "people who are rich." I asked her to name people in Boonville that she thought were not common. Mr. Pratt (the millionaire miser) and Colonel Best of a very old local family and the President of one of the Boonville banks. She added, "I don't think you're quite common."

The old G—— house at Collinsville. Seeing it so dark and Victorian among its gigantic elms, I had always been curious to go inside. Now old Mrs. G—— is dead, and her son wants to sell it for $10,000, with everything that is in it. I went over with the Loomises to see it, and the younger Mrs. G—— took us around. It has not been painted lately and has an ironlike neutral color. It is one of those old square affairs, built in 1852, and perhaps what is meant by Hudson River Bracketed, for the long upstairs windows have ornamental supports. The roof of the porch has a kind of row of teeth that give it a sinister look, and the porch itself, with slender pillars that are joined at the top with arches, is masked by a great growth of spruce and a spread of Virginia creeper that hangs from the top. At the back of the house, a gray stone smokehouse, also more or less enveloped in greenery; and parallel with the house, a stable, on top of which —one can't imagine why—is a little flat square turret with windows. Woods beyond this and a stream—"G—— Glen" —on which used to stand a gristmill. The gate is an iron-work grill, the black bars and spokes of which give it, too, a forbidding look; a narrow stone-paved path leads to the broad stone steps of the house. The interior is most un-attractive but a not uninteresting example of the taste— the bad taste—of that period. Little seems to have been changed since it was built. It has a curious unlived-in air. The Brussels carpet with a rose design that completely covers the floor of the enormous living room on the left as you come in the door is faded and worn at the end toward the front, but this was done, it seems, by skiers—to the indignation of old Mrs. G—— —who rented the house one winter and gave a good many parties. This room has upholstered Victorian chairs, including one that is covered in dark red plush with elaborate lace "tidies", from which long tassels hang, protecting the arms and back; an otto-man near the fireplace, with embroidered flowers on the top. Extravagant drapes on the windows—one set at the

opposite end of the room has at the top a scalloped canopy
and, hanging from below this, in the middle, a kind of
great tongue of cloth; at the side, august curtains which
are caught up, near the bottom, with ropes. To one side
of this stands a whatnot, with conchshells and china ornaments. A piano, facing the fireplace, with an old-fashioned
black piano stool; above it hangs a large boxed picture,
painted in 1876, by someone with a foreign name and
supposed to have originally hung in the house of a New
New York City G_____. This picture is called *A Musical
Party* and depicts a group of ladies, one of them seated at a
piano, in the hats and bustled gowns of the seventies. Other
pictures are uncolored family portraits that have almost
the look of engravings but must be monstrously enlarged
photographs; an engraving of a village blacksmith and a
painting of a horse by some relative (there are other
horses and cows by this artist in some of the other rooms).
A white marble fireplace and a great low-hanging and
wide-spreading gilt and black gas chandelier, which has
been fitted with two tiers of electric bulbs. There is a
cornice of gilt leaves. (In one of the bedrooms there is a
frieze of wallpaper as old, it seems, as the house, of classical figures in blue and white—unpleasing like everything
else.) The front room across the hall is somehow especially disgusting: a mantel of black marble with white
mottlings, perhaps imitation marble, on top of which,
beside the mirror, there stands a dark structure of wood
of which one cannot imagine the use unless possibly to
contain ornaments; a blue velvet and wicker chaise
longue; a low bookcase darkly crammed with cheap sets
of Scott, Bulwer Lytton and Thackeray—the old two-
volume edition of Grant's Memoirs was lying on the floor.
Upstairs in one of the bedrooms, a small bookcase of
books on agriculture. The only at all attractive feature
was the hallway when you came in the door: the old

red-and-yellow stair-carpet ran rather steeply up to an ornamental window with a scrolly design of yellow and brown and white-clouded glass, through which the afternoon light—the only bright element in the house—fell on the old chairs. When I first came into the place, I thought it might prove enchanting, and if there was going to be a sale of the things, there might be some I should like to have, but the more closely I scrutinized them, the less attractive they seemed. Even a little gilt mirror that I had at first thought pretty now seemed to me second-rate. When I went a second time with the Fentons, the effect was actually sickening. I don't want to go there again.

There is a scandal about old Mrs. G——. Homer Collins, who was related to her in some way, did not like to be kidded about it. She is supposed to have had a baby by a man in Boonville, and this man is supposed to have bribed his wife to bring up the little girl as his own. The bribe was a grand piano, which it was noticed that she acquired soon after the appearance of the baby.

The younger G——s live in a much older family house built in the eighteenth century and afterwards added to. Mrs. G——, an amusingly tough-spoken and very likable woman, showed us around and offered us a drink. A few days later, I saw her again when I took the Loomises to dinner at an old summer hotel at Brantingham Lake. She came over and sat at our table. She started to say something about her grandchildren, then explained to me, "I've got more goddam grandchildren!" I asked how many, and she held up all the fingers of one hand and one finger of the other. I said that I was sending somebody from the Utica museum to look at the portières in old Mrs. G——'s house but I doubted whether they would buy them: "They goddam well better!" Later, when two daughters came over, she announced, "I've got more goddam daughters!" She had rather shocked me by telling me that in the old days, when an Indian turned up, the man of the house threw him out. This would have been contrary to the then accepted law of reciprocal hospitality. Dorothy Mendenhall had told me that when an Indian appeared at the Stone House, he was given some supper as a matter of course, and lay down to sleep in front of the fire.

Beverly says she has always said "youse" for "you" and "witjus" for "with you", and she doesn't know where she got it. When she was going to school, they tried to correct it, but did not have any success. She used to write it in compositions—spelling it "you'se"—and this was one of the causes of her getting low marks. I tried to interest her in some book, and she said that she had never been able to get interested in books.

Old Fred Reber, now in his eighties, seems still well able to do anything. His wife forbade him to undertake to paint my ceilings, but he cheated by getting an old Texan from Boonville and then working with him. He called the old Texan "Grandpa"—also calls me "Grandpa." I think he likes to call people "Grandpa" in order to bring out how young he is himself for his age.

Vista in the house I like best (August 8, 8:15 p. m.): to sit in the long chair and look across the hall into the smaller living room, at the slim legs of the chairs and of the phonograph table—with the patch of plush visible of the newly upholstered rocking chair, the gray floor and the gray shadow behind the white curtains where the shade is down. It is dark in that room: chairs and tables dark, even the gray floor; the curtains below the shade only glowing dully.

This summer, in relaxation from my historical and anthropological reading on the Civil War and the Indians, I have fallen into the habit of going to bed or amusing myself at breakfast with the memoirs of the literary life of the late eighteen-hundreds and the early nineteen-hundreds, the period in which I suppose I am most at home. It rests me and entertains me: the volumes of Max Beerbohm I have here, Shaw's correspondence with Ellen Terry, Lionel Stevenson's biography of Meredith, Edward Marsh's *A Number of People* and Christopher Hassall's biography of Marsh. These books by and about Marsh are delightful till his so constantly telling anecdotes may become fatiguing: clear well-bred English style, background of classical studies, associations that combine the political nobility with the cultivated professional class, personality good-humored, conscientious, generous, great love of poetry and painting, the best of the life of the British upper classes in the period before the first war—good living, good stories, good jokes, endearing eccentricities. Marsh had had a serious illness at the moment of adolescence, and on this account neither his voice nor his sexual organs had ever matured. He never had to worry about love or a family. His crushes on Rupert Brooke and Ivor Novello were absorbing while they lasted, yet they do not seem to have involved him deeply. And he worked as a civil servant under Liberals, Tories and Labour—Churchill, Thomas and the Duke of Devonshire—without apparently ever worrying very seriously about what they were politically up to. When he comes to the first war, he says in effect, "I might as well skip it—I don't want to bore you with it."

In regard to other events, he is likely to dispose of them quickly: "It is written in the Book of Chronicles."

I had by this time come to know the Crostens. Loren Crosten is a musician, who is head of the music department at Leland Stanford University in California. Loren and Mary both come from the Middle West, but have acquired a strange fixation on Boonville. They got to know a Boonville native, Jessie Laing, now Howland, when they were all students at Columbia, and Mary Crosten, when Loren was away in the last war, had her first baby up here. Ever since they have been coming here every summer, driving the long trip across the continent.

The day before the Crostens left, September 7, they took us to the place they had been telling us about, where Sugar River, after going underground, gushes suddenly out of the hillside. It is strange that I had never before known about this. I had always assumed that the trickle which runs down to the Black River was all that was still flowing of the sunken water; but actually the main stream turns sharply east and runs for about a third of a mile completely concealed under woodland. You pass an abandoned quarry and pick your way through a queer broken-up terrain: great square blocks of stone, like the bed of Dry Sugar River, with deep straight-fissured crevices between them, but here disguised by having been grown-over so that the crevices have grassy lips and from a distance look like a field. This formation continues through more woodland, in the open places sprigged with everlasting—after which you come to a clearing partly framed by big maples, but lined on one side by a row of cottonwoods diffusing a pleasant fragrance. Now appears a great pit, from which rises a kind of rock pyramid, made of more or less square-cut blocks. One cannot tell whether this object is natural or erected by human hands, somehow in connection with the quarry. Traversing this field to the left, you soon hear the roar of the river. You find yourself at the top of the glen, at the bottom of which the stream gushes out in what is at first a small torrent. But when you look down at it the trees that grow out of the walls further along conceal it. You descend by a kind of flight of wide stone steps that present themselves on the slope at intervals. On the left of a path are large rocks speckled with black lichen; on the right one finds a higher wall of ledges, with rusty ferns growing out at the base. At the bottom, you stand at the edge of a stream, but, on account of the bushes and trees and the lovely bends of the river, you still are unable to see—which makes it even more mysterious—exactly where the stream gushes out. You would have—as I once did—to wade up to the mouth of the cave. To one side, in a little cove, there is a pool, brown and flecked with foam. But the river is very active: it twists and turns, spreads out into a wider bed. It goes under a crude bridge, over which, as one sees from a layer of their dung, a herd of cattle passes. This bridge is propped up by trunks of small trees, some with the bark still on them; it has at one time been faced with concrete, but has no railing, and the edges are grassy. One can never see ahead where the stream is going, but eventually, it, too, runs into the Black River.

There are the ruins of an old stone mill, which is roofless and which one can enter through a very low door like the entrance to an Egyptian tomb. Not far away, sunk level with the ground, is a millstone of huge size, grooved from its center with curving rays. There is also an old rickety picnic table, with rough benches, knocked together from boards, now gray and leaning askew but braced with small boulders to keep it from collapsing too easily. It cannot have been used for a long time because, when I tried to sit down there, I found that the bench wouldn't hold. There is a fenced-in pasture, with a great bank of lilacs along the fence that must have been planted long ago, and beyond this, one comes to a collapsing barn, with an old-fashioned stone foundation, inside which the ancient hay drips down through the cracks in the mow. Through the planks that barred the door, I saw a carriage wheel of large circumference standing upright embedded in the dirt floor.

Strange that, with all the time we once picnicked at Dry Sugar River, I never should have known about this place, which is hidden not far from the road. Crosten says that he doesn't believe that very many people in Boonville now know it exists; he and Mary discovered it when they were camping on the Black River and used to take long walks of exploration. The old mill and the underground river seem to concentrate an essence of the curious magic that one still feels in this part of the world—not so long ago humanized and lived in, then abandoned except for some cattle and a silo in the distance, and completely disregarded. For myself, I was a little troubled, in connection with this romantic spot, by the feeling that I had found it too late—too late for children's outings or for youthful love affairs. What could I do about it except describe it, and hope that my children and grandchildren might someday enjoy it more?

XV

1960-1961

Talcottville: a *pied à terre* in stability.

But the winter of 1960-61 was overshadowed by worry
about the income tax. I came on to Utica sometime in
November, '61, and was fined $7500 by Judge Brennan,
about whom, in my *Apologies to the Iroquois,* I had at
least implied some criticism of his handling of a case in
which the Mohawks of the St. Regis reservation were
opposing the right of the State of New York to dispose
of a point of land in the Saint Lawrence for the purposes of the new Seaway; but his sentence was not, I believe, influenced by any prejudice. He knocked off on
the same day a number of similar cases. I borrowed the
money from Roman Grynberg and Barbara Deming, and
paid it back by selling my papers to Yale. I was gouty and
began to realize that I had something wrong with my
heart. The doctor told me it was "a touch of angina."

The summer of 1960 in Talcottville was uncomfortable
and very strained.

Beverly Yelton was married on June 25, just before I

arrived, to a perfectly sound young man, who works in one of the garages, a contrast to her former fiancé who made her pay for a new car, then took it for his own use. But she went on working at the Park Market till she had her first child.

Barbara Deming and Mary Meigs came to see me just at the moment when there was an income tax crisis; most of my other guests mostly in August: Bill Fenton, Stephen Spender, Sam Behrman, the Marcelins. Without Elena to help entertain them, I could hardly do them all justice. I saw Stephen at, I think, his best. He likes to be encouraged and reassured; is better, perhaps, alone when one can give him all one's attention. He inscribed one of his poems on the hall window at the top of the stairs, the one that begins

"I think continually of those who were truly great . . ." and ends

"Born of the sun, they traveled a short while toward the sun

And left the vivid air signed with their honour."

I don't have a curtain hung over it, and it comes out brightly and appropriately in the light of the late afternoon. He also did a quatrain especially for me, which I have set in one of the front windows of the big downstairs room. A pleasant picnic at Independence River, with sandwiches and a bottle of wine: blue closed gentians and red cardinal flowers, little boys diving and swimming, with a dog that got worried and barked when he had difficulty in going after them across the stones. Stephen thought that it was all "very *Huckleberry Finn*."

Albert Grubel was much gratified this year by the highest death rate yet for the 4th of July.

He is getting rather feeble but still drives me to Boonville.

Everett and Mabel Hutchins; Kay Hutchins (Widnik);
Beverly Yelton and her husband George A. Wheelock

There is a house on the left when you are entering
Boonville in which a woman, as he tells me, shot her
husband last autumn. He had bet on the World's
Series and lost, and came home and got rough with his
wife. She was pregnant, and he kicked her in the stomach
and threatened to shoot the children. She peppered him
with a shotgun while "he laid right on the bed." She
appeared in court in Utica, and was let out on bail and
had her baby. There have been, I think, two other cases
lately of women who shot their husbands and went scot-
free. This seems to me characteristic of the local independence of the letter of the law. I was told about two
Boonville men who decided to swap wives without the
formalities of divorce. The one who had the less attractive
wife is supposed to have made it up to the other man
by throwing in a sack of potatoes. So long-illicit relations
are overlooked. And there is a legend of a house in Talcottville to which the husband came from work one night
—according to one version, after having been away for
some years—and which he was never seen to leave. The
story is that he was murdered by his wife and buried
in the cellar.

Albert said that some people thought that there had
been something kind of funny about that boy who got
lost and was never found. They drained the lakes. "The
boy hadn't been quite right, and the family may have
done something to him."   *Patriotec Pore, Sanseme*

⎡I spent all last winter in Cambridge finishing the Civil
War book, did not even write in this journal. I got bored
in the long run with my political and literary history and
with the limited resources of my own vocabulary in dealing with this sort of thing, at which I don't think I am
really at my best.⎤It is a relief to get back to this journal.

Last summer Bill Fenton brought me in touch with a
state zoölogist who was studying the small mammals of
Tug Hill. An enthusiastic able young man, excited at
having found water-shrews of a kind that Audubon does
not include in his *Quadrupeds of North America* and
about which not much has been known. They have a
fringe on their hind feet, and are the only animals known
which like water bugs can skate on the surface of the
water. He had found one that had been maimed but not
killed in one of his traps and was still able to "skitter
around" on a pan of water. When they dive, they secrete
bubbles of air in their fur that enable them to rise to the
surface. They flourish here in abundance, and this young
man was delighted by the unexpected opportunity to
study them. He had a laboratory in a little old schoolhouse that had been turned into a camp, and an assistant
who knew how to dissect the animals, but didn't know
what such a word as *placenta* meant. The little pelts were
all mounted, and some of the little organs preserved in
jars. He explained to me the various species of mice, of
which there are more than I could have imagined, the
shrews and the flying squirrels. It made rather a pathetic
impression: among the fresh specimens, one of the
females was pregnant, and the pale tiny penises of the
males stuck out in a frustrated way that also testified to
the determined persistence of life. From there we went
to visit the traps—which he does early every morning. I
had never been off the road in that wild part of Tug
Hill before: unfamiliar birds, animals, flowers—yellow-
beaked cuckoos and a huge blue crane; the usual closed
gentians and cardinal flowers; a bright reddish pink water
flower, floating in a web of stems in a marsh, which I
later identified as "amphibious knotweed"; the insect-
trapping pitcher plant, with the red-veined green pitchers

of its leaves, which look as if they actually contained arteries, and its startling rosettelike red flowers. These last in a sphagnum swamp, where they gave an uncomfortable impression of being actually voracious in a carniverous animal-like way. As one walked on the sphagnum—which is a heavy kind of moss—it gave under one's weight like a hammock. (Darwin, in his book on Insectivorous Plants, knew about our pitcher plant, Sarracenia, and the so-called cobra plant, Darlingtonia, that grows in the Sierra Nevadas. He mentions them, but does not describe them, having apparently never been able to examine them.) The zoölogist did his trapping with mouse-traps and rat-traps, but mostly not far from the road. Beyond is the forest, a wilderness in which there are wildcats and bears and in which it is easy to lose one's way. But he says he never carries a gun. Many water-shrews and mice in the traps. It gave me a new satisfaction to go into the woods with someone who could tell you about not only every animal but every bird, every tree, every plant. He knew what each of his little animals ate, where it would be likely to live. I had mixed feelings of admiration for the techniques of zoölogical science and of pity for the poor little beasts. They don't, however, have much mercy on one another: a shrew, it seems, will eat another shrew if it finds it caught in a trap. On the way back, the young man confessed that he felt rather bad about killing his specimens. He took me to his house for a drink. He and his wife and their children seemed a little like small mammals, too. I have felt that this was a kind of law among people who study wild life. Ornithologists are often birdlike; and I remember how Carl Akeley, who wrote about pachyderms, used to come charging into the *Vanity Fair* office, giving the impression, with his gray skin and heavy build, of being himself a rhinoceros.

The young zoölogist's stay was curtailed when his

department transferred him to Long Island to find out whether the cases of hookworm which had been appearing there had been due to infection from any small mammals. I was sorry to have him go, and for him to have to drop his study of water-shrews.

Two of my plays had been translated in Hungary, and a volume of the Hungarian translations reached me in Talcottville in the summer of 1960. I gave a copy to Mary Pcolar, who works in Kramer's pharmacy in Boonville and who is the only Hungarian here I know. I found that she was perfectly literate in Hungarian as well as in English. She is a very handsome girl in whom the Mongolian stock is evident: high cheekbones, slightly slanting gray eyes, set rather wide apart, a figure erect and well built. I asked her to teach me Hungarian, and she said she would if I would teach her French. I made a couple of appointments with her, but she always later got out of them. When I knew her better, she told me that she had been afraid that she didn't know the language well enough to teach it to someone else, and that she had heard that I might be a dangerous character because I had a cellar of wines and had been married four times (the rumored cellar consisted of three or four bottles which I sometimes purchased in Utica and kept on the window-sill).

But by 1961, she had left the pharmacy and for the moment did not have a job. She suddenly appeared at the Stone House one day, leaving her children in the car as chaperons, dressed in white shorts and looking very attractive. She said, "All right, I'll teach you Hungarian." She turned out to be very intelligent. It is not likely to be the case that children who have grown up in foreign-language-speaking households really understand the language of their parents in such a way as to be able to explain it from a grammatical point of view. But Mary was able to analyze the structure of these agglutinated Hungarian words. She has natural qualifications as a teacher, and has always had the ambition to be one. It has been the tragedy of her life that she was not allowed to go to college. The superintendent of her school recommended it to her parents; but they, European peasants, had no idea of higher education for women. She had taught herself literate Hungarian entirely by studying the Hungarian papers from the point of view of literate English. Though she understood the structure of the words, there was one thing she could not explain. The language has a peculiarity, apparently derived from its oriental source, that does not exist, so far as I know, in any European or Slavic language: the form of the verbs is determined not only by the subject but also by the object—that is, if the object is "specific," the verb has a different ending than if the object is something general. There is a difference in the form of the verb between "I want eggs" and "I want that egg"—though the Hungarian idea of what is specific and what is general does not quite correspond with ours. There is also a distinctive form of the verb in the first person with a personal object in the singular second: *szerelek, I love you,* and *kérelek, I beg you,* do not need any pronouns at all; the form of the verb is enough. A literary Hungarian who has a French wife tells me that this is the only feature of the language that she has not been able to master. And I found that Mary, when I began to be puzzled by two forms which seemed to mean the same thing, was not able to explain that for every verb you had to learn two conjugations— though of course it would have been impossible for her ever to have used the wrong form herself. An English-Hungarian grammar saved the situation.

That summer, when Mary was out of a job, she became indispensable to me. She not only worked with me at Hungarian, she drove me around, typed my manuscripts and letters, and provided me with a pleasant companion who never got on my nerves. She has a remarkably many-sided competence. She makes all her own clothes and does gardening and carpenter work on her house. She takes courses in cosmetics to qualify herself for work in drug-stores and does the make-up for the amateur theater at Lyons Falls. She has written poems and children's stories, and she still, when there is nothing more urgent to do, paints not at all discreditable landscapes. She has brought up her three children so that they are much better trained than many of the children of my literary and academic friends. She has had each of them learn to play a different musical instrument, and restricts their watching television to the weekends. She was secretary and treasurer of the local Parents and Teachers Association and president of the Alumni Assoication of her school. She belongs to a large family. Her father had acquired in West Leyden a farm of a hundred and seventy acres, which he seems to have worked with remarkable success in handling the difficult soil, and Mary, who adored him, grew up learning how to do all kinds of farm work. After school, when she could not go to college, in order to get away from West Leyden, she went to live in Perth Amboy, New Jersey, where there were already many Hungarians. There she worked by day at the Vogue School of Fashion Modelling in New York and at night as a telephone girl. The horrors of living in Perth Amboy I can imagine from having had to pass through it on my way between Red Bank and New York. The New Jersey heat in summer is bad enough, but in Perth Amboy she had to endure it in uncomfortable living quarters in the bad-smelling factory town. She married there a young Slovak, an ex-war hero who

The Pcolar family (from left to right): (standing) Janet, Edward, Susan; (seated) Mary, George

had been decorated for distinguished service in the Forty-Fifth Combat Infantry in Germany. Then her father died unexpectedly of a heart attack, and her mother was about to sell the farm, but Mary hurried back and prevented this. She took over the household and has run it ever since. Her husband was at first reluctant to come but very soon got to like the country. He is a steel worker in the Revere Copper and Brass works in Rome.

Mary is in some ways more European than American, and it is interesting to hear her opinions of the way young Americans live. It seems to her odd that there should be a convention that, when children get married, their parents must give them a car as a wedding present instead of their working for one. I became very fond of Mary and followed her further career, as if she were an interesting niece, and I always felt regret that there was so little I could do to help her.

I find that I sometimes feel nowadays, as I did in the Soviet Union, when I first got out of the hospital, that I have to recite my poetry or reread something I have written in order to assert my identity against the income tax and Robert Moses and all the rest of our obliterating bureaucracy.

Death of Hemingway. This has very much upset me. Absurd and insufferable though he often was, he was one of the foundation stones of my generation, and to have him commit suicide is to have a prop knocked out. I am told now that his mind had been going and that he had been given shock treatments in Rochester; I hear reports that he was quite demoralized and could sometimes hardly talk intelligibly. But at the time of his death I was much depressed to realize that, after exhorting writers "to last and to get their work done," he should

have [died in such a panicky and undignified way] as by
blowing off his head with a shot-gun. The desperation
in his stories had always been real: his most convincing
characters are always just a few jumps ahead of collapse.
It is a wonder that this was not more noticed. The press
and the public, instead, took their cue from his public
show of full-blooded and triumphant vitality. Having
created this delusion himself, he fell in with it enthusiastically. It began to get into his work in the interludes
to *Death in the Afternoon,* and it became after this quite
rampant—although mostly in magazine and newspaper
stories which he afterwards did not reprint—and one
gets the impression that the serious artist had actually to
struggle against it. The thing about the two rival bullfighters—parts of which came out in *Life*—looked to me
perfectly awful; it was the only thing of Hemingway's
that I felt I could not read. *Life* was exploiting him
for all he was worth, and he was collaborating on all this
publicity. There was a picture of him in *Life* on every
page: Hemingway towering over the bullfighters, Hemingway dining with Spanish friends who adored him—even
the bulls seemed to have his face. Something he said
about this work in an interview or a statement made
me think that he recognized its badness, that he did not
want it published in that form as a book. In any case,
it has never appeared.

As a character in one of Chekhov's plays, speaking in
the late nineties, says that he is "a man of the eighties,"
so I find that I am a man of the twenties. I am still expecting something exciting: drinks, animated conversation,
gaiety, brilliant writing, uninhibited exchange of ideas. I
have never had quite the expectation of Scott Fitzgerald's
character that somewhere things were "glimmering": I
thought life had its excitements wherever I was. But it

was part of the same *Zeitgeist*. Now I try to discipline myself not to be so silly in depending for really deep satisfaction on things that are transitory and superficial. I try to diet and cut down on drinking and not to look forward to sprees. I hope I am well on the way to becoming a sedate old gentleman.

It is a sign of Mary Pcolar's genuine sensibility that when I gave her two of Hemingway's books, she should have noted with special appreciation the moment in *Big Two-Hearted River* when the boy, having just caught a magnificent trout, delays, before cleaning and cooking it, to savor his high satisfaction.

Helen and I went to the county fair at Lowville (August 17) with Mary Pcolar and her two little girls—a more enjoyable day at a county fair than any I have had since my youth. There was a better sideshow entertainment than has been usual lately—this kind of thing seems to be dying out. It included a magician and sword-swallower and one of those manufactured monsters, a supposed baby with a dog face. The magician got Helen on the platform, and—somewhat to my surprise—she seemed to be enjoying her own performance. He had also a really pretty and young assistant. As we were walking later on the fairgrounds, I met the magician from the sideshow. I explained that I was an amateur magician myself and complimented him on his coin tricks, said that there were certain things he did that I couldn't understand. He said, "I can see you're a carnival man"—I was carrying a hooked cane and had an old shapeless panama hat with one side of the brim torn—and he showed me how to perform a palming sleight that I have never seen described. You catch a quarter between two folds of skin at the top of the wrist below the thumb. He had specially developed the two folds for this, and this was how he had made his coin disappear when I couldn't see where he was holding it. "I taught Indian Jim that," he boasted.

It was all very quiet and pleasant. Helen inspected the horses with a more or less expert eye, and took the little girls on the Ferris wheel and merry-go-round and bought them candied apples with nuts stuck around them, which, however, turned out to be rather green. The Pcolar children are so well trained that they never ask for things or interrupt. The younger gray-eyed blonde —a little more assertive than her shy brunette sister—did, however, at one point, declare that she "didn't feel like seeing that exhibition." Mary ran into her former art teacher, now studying at Syracuse, who told her that she and a co-worker had won the second prize—$8—for a booth that they had arranged for a Home Demonstration Unit of which Mary is the president. This is an agency for improving the domestic arts which has been organized from Cornell. Mary's exhibit dealt with the problem of removing spots not by cleaning fluids but by the application of starch and other domestic staples. The various possible kinds of stains were illustrated by a cake of wax, some artificial apples, a bowl of ordinary grass (she was humorously proud of this), and several other things. The whole occasion was comfortable and local.

The big old Merriam mansion that stands rather far back from one of the country roads is being sold by the last of the resident Merriams, a Mrs. Sally Trube, who has gone to join a sister in California. The most distinguished of the family was a Dr. C. Hart Merriam of Leyden, a scholar of some importance, who wrote on "the Natural History of the State of New York." When Mrs. Trube left, she took most of the furniture and ornaments with her, but an auction is now (during three days in August) being held in the Merriam house by a New York dealer in antiques, which is an almost complete fake. We went one day with the Loomises. It was disgusting. The men from New York had brought with them a lot of cheap and ugly stuff such as the Merriams would never have touched, and were selling them as the genuine contents of the house.

During a trip to New York, I saw three old friends who seemed to me all to have a kind of nuclear age jitters: Thurber, Janet Flanner and Morton Zabel. Morton gave me a travelogue on his five months in Europe which sounded less like his usual conversation than like one of his interminable compulsive letters. Janet had in some strange way severely injured her hand—as far as I could make out, by picking some kind of sharp-leaved plant. I couldn't understand her at first, her utterance had become so rushed and blurred. But then she more or less cleared up and became as amusing as ever. She said she was going to Italy. I ran into Jim Thurber's wife in the lobby of the Algonquin. She said that he was in very bad shape, but not to tell him that she had said so. I had a drink with them in the dining room, where, as usual when he drinks, he was throwing his weight around. He was haunted, as a good many writers are, by the idea of getting the Nobel Prize: they might give it for once to a humorist. I used to feel with the exiled Russian novelist Aldanov that I could see it, hanging in the air before his longing eyes as if it had been the Holy Grail. I ran into Thurber again the day I was having drinks with Janet, who said he was drinking himself to death, though I'm not sure he was drinking more than usual. Again, when I was dining with Mike Nichols and Joanne, Jim told me he had been having "vastations." "Why," Mike asked

at dinner, "does Mr. Thurber feel that he has to tell us
about the people who came backstage to see him?" (Jim
had recently been acting in a Broadway show made out
of his own writings.) I answered that, depressing though
it might seem to him, getting older, for a writer, did not
necessarily give you self-confidence. I told him that I
sometimes got up at four o'clock in the morning to read
old reviews of my books. Mike asked what Jim had meant
by "vastations," and I explained that he had found the
word in Leon Edel's biography of Henry James. The
elder Henry James had used this word for a kind of
blackout that he sometimes had, when his mind had
simply gone blank, and he hadn't even known where he
was. Mike said, "I'm in that state a good deal of the time."
He told me about the play that Elaine May was writing
for them and that they hoped to have open in February.
It was about a Jewish family. He was to be the husband,
and the main action seemed to hinge on the unsuccessful
attempts of the wife to make him get out of bed. I said
that I hoped she got him up at the end. She was rewrit-
ing the end, he explained, and he didn't know yet what
was going to happen. He was supposed to go around to
see Elaine after dinner; but he evidently stayed longer
and drank more than he had intended, for he finally
declared that he didn't feel able to cope with the situation and that he would go home and go to bed.

I felt that my friends were demoralized by the atmosphere of insecurity in which we are living at present—
as I, of course, have been myself; perhaps, if they felt
as I did, by a suspicion of the ultimate futility of the
work they have been doing all their lives, of even the
prospect of its ultimate annihilation. Mike Nichols, who
had had to face the menacing situation in Germany at
an earlier time in his life, said that he was reconciled to
the present one in the sense that one had to be reconciled,

in any case, to the prospect of one's own eventual death, whether or not this occurred as an incident in the more general destruction of humanity.

Not long after, Jim Thurber died. This depressed me: he was just my age. The "vastations" of which he had spoken had been evidently very real. They must have been genuine blackouts caused by the cerebral tumor for which he had been operated on.

Utica and Talcottville, November 30-December 3. Usual gloom and strain of tax business with Penberthy and tax people. Spent Thursday night at Fort Schuyler Club; comfort at least of good breakfast in a well-served old-fashioned club. Mary P. met me there for lunch and drove me to Talcottville. She came in through the front door instead of the ladies' entrance. From the moment she talked to the man at the reception desk inside the door, she recognized him as a Hungarian and established an understanding with him. When I came out and met her, he was taking her through the ladies' dining room. On the way to Boonville, she told me at length about the situation at the pharmacy. When she had first left—on strike she said: she had been getting only $1.25 an hour—she had gone to work in a restaurant; but they had paid her only $1 there, and she had very soon gone back to the pharmacy. Out of $36 a week, she has to pay $8.50 for taxes. It was warm for that time of year—no snow. But it was gray and rather sad—I felt that the people were lonely. It would have been more cheerful if the ground had been covered with snow. The bears had been moving in on the towns, because the beechnut crop had failed them. In Boonville, a bear had got into a garage, and in Talcottville one had been seen on the bridge that goes over to the "island" in Sugar River.

Walter Edmonds saw one in a tree and met a young one during a walk on his place. His retriever had run off barking, no doubt in the direction of the mother. I am sorry not to have seen these bears.

I told Mary about my weekly Hungarian sessions in Cambridge with my friend Zoltán Haraszti, former librarian of the rare book department of the Boston Public Library. They are invariably so tumultuous that Elena calls them my "Hungarian rhapsodies." All Hungarians of Zoltán's period have been deeply "committed" patriots, and to ask them any question about Hungary is to bring forth a torrent of information; to mention the poetry of Ady to Zoltán is to set off a spate of quotation. Zoltán would go on so long about Hungarian politics or literature if I asked him some question while we were reading a poem that I would have to make an effort in order to get him back to the text, and he would continue to talk so much at dinner that he forgot to eat or drink. I suppose that they are not encouraged often to talk about the Hungarian past, that a sign of interest in Hungary releases old stored-up emotion. And the idea that everything in Hungary is of so very special a character that for everybody not Hungarian it requires special explanation and leads to long emphatic lectures. Zoltán was always so anxious that I should get the point of what we read that, with Móricz's story *Hét Krajcár,* he was constantly afraid, in the early part—as I myself had been—that the joking and excessive laughter of the poor boy and his mother were merely silly. "I think," he said, "that this is hysterical"; and when we came to the end of the part we had read, he said, so that we should not leave the point in the air, "Let us go on to the end—my honor as a Hungarian is involved!" When it ended with the mother's coughing blood, he triumphantly expounded this climax.

So Agatha Fassett would keep telling me that the dialogue of a Molnár play was not the way people really talked. With Petőfi's well-known poem *Befordúltam a Konyhara . . .*—the point of which couldn't be clearer—Zoltan impressed it on me, springing up and violently gesticulating: "Do you see? His pipe goes out, but at that moment his heart, his sleeping heart, awakes!" I asked, at that time being only a beginner, why *megláttam* was used instead of simply *láttam,* when he sees the beautiful girl in the kitchen. "*Megláttam!* It is something almost physical! It is sensual!—he *touches her* with his eye!" I asked Mary what this really meant—the dictionary simply gave *glimpse.* "It means what he told you," she answered. "It's something very special, very personal." I asked her to give me an example. Her reply was a stroke of that flattery in which, as in other ways, the Hungarians resemble the Irish: both have been living so long under alien domination that they outwardly propitiate while they inwardly defy. "If I went to New York and came back and told my mother about it, I'd say that I saw this or that—*láttam*—but '*megláttam* Mr. Wilson.'" Neither she nor Zoltán, I found later, had quite the right idea in explaining this form: the common prefix *meg* can more or less be counted on as changing the imperfective of a verb to the perfective aspect, that is, continuing to completed action. I purposely had Mary read with me Ady's wonderful winter poem, so full of the terror and mystery of a wild Hungarian forest, *Az Eltévedt Lovas,* which reminded me rather of upstate New York. I did not mention this, but when we afterwards drove to Glenfield, she spoke of the resemblance herself, as we approached the Adirondacks, in the bleak and misty landscape beneath a completely ashen sky: "Köd-gubában jár a November," "November goes in its peasant's overcoat of fog." Then,

Alusznak némán a faluk,
Multat álmodván dideregve,
S a köd-bozótból kiroban
Ordas, bölény s nagymérgü medve.

In silence sleep the villages
They dream, and shudder, of the past,
As from the fog-bound thicket breaks
The aurochs, wolf and angry bear.

This seemed particularly appropriate in view of the emer-
gence of our local bears. I thought, too, of the gigantic
and frightening bears that figure in the Iroquois legends.

We were going to see Mr. Mihály, the biggest dealer
in real estate in this part of the Adirondacks, who is
director of the Hungarian Center at Grieg and more or
less the king of the Hungarian community—though the
Hungarians, from a long experience at home, do not
readily accept a ruler. He is probably more responsible
than anybody else for bringing from the Pennsylvania
coalfields both the Poles and the Hungarians here, and
he presides at the Hungarian Center over the Saint
Stephen's Day celebration in August, where he dances
the czardas with Mary, to whose father he sold their farm.
This celebration, to which Mary had promised to take
me, was not long afterwards discontinued and the building of the Center sold. The young people no longer speak
Hungarian. Even, however, after the sale of the building,
I saw people gathering there, when I passed, on Saint
Stephen's Day. Mr. Mihály is in some respects a remarkable man. His real interest is not real estate but numismatics. He is said to have made the most complete collection of Hungarian coins outside Hungary and has been
awarded all kinds of honors from the American numis-
maticians. He has also a collection of American coins,

and I brought him a box of these, which had been collected by my father's brother. There were pennies of
almost all the years of the Republic, mostly given my
uncle by the sexton of my grandfather's church in Shrewsbury, New Jersey, who had found them in digging new
graves. They had been used to close the eyes of the dead.
Mr. Mihály scrutinized them through a magnifying glass
and sorted out those that had any value. They were most
of them defaced from neglect. There were also Civil
War tokens that had in those years been used for money.
Mihály has a room in his house of built-in drawers, in
which the coins are professionally polished and labelled
and wrapped up in cellophane. He is an able tough short
chunky man, with the characteristic Hungarian energy
and propensity to talk uninterruptably. He has accumu-
lated on the top floor of his house a museum of all sorts
of curiosities: stuffed animals and birds, old army equipment, scraps of minerals, Hungarian books. He owns a
considerable tract of land, on which he has created a
small park.

The Hungarians, though they have had to learn other
languages and although they are so diffused, seem always
to remain rooted in Hungary and never to lose their accents. Zoltán, who writes admirably in English and who
has been in America thirty years, confesses that he still
has a heavy accent, and says that he cannot talk to another Hungarian without being immediately recognized
as coming from the region of Eger. When he heard me
read Hungarian, he said he guessed at once that Mary's
parents must have lived near Russia because I had acquired from her a Slavic intonation. It was true that her
father had come from Unwar, near the Russian border,
which is now in the Soviet Union. So Mr. Mihály said
that he had met a Hungarian who had told him at once
what town in Hungary he came from. The man knew

because he came from the same town. When later I visited Hungary, I brought back a book of reproductions of the paintings in the National Gallery. I lent it to Mary, and she soon returned it; but I was rather astonished when she showed me a landscape she had just painted, copied from a colored picture in an ad, which had exactly reproduced the typical Hungarian palette—turbid browns, greens and grays. I was even more surprised when I found that the commercial picture she had copied from—a meadow, a woodland, a gate, a man in the distance beyond it—was cheerful and sunlit and green. Mary had suppressed the man and turned the gate to an iron barrier which seemed to stand between the spectator and freedom. It could not have been more Hungarian.

We had to leave rather early because Mary was driving me to the Gauses for dinner and had to get back herself for her Saturday night bowling at 7. She is a champion and very keen on it. She was anxious and I was nervous. We several times lost our way in the now darkening mist.

XVI

1962

On May 16, I flew up to Utica from New York, spent
the night at the Schuyler Club and had dinner with
Cecil Lang, the editor of Swinburne's letters, who is now
teaching English at Syracuse University. When we were
sitting around after dinner, an elderly man, very tight,
came over and talked endlessly and bored us. He was an
old Utican, who knew the Harts. He said that Merwin
was eighty and in bad health, and that he lived in New
York but made visits to Utica. He thought that Merwin's
ideas were fine and wished that they could have been
made to prevail. He said that he had sat for forty years
on the election committee of the club and they had never
in all that time admitted a new member. He then—what
delighted Lang—complained that the club was now doing
badly, had in fact to struggle now to survive. When I
afterwards asked Penberthy about it, he said that this
man was a member of one of the rich old Utica families
who had owned the "knitting mills." He had never done
a stroke of work in his life. It was possible that for a time
those original Utica families had kept everybody else out
of the Schuyler Club; but that there were plenty of new

younger members. (Nevertheless, I have always been struck by the predominance of elderly men.) He said that the club was not badly in debt, was in fact doing quite well.

Coming back here, I don't any more think much about the past, although it is always there. I am now living a new chapter. The income tax business, the Indians, what I see of the life of the Munns and getting to know the Hungarians have brought me into contemporary New York State. Also, Glyn Morris's problems. He is an ordained Presbyterian minister, who went to Union Theological Seminary in New York—born in Wales and married to a Welsh first cousin. Though he boasts that he is capable on occasion of the Welsh inspirational eloquence called *hwyl* and I don't doubt is an excellent preacher, he has devoted himself largely to education and evidently likes to meet the challenges afforded by obscure unpromising localities. He spent eleven years as a schoolteacher in Harlan County, Kentucky, that primitive mining community where the labor agitation is mixed up with the mountain feuds, and says he looked under the hood of his car every morning before he went off to school to be sure there was no dynamite under it. He finds Lewis County congenial and claims to have made Lyons Falls, where he lives, what he says it had already been in the past, the cultural center of Lewis County. He has obtained a good allowance of federal money and has transformed an old Lyons Falls store building into what he calls a "gadget factory," known officially as a Learning Center, for the benefit of local education. It has a library of prints and documentary films, a video tape studio, a reading clinic for retarded children and a child guidance clinic for mental health. I have learned a good deal from Glyn about the condition of the local children, for whom he arranges trips to places of interest in New

York, Massachusetts and Canada. He has also arranged
first-rate concerts. He tells me that when a production of
Fiddler on the Roof was brought on with half the expense
paid by the state, the entertainment-hungry audience applauded so enthusiastically that the cast were reduced to
tears. Glyn has published professional reports and general
books on education, and has become rather widely known
as an authority on his subject. He is interested in literature, theater and music, and is intelligent, imaginative
and amusing. He thinks about fundamental questions
and is nowadays the only person with whom I discuss
religion. I confine my opinions on this subject to my
books, and never argue with people about them. There
is no point in this with people who are really religious,
with whom it is quite impossible as well as undesirable
to argue. Glyn's wife is a delightful cook and has provided a welcome relief from the chipped beef, canned
hash and canned baked beans which, when Elena is not
here with me, are usually all I can think of for dinner.

Glyn points out to me the traces of the Welsh population here of which I had not previously been aware—a
Welsh graveyard with inscriptions in Welsh and stone
cottages which, he tells me, are replicas of such cottages
in Wales.

Albert Grubel can't drive me any more. He is too old,
has a bad back. Huldah Loomis has been miserable, she
says—in the Utica hospital with flu, and the bad eye
from which the cataract has been removed. Beverly is
about to have a baby. I called on her at her house in
Boonville. She is living next to her sister and has an
attractive long stretch of back lawn. Her husband, who
works in a Boonville garage, is shy but, when I catch his
eye, there is something not so simple and not unrespon-
sive in its green-shielded coruscation. Fern has a political

job in Lowville. She came to see me, very smartly dressed, with lilac gloves and patent leather shoes.

Whisky in the morning:

> The mist that lies before my Eastern door
> And morning's golden kingdom of the light.

I had a complete collapse, got some kind of flu that has been going around. I ran up a fairly high temperature and, on top of that, had a terrible attack of gout—while it lasted, one of the worst. Instead of finding relief in lying down, I was writhing all one afternoon and couldn't even get to the bathroom in order to take my gout medicine. Mabel Hutchins waited on me, Mary bought me things in town, and Dr. Smith attended me. He seems to me a model of the country doctor, completely at the service of his patients, who are very dependent on him, and he is kept extremely busy. Once when my heart was giving me trouble, he paid me a second visit although I had not telephoned him. On the occasion of this attack, I had told Elena on the phone not to come, but in the evening I got Mrs. Hutchins to call her and tell her how ill I was. She flew over and arrived early Sunday afternoon. I had moved out of the front room into the bigger and quieter back corner room, which is my favorite place to sleep, and this somewhat improved my morale. It seems more spacious—perhaps on account of the high old-fashioned wardrobe and the big bed with the Columbus head from Minnie Collins's house, in which my parents used to sleep and for which I have bought a new springy mattress. I read Diderot's *Bijoux Indiscrets*, which amused me and took my mind off my troubles. Elena stayed for two days, then went back again on account of Helen; but by that time I was on my feet again.

It was a good thing she came at that time for other reasons beside my illness. We went to the mat with Penberthy on the income tax matter and had him submit another offer, and I got him to take me to Syracuse to talk to the tax people there. They were decent and, I thought, quite intelligent. When you deal with the underlings in the tax department, you are appalled by the vision of a federal bureaucracy that opens up for the future. They have to make a show of severity. It is the higher-ups who actually decide things, but these, of course, are bureaucrats, too.

Mary Pcolar, driving me back from Utica, talked at length about the local schools. They give them what sound like ridiculous courses in "Home-Making" and Sex Education. In the Home-Making courses, it seems, they don't teach them to cook or sew. The young women are likely to get married without knowing how to cook a good dinner, and as for sex, Mary told me a story about a girl who had been a Home-Making teacher and who, in preparation for getting married, was studying a manual she had been given at school. It taught her all about a thing that was called a "basal thermometer," which showed when ovulation took place. A woman friend became anxious about her and asked whether she were sure that her wedding day would not coincide with her period. It turned out that the girl was quite ignorant about these fundamental matters: she thought that the period always occurred on the first of the calendar month. "You'll be settin' there," the friend had said, "readin' that little book, and your husband will be lyin' in bed waitin' for you."

When I came out of my collapse, I felt better and more cheerful than I had all winter at Cambridge. I am

able now to get around, and the weather has been wonderful. I set out to look for the Showy Ladyslipper. I have
never seen this flower, which has become very rare. It is
now against the law to gather it. The children in the
Berkshires and elsewhere would pick it and sell it at the
roadside and almost exterminated it. I have never seen
one, but I know that it is found in this region. I had
nothing to guide me, however, except a state botanical
report made in 1932, which indicates several places in
which the orchids were then to be found.

Mary and George drove me, and this gave me a chance
to see the Pcolar family at home. They made a very
pleasant impression. George was playing outside with
the children. There were the ginger cat named Ripple
we had given them and a much beloved beagle bitch who
is about to have puppies. The old Hungarian mother
lives in a little out-building that Mary has fitted up, so
that the two generations of the family need not interfere
with one another. I was taken in to see her, as if she
were, as she evidently is, the official head of the household. Her little house was as neat as a pin: small bed
with an old-fashioned white coverlet and a colored picture above it of the Mother of God; an English Bible, a
Hungarian prayerbook. She came over when she was
only fifteen but still speaks with a strong accent. I told
her that I thought her daughter an exceptionally bright
girl. "Do you think so?"—she looked at me intently and
shrewdly. "She wants something more, but she can't
reach it." I regretted her taking this attitude—I know
from experience that a mother's predictions may leave a
lasting impression—as when my mother told me at an
early age that I "didn't have it in me to write a play."
Mary showed me, in a little cemetery, a towering white
crucifix. She told me that when her father had suddenly
died, eight years ago, of a heart attack in her mother's

presence, it had been such a shock to her mother that she had not recovered for years, suffering from heart trouble of her own combined with rheumatism. She had prayed all the time and quite recently had begun to have visions. One day in winter when she was looking at the window, which was partly coated with frost, she saw a man outside and was frightened. But then the window began to take on colors, and she saw that it was a stained-glass window which made the room holy, and that the man was Jesus Christ. She had other visions, too—Mary became worried about her sanity—and entirely stopped taking the pills to which she had been addicted. She had had a memorial cross erected in the cemetery—it was imitation marble and had cost four hundred dollars—in gratitude to the Savior.

They seem very old world this family. They are closely bound up with one another and have a good time together. George and Mary and the children kid one another amiably. They know intimately all that goes on on their hundred and seventy acres: birds, animals, plants and trees. Her father used to trap mink, weasels, rabbits, etc. This was something in common, I think, with life in the early days. Agatha Fassett has told me how self-contained and self-sustaining the Hungarian communities had had to be. They did everything for themselves—amused themselves, made their own music, had rhyming and joking conversations. The Pcolars make a separate unit. Mary does not talk as if she had close woman friends and is very much devoted to her children.

Having failed the first time to find the Showy Lady-slipper, we made a second expedition equally unsuccessful. But George and I spent the rest of the afternoon fishing. He caught a perch and a small brown trout; I caught a small catfish. The attractiveness of Mary won her a present from one of the other fishermen there: a rockbass and a rainbow trout. I thoroughly enjoyed the afternoon. It was so long since I had done anything out of doors. I had never been much in that part of the world—we were not far from Pulaski on Lake Ontario—where it is wild and there are few people living, only a scattering of summer camps. It is almost like being in a foreign country—so fresh and unmodernized, so far from the filing cabinets and overhead lighting of the tax officials' and lawyers' offices. I was tired when I got back in a healthy physical way and sleepy during dinner with the Munns.

Fern, in her present function of Commissioner of Elections, had been recently in the even wilder country north of Osceola—Montague and Pinkney—which she herself had not known. She says that the people there are still on the level of the early settlers. The older men have long beards and wear mackinaws. She went to a town meeting which consisted of six men, at which the Town Supervisor all through the proceedings, while other people were talking, was reading a book of comics—occasionally interrupted when somebody else spoke to him and giving a signal of permission when somebody wanted to take the floor. One man was lying on his back on a bench, with a jug of liquor beside him from which he would take long swigs. He would hold it out to others when they entered, but still remain on his back. Fern has to check on the voting machines after an election has taken place. She says that in this kind of country there is no possibility of fraud unless everybody, including the sheriff, should engage in such a complete conspiracy as those people are incapable of organizing.

The Pcolars told me that the woods around Osceola have been swarming lately with wild cats. People shoot them for the bounty, and they sometimes get badly chewed up. They find deer that have been killed by the cats, which leap upon them and bite through the jugular vein, but have been left by their predators uneaten. Of course, a wildcat cannot eat very much of a deer. They may leave them for provision later on or merely kill them out of the hunting instinct, just as human beings kill so many animals. In proportion as the human population here is giving up and abandoning the countryside, the wild beasts seem to be moving back in.

Mary's language: her vocabulary is sometimes a little pleasingly unexpected. The children had "spied" a package in which I had sent them a book, so she couldn't keep it for Christmas. When I asked her whether she read a paper, she said that they took the Rome *Sentinel* and that she at least every day "scanned" the front page. When I see her with her family, she speaks like them; when she tells me about the pharmacy, it is all "she said" and "he said" and "I said," on the level of the Boonville store people; but when she talks to me about current social problems, she has the language of a fairly well-educated person.

I went back for a time to Wellfleet on account of Reuel's coming on, and found it rather demoralizing. I decided that, except for Reuel, I should be better off in Talcottville, now that the Sharps were there.

But when I got there, I found the Sharps quite miserable. Dorothy, who has had a bad fall, is only learning to walk again; if she makes any special effort, she seems invariably to sprain a wrist or throw a toe out of joint. I have some idea, on account of my gout, of how it feels to be crippled and uncomfortable most of the time. She says that her breaking her hip and all the confinement that followed has had on her a bad psychological effect, it has made her morose and irritable. She dislikes almost everything that is going on—as I do, for that matter, even when I am well. She is annoyed by a radio and a barking dog that are new in the house next door (where in my boyhood the pretty Smithling girls used to live—one of them worked for my Aunt Addie—and which is now a ghastly mess). She has always been apprehensive and seems to be losing her capacity for enjoying life. Malcolm is invariably attentive and patient, almost never leaves her alone in the house. They have been over here together only twice, and he very rarely comes alone and never for very long. He will not even take a drink. It is impossible for them to go out for drives or dinner, and I feel that I mustn't stay long with them: it tires Dorothy and wears on her nerves.

Beverly, who had come to see her Aunt Mabel, brought over her baby to show her to me. She is touching and sweet, looked quite pretty after her pregnancy and is crazy about the baby. She said that Elena had told her that what she needed was a baby to occupy her, and she now thinks Elena was right—though she had had a hard time giving birth and still has to wear some kind of brace for her back.

It is sad for me up here this summer. Mary P. has had partly to desert me. She now has a job in Rome in a new drug store in which she manages the cosmetics department and is, she says, "on the crest of the wave." She has resolved to get a degree from Utica College, a newly organized offshoot from Syracuse University. I encourage her in this; the project has contributed to bucking her up. She came here this morning (Saturday), and she is coming tomorrow afternoon to type letters and do Hungarian. I miss having her with me almost every afternoon as she was able to be last summer. I like to have her around, she is so capable and well developed. I had her take me to the Boonville greenhouse to get some geraniums and petunias for the old stone receptacles along the porch, and she said suddenly, "Why should you buy petunias when I can give you some?" She then brought me some huge ones and some ageratum. I said to Rosalind that those were Hungarian petunias, and she commented, "They'll make trouble!" Mary also brought me vasefuls of her magnificent gladiolas, purple, yellow, blue, scarlet and pink—as well as a great glass jar of excellent Hungarian stew.

Rosalind came up here from Wednesday to Saturday (August 15-18). The only time I really get to talk to my children is when they drive me around, and then we do have long conversations.

We made an expedition to Tug Hill by the road I had gone with the zoölogist. Rosalind was bored at first by the monotony of the narrow bushy road, but then when we got to the wilder part, discovered it was quite beautiful. The fireweed was past its prime, but the last blossoms and the pinkish stems made a curious screen of pink, and the road was lined with goldenrod, which, like the fireweed, had grown to an enormous height, Joe-Pye-weed and low yellow St. John's-wort. A few pink roadside mallows were rearing themselves and exulting in their beauty as they do not do in the fields. Like all jungles, this terrorizes one a little. The road is full of horrible holes, and in one place impassable to a car, because a plank bridge has broken down. That wilderness was rather eerie. One felt that the plant life was master here. It made for us beautiful smears of color, but it did not have to bother about us. Even the flowers could overtop us.

Elena and Helen arrived on August 24.

Elena says that the plastic flamingos that one now sees so often in front of the houses have become "a status symbol." It shows you can afford an ornament that doesn't have to be planted or have the soil prepared for it or watered.

The Players Guild of Collinsville, coached by Glyn Morris, did Noel Coward's *Blithe Spirit* this summer. Jane Klosner of Boonville, who has been their main attraction for years, played the ghost of the first wife. I had not seen her before and was astonished at how good she was: so different from the heaviness of the rest of the cast—lively, amusing, pretty, full of *espièglerie* and charm. She is Scotch-Irish, her maiden name was Galbraith. I invited her and her husband for drinks. Elena had her usual stiffening that was stimulated by my having her meet any woman that I had talked about with admiration—"When is your Sarah Bernhardt coming?" But she liked her, too, and said, "She's straight." Jane's husband wasn't well, so she came alone. It turned out that she was so conventional in terms of her local milieu that she had felt some hesitancy about going out without her husband—but, she said, "I thought if Jackie Kennedy can, I can!"

(The Players Guild didn't survive, though its performances, I thought, were excellent. The production, under Glyn Morris's direction, of O'Neill's *Ah, Wilderness* seemed to me much better than the Theater Guild production in which George M. Cohan played the father. I think that these amateur performances are a very good thing for provincial communities. We also used to have them at Wellfleet. But neither of the groups that put them on is any longer active. I suppose that the movies and television have thoroughly discouraged people from doing anything for themselves—though they still have theatricals in Rome, and Jane Klosner, I am told, takes part in them.)

Elena's stay this summer was not a success. Things came to a climax on August 27, after a celebration of her birthday, and we had a rather bitter quarrel. The next morning, she had packed her belongings and drove Helen and the dog back to Wellfleet.

That night Mary came to do my letters. I had had most of a pint of Scotch by the time she arrived. I asked whether it wouldn't be possible for them, on Saturday or Sunday, to drive me over Tug Hill along that washed-out and car-jolting road; but she didn't seem to think it would. I dramatized it, telling her how terrible it was, and she said, "You're building this up." Then I described the sphagnum swamp and said that it might be safer to go in with a rope. The Mayor of Constableville, when he had given me the key to the gate across the road that led to the camps, had warned me that there were "some pretty bad holes in those swamps." Then she began to talk about the swamp in what I thought was a peculiar way—though it may have been just the whisky. "Have you got a rope?" she said.

August 30. A telegram from Elena: "Arrived last night very sorry have written love."

That night I had dinner with the Crostens on their usual lavish scale. Their attractive children are away, and one misses them. Jessie Howland was there and had arranged to take us to an old house between here and Utica. It is an old stone house, somewhat bigger than this, and with a stone extension at the back. I had wondered about it as I passed it. It has been bought by a retired dentist and his wife, who has interested him madly in American antiques. He took us from room to room, explaining in a loud voice how rare and precious everything was: lusterware pitchers, candelabra, highboys, bas-relief hunting pictures with dried grass for the foliage (this kind of thing I had never seen), embroidered Biblical pictures with painted paper faces rather like those that my Uncle Charley Corliss's mother used to make. He had collected all this for himself. There was almost nothing left from the original family, the founder of which had been a Dutchman with a grant from the Holland Land Company. The house was built in 1802. It is not unlike ours, but somewhat grander and fancier—white fireplaces all carved differently like ours, but with classical Georgian designs. As they took one around among the four-poster beds, the pianos, desks and grandfather clocks, one wondered how and where they had their daily existence. Jessie, as we were waiting for drinks, hesitated over an ashtray and asked, "Is this supposed to be used?" It seemed to me rather significant that a man who had evidently never before possessed or lived with such things should now have such a passion for them, such a nostalgia for something he had never known. How far we have come from the era when houses were furnished in this way is shown by the prestige and value now attached to such household objects, most of which in the period to which they belonged were common enough conveniences of a modest enough elegance.

Elena and I became reconciled when I made an expedition to Canada and had her meet me in Montreal. This trip was immensely interesting to me but I omit my description of it except for a few general observations:

The people in Toronto, although no great beauties, seem healthier and better set-up than those in New York and Boston. Not so driven and not so cramped between big buildings and in narrow streets, they seem to be more good-natured, and they probably enjoy themselves more. In Canada, after coming from the States, one is to some extent able to relax. One feels off on the margin of the continent. The Canadians are not under the same pressure as we are, do not have the same responsibility. Their semi-dependence on England has been in some ways an advantage. They have not had to save the Republic, to justify democracy to the rest of the world. They have been able to remain à l'abri, to watch the United States from the sidelines. But, having so far escaped our panicky crises, they seem now to be having something of a crisis of their own. The recent inroads of the U.S., which now apparently owns most of Canadian industry, have stimulated an anti-"American" nationalism at the same time that they cannot see how they can avoid a kind of union with us. Then the resistance of the French Canadians to British Canadian domination has been stiffened to a point that, in its extreme form, it has produced a "separatist" movement, demanding complete independence, a parliament of their own: like Iroquoia (the country of the Indian Six Nations) and the American South of before the Civil War. In spite of Elena's two years in Canada, she said that she now for the first time, except for official occasions in the past, was meeting French Canadians. I took her to Quebec City, where she had never been before.

A certain sound residue of the English tradition: better service in hotels and at airports. The people are more

polite. Our bewildered and terrified state of mind is seen
in our administrative inconsistencies and operational
messes. But in the hotel rooms the nuisance of television
is equally inescapable and the business men's conven-
tions are just as noisy.

Strange how different Talcottville looks from Canada,
which is another country, dark and special; our stone
house seems something quite alien to the Canadian stone
houses, which are tighter, blanker, narrower-windowed,
with no front porches, with for me no physiognomies. It
is almost as if down in New York State they were having
a different autumn. Our people are enclosed in a separate
countryside and have a separate orientation. There is all
the difference between a place in which one feels the
fibers of family and a place in which one is totally unaware of other peoples' similar fibers.

The literary and academic people are interesting in a
way quite distinct from ours. Hugh MacLennan has had
international experiences—including Princeton and Oxford—but at the same time manages to be a Scotch-
Canadian patriot; John Buell is now preoccupied with
working for the Catholic Church in Quebec—I met at his
house a Jesuit of Loyola University who had encouraged
him in writing at college; Morley Callaghan may seem,
like his novels, commonplace when you first encounter
him, but, like them, he is deeply sensitive and understanding of human processes; young Marie-Claire Blais, who
writes such gloomy and eerie novels, is an altogether
unique phenomenon, who, in spite of her present reaction
against her clerical education, has perhaps the possibility
of becoming one of those convent saints for which French
Canada has been distinguished; Père Lévesque, who discovered Mlle Blais when she was only nineteen, is a

cultivated and highly intelligent Dominican. He was eliminated from Laval University as the head of a department
of sociology on account of his advanced views, and has established at the Maison Montmorency a refuge for scientists and artists of all denominations as well as a resort for
Catholics who are making their retreats; Jeanne Lapointe,
who teaches at Laval, is a genial and witty Frenchwoman,
who occupies herself with the problems of French Canadian education; she believes—I assume, rightly—that these
ought to take precedence over political problems of French
independence. None of these people seems to me in the
least to resemble any type in the United States, which
they usually regard from a remote distance and of which
they are often surprisingly ignorant.

Elena went back to Wellfleet and I to Talcottville. This
almost a month in Canada from September 14th has in
several ways done me good—restored my relations with
Elena, and got me away for awhile from myself and the
damned American problems.

Return to Talcottville, October 2. A perfectly marvel-
lous day. Everett Hutchins picked me up at the airport
in Buffalo, and we came in through the Boonville Gorge,
which is now all rose and yellow and orange and crimson.
I like to see this country here at different times of the
year and to think that it must have looked so to my
relatives when they were living—pathos of feeling this.
The next day was also beautiful. The maple in front
of the house is now all rose madder and gold, with a little
light green underneath, and in the lot across the road in
which it stands, the young sprouts of trees looked like
goldenrod and the milkweed was wearing white puffs.
It seemed a pity then to have to leave; but the next
day, Thursday, was clouded, and today there is nothing

but dreary rain. The colors of the trees are rusted, and the leaves are falling away. In the old days, I suppose, they were kept so busy that a merely rainy day could not have depressed them much.

Dinner with the Morrises last night, and our usual animated conversation. Their friend Barbara Erwin was there, the nice somewhat unconventional schoolteacher, who, I take it, is one of their only "kinspirits." She kids Glyn, and I try to discourage him, when he gets on the subject of Calvin, who seems to have haunted him all his life: he is deeply convinced that anyone who has come under the Calvinist influence must suffer from a conviction of guilt. There is an old lady in the neighborhood of a family made rich by the paper mills who, I imagine, is perfectly self-satisfied and has never felt a twinge of guilt in her life; but Glyn thinks she is driven to go to church simply by a conviction of sin at not having contributed money to the kind of benevolent projects that he himself tries to promote. (When she died, however, it turned out that she *had* left money for such causes.)

At one point after dinner, Glyn questioned me—"It may be impertinent to ask you this"; but didn't I feel that there was something behind our lives that would make things come out all right. He approached the subject so discreetly that I did not at first understand that he was talking about God as a power and purpose in the universe. He has mainly dropped his Protestant theology, but he still feels under the necessity of keeping hold of this belief in some divine intention. Since I have never had to think in these terms, I did not grasp at first what he was getting at, and so my answers must have been unsatisfactory.

 I don't believe I have noted Glyn's excellent remark that "a language is really a way of life." He was born

in Wales and used to speak Welsh, and Welsh conceptions with the words that express them still play some part
in his thought. *Hwyl,* for example, which means a gift
of eloquence that descends on the Welsh orator and sometimes carries him beyond his comprehension.

I saw Mary only once after I got back from Canada.
She now goes two nights a week to Utica College, driving
there from her job in the drug store in Rome. In order
to get some kind of certificate, she has to have thirty
credits, but she has already so convinced them of her
competence that they are going to let her skip English
I and II.

She said she had once delivered a neighbor's baby.
They had been caught on their farm in a snowstorm and
had not been able to get anyone in. She herself had been
delivered by her father.

Mabel Hutchins drove me as far as Helen Muchnic's at
Cummington. Her sister, Beverly's mother, went along
to "visit with her" on the way. It is not true, as Loren
Crosten thinks, that the natives do not appreciate their
landscape. Mrs. Hutchins and her sister were in ecstasies
about the colors of the trees. Elena met me in Cummington.

XVII

1963

I got an April Fool telegram concocted, I found out, by the family: "We request the honor of your presence at banquet and would like you to judge beauty contest of New England chapter of Magyar women."

Dreams about Talcottville. As always, there is something in the house that I don't expect. The commonest kind of dream is one in which there are strange intruders that I have to expel. This, I suppose, is partly due to the actual intruders who, when my mother left the place vacant, burned holes in the upholstery with cigarettes. In the first of my recent dreams, I went into the east front room and saw what looked like the profile of a person in the corner against the light; then I saw that it was not real, a dummy. Then I noticed other things to the right: those creatures like salamanders or hellbenders which I sometimes see in my dreams, that have previously taken the shapes of other objects or even people. There was one that had the shape of a particularly unpleasant bright red worm with a head like a caterpillar; it had attached itself high on the wall. I knocked it down with my cane and was beating it to death when I woke.

249

Two or three days later, I dreamt again that I had come back to Talcottville and found a couple of men working on the house that I did not remember to have told to come. They were not, however, hostile, and they showed me a part of the house that I had not known existed. It was up a rather hidden stair through a narrow little hallway near the front: a living room with furnishings of an elegance such as otherwise is not to be found in the house—a kind of highboy made of inlaid wood, books with fine bindings, etc., and, opening out of it, a bedroom with a beautiful old bed. I was, of course, delighted. It was what I had wanted the place to be.

I came up to Talcottville June 9, and have been writing my diatribe of protest, so have not kept up this journal, am only now bringing it up to date.

I had been sitting alone here in my two-piece chair in the summers reading the papers and getting more and more indignant at having my income bled by the government in the interests of the war in Vietnam and the constantly increasing funds for "defense." I have finally produced a pamphlet, *The Cold War and the Income Tax*. Arthur Schlesinger called up to ask whether I would accept from Kennedy one of his new series of "Freedom Medals." I sent Arthur proofs of my pamphlet and asked him to be sure that Kennedy knew what was in it before he decided to give me a medal. Long afterwards, I learned that a newspaper man had asked an Internal Revenue official what they were "going to do about Wilson." The official had answered, "Shoot him, I guess," then explained that when the award had been proposed, they had submitted in opposition a sixteen-page memorandum. "Unfortunately it didn't stick." But Kennedy, since I had had him informed, had known what was in my pamphlet before he got the memorandum. I learned from another source that when Kennedy saw the man who remonstrated, he said, "This is not an award for good conduct but for literary merit."

In my boyhood, I read Maeterlinck's plays up here, having found them in some upstate bookstore. (I still have the volume, published in 1911.) I read somewhere that whenever he had finished some work at the castle (I think it was) in which he lived, he would invite all his friends in and celebrate with a rousing party. While working, he had shut himself up and lived with the utmost asceticism. This made a great impression on me, and, in spite of the fact that I do not take Maeterlinck very seriously as a writer and think that his celebrations were bought rather cheaply in terms of accomplishment, this festive practice of his may have influenced my own habits: first the "dedicated" toil, then the orgy. Maeterlinck had been at that time associated with the actress Georgette Leblanc, and when I lived in Greenwich Village in the twenties, I was somewhat shocked to find her an aging and rather stagy large woman of Lesbian reputation, on the fringes of the Provincetown Players. I had had such a vision of her, in trailing robes, as the mistress of a wide-lawned château.

The knowledge that death is not so far away, that my mind and emotions and vitality will soon disappear like a puff of smoke, has the effect of making earthly affairs seem unimportant and human beings more and more ignoble. It is harder to take human life seriously, including one's own efforts and achievements and passions. In my tendency toward this state of mind, I have found Pope John fortifying. When over eighty and knowing he is doomed by cancer, he gives all the energy left him to the council whose object is to modernize the Church,

Pope John

then dies with a perfect dignity: "I am watching myself die, step by step." I am told by a Catholic in a once high position that those who appointed him Pope were counting on his imminent death, on his filling a gap as an interim nonentity, then were astonished to find that he was really a man of strong character who would work for fundamental reforms. He was that very rare phenomenon, a professional ecclesiastic who was trying to be a Christian.

heaven' During the first five weeks I have been up here, I have lived virtually the life of a monk and have succeeded in getting my pamphlet written. I have had perfect quiet and freedom: no family, few telephone conversations, no newsstands and bookstores to visit, no temptations to social life. The Sharps had not been here; the Crostens had not yet come; the Gauses were still in Europe. The house is now homelike and well taken care of. Mabel Hutchins gets me breakfast and supper.

I am glad to have got that pamphlet off my mind and conscience—for several years now, it has been rankling with me, poisoning me, depressing me, creating conflicts of purpose of a kind to which I am not accustomed. Not to have decided something, not to know what I am going to do and to be able to go about doing it has always had a demoralizing effect on me. My sleeplessness at Red Bank in 1917 when I could not make up my mind what to do about the war. I have been thoroughly enjoying my solitude, am not lonely and do not suffer any longer from those dreadful depressions that I used to have here and in Cambridge. It is partly that I have settled down to growing old, which in a way makes one feel one's depressions less; and my gout seems to be almost cured. I have not lately had bad angina attacks, and though I was miserable on my way here and after I first came back, on account of having had five teeth pulled and the painfulness at first of my bridge, my mouth is quite comfortable now, and I find that it is reassuring to be able to chew again.

I went to the Players Guild play at Lyons Falls and saw there Helen Johnson, the nurse who stayed with Father in Red Bank, that ghastly summer that Mother had taken a vacation and I had to spend some time there. Encountering Miss Johnson gave me quite a turn. I had seen her again before, several summers ago, but she is now very old, over eighty, and it brought back again out of the past an experience that my memory had tried to suppress. It had been in my later years of college when I was full of intellectual excitement and my varied social life with my friends, and my poor father was buried there, in the uncomfortable Red Bank house, in the hypochondriacal gloom which prevented him from taking an interest in anything and which blanketed the future with darkness: no real desire to live, to hope of doing anything further. It was strange and repugnant to me, on meeting the old nurse, to realize that a witness to all that was still alive.

Mary is evidently enjoying her new job in the drugstore in Rome. She is on excellent terms with her boss, who is going to run for mayor. He pays for her Utica nightschool and has given her a one percent interest in the business. She is proud of having had all B's on her Utica exams and has evidently got a lot out of her courses: has learned about Evolution, has had to read and discuss that, it seems to me, very foolish but certainly discussion-promoting book, *Lord of the Flies.* It is touching and worries me to see how anxious she is for an

education and to make possible for herself some better
kind of employment.

Trip to Tug Hill with the Pcolars. Many pheasants, a
snow rabbit in its brown summer coat, which George
identified by its size. We found the sphagnum bog behind
the gate, abounding in pitcher plant in full bloom with
its leathery maroon flowers that have a rather sinister
look. George and I felt a certain interest in finding out
where the road led to—though rough and unfrequented,
it seemed to go on interminably; but Mary, who was
doing the driving, after crossing the bridges of rotten
plank and plunging through the flooded holes, became
more and more reluctant. We were finally stopped by a
stream over which the bridge was completely broken
down. We brought home some pitcher plant and arum
lily. I have been keeping them in basins of water. The
flowers are now fading, but the pitchers seem to be
multiplying and now fill the basin. The local kids at
one point seemed to think it a good joke to upset the
whole thing on the lawn.

I discovered a nest of robins outside one of the third-floor
windows. When they left, I found a baby bat. It looked
like a gray baby demon; its wings were too limp to fly,
and it was groping with its little paws trying to climb up
the glass. The orioles have pathetically built their nest
in the old dead tree back of the house, where they have
had no protection from the leaves. One of the trees on the
street beside the stone barn was rotten in the crotch
between its two prongs, and another came down in a
heavy wind. I have had to have them all taken down.

The young people don't know what to do with themselves. They hang around in the evenings on the corner
next to our house or sit on the stone front steps and make

so much noise that I have to drive them away. Last winter
some of the boys broke the windows in Carrie Trennam's
house and Aunt Addie's old house, and wrecked the pop
machine on the front of the Roches' store. Fern says it
is the boys of two families who are recent newcomers to
the village. We once picked up one of these boys who
was hitchhiking his way to Boonville and noticed his
confirmed sullen look. The cheapness of property here,
due to there being no general water supply or any
general sewage system makes it desirable to poor people
who are living on welfare. In two of these families, the
fathers are dead and the mothers have jobs in Boonville,
so there is nobody to control the children.

Cecil Lang came over for a night. We sat on the
back porch and talked. He comes from North Carolina
and was interesting about segregation. I said that I had
a certain sympathy with the Southerners, but he said he
had none at all. He was careful to add, however, that he
could not feel at ease with Negroes socially. I said that
the Southerners were scared of the Negroes just as they
had always been. *"I'm* scared of them," he confessed.
On his last visit home, a big Negro had come to the door
and asked, "Is Milly here?" He was frightened, but then
it turned out that the Negro had got into the wrong
house.

Canadian authors.

The days when I was looking up bacteriological warfare in connection with my income tax pamphlet were
also the days when, in connection with Canada, I got
around to reading Anne Hébert, Jean Le Moyne and Saint-
Denys-Garneau, and this combination of subjects rather
got me down. These denizens of old French-Canadian
"maisons seigneuriales," who exist in a damp murky at-

mosphere of Jansenist religion and incestuous relationships—they chafe at the narrowness and puritanism of
their Church and the imprisoning walls of their families
but they are powerless to liberate themselves. Saint-Denys-
Garneau and Le Moyne cannot even get to the point of
being explicit about what it is that worries them. If you
knew nothing about French Canada, you could hardly
guess what it is they are writing about. Clotted and
clumsy prose. I fell back on my usual resource of reading
books by and about Bernard Shaw, Max Beerbohm and
Oscar Wilde—also, a new biography of Huneker.

Bette Mele's visit. She is a Seneca woman, connected
with the Krauses and all those Beaver clan ladies, who
comes from the Allegheny reservation and went to the
Indian school, but is now married to an Italian psychia-
trist, who graduated from Princeton and now practises
there. Her family, Fenton tells me, are noted for their
beauty—the Seneca women are in general very handsome
—and Bette is extremely attractive. She had her three
children with her and a tall good-looking German girl,
a student from Berlin who was qualifying for some degree
that would enable her to teach English, by spending two
years in an English-speaking country. She had a job
taking care of the Mele children. As Bette said, a curious
combination: an Italian doctor married to an Indian princess, whose children were being looked after by a well-
educated young woman from Berlin. The girl talked
about Proust when she saw a volume on the table but
was otherwise running after the children when they were
scampering about the lawn. Bette apologized for calling
herself a princess—this, she says, is how her husband
introduces her. She knew this was not quite right, but
it was too much trouble to explain that she belonged to
one of the families which for nobody knows how many

hundred years have enjoyed the exclusive privilege of
having the chiefs chosen from among them.

  Bette had tried to adapt herself to take a place in the
white world, but this she had found very difficult. She
had had two years in a white school and felt that what
they had taught her there had not been of any use to
her. She had trained to be a nurse in Rochester and had
met her husband there. [She had known there was something wrong with her and had gone through two years
of psychoanalysis, which had not cleared her up at all.
Then coming back on the train from New York to Princeton, she had happened to read in the *New Yorker* one of
my articles about the Iroquois. She had recognized some
of the Senecas that I wrote about without naming them
as relatives or people she knew, and she suddenly burst
into tears. She said that my book had done more for her
than two years on the analyst's couch. She realized that
the trouble with her had been that she was altogether an
Indian and could not be anything else.] Since then she
had taken part in the women's peace movement and had
tried to help the cause of the Senecas, who were fighting
to prevent their settlement at Quaker Bridge from being
flooded by the Kinzua Dam. She had got into correspondence with me, and her letters had interested me: they
were obviously those of an intelligent woman who was
competent to write in English. She had just been to an
Indian School reunion at Onondaga and brought me a
container of their ceremonial corn soup. In visiting her
reservation after so long an absence, she had feared that
she might not be well received, and she had been very
much gratified to find that she was warmly welcomed.
She had also been visiting her brother-in-law at Barne-
veld. She said she had difficulties with her husband's
family, because, just having come from Italy, they would
insist upon trying to persuade her that she ought to

become "Americanized." She told me that her father had been a Christian, but her mother was a Longhouse woman, who had belonged to the Little Water Society. In reading my articles, she had been astonished to find me describing the ceremony, which she had never been allowed to go near. And when the Dark Dance had been "put up," in her house, she and the other children had been sent upstairs and were frightened at what they heard going on below. Accompanied by William Fenton, I had been admitted to both these ceremonies and had described them in my *New Yorker* articles.

She and her children, when they came to see me, were on their way to Blue Mountain Lake to call on some people she had once worked for. On the way back, she dropped in again and said that she had found her visit disappointing. I think that it is difficult for her—from what she tells me of her life in Princeton, too—to establish close relations with non-Indians. This willingness of hers to visit white friends is very rare on the part of the Indians. The Fentons, who have really close Indian friends and are honorary members of a clan, tell me that they can never prevail on these Indian friends to visit them. I wonder whether the reason is that they don't want to be beholden to us. But my relation to Bette is special. On this visit, besides the corn soup, she brought me a box of English candy, a bottle of Moselle wine and a bag of cherries and peaches.

I once thought I was safely remote up here from the dangers of atomic warfare; but I have come to understand that I am only a few miles from the air base at Rome, which would be one of the important targets. This air base, I am told, supervises the equipping and dismantling of the bases all over the country, and it maintains a squad of pilots on duty around the clock who fly off at intervals in the direction of Russia and then come back again. This has only recently been given publicity after having been kept secret hitherto. The men, to prevent them from being bored, are encouraged to do water colors.

Three peace marches converged at Rome, and I went over to see A. J. Muste, whom I had known in my radicalizing and labor-reporting days. He is aging—seventy-six—and they told me he was having to slow down. The peace marchers were standing with banners at the gate of the Air Force camp, and committing acts of "civil disobedience" by making forbidden entrances and getting themselves removed. One woman who did this was arrested. Muste seemed rather worried. A young man came over and asked him whether they could call it a day. Muste looked at his wrist watch, and said that since they had publicly declared they were going to stay till 6, he thought that they ought to stay. It was pointed out that the marchers seemed somewhat to be losing their discipline. Some were now singing folksongs, and others were lying on the grass. They should have been standing in ranks. The woman who had driven me up to the gate did not approve of this sloppiness. A good many of the young people, including herself, I was afterwards told, are anarchists and do not submit willingly to discipline. What does it mean to be an anarchist nowadays? Muste had told me, when I saw him in New York, that he regretted the beatnik beards, and I did not see any among these marchers except a very well-trimmed and decorative one worn by a young minister.

Dinner with Walter Edmonds at the Towpath. He says he doesn't know any writers except me, whom he regards as "a local character." He is really, as I was told, very shy, and he leans over backwards not to make any pretensions. He seems to me a curious person. He will admit to no real interest in literature, seems to read only historical novels, as if following the stock market of his own investments. And he seems to have so little desire to see the world that I was surprised at his going to Iran at the time when his son was in the Embassy there. He claims that he does no research in preparation for his New York State novels, but gets them all from old anecdotes that the local people have told him; but I know from the people at Hamilton College that this is not quite true.

He said that when he first got to know Grace Root, she offered him what she said was a new kind of cocktail called a "martini."

Six days in New York, July 9-14. A very satisfactory visit. Arranged with Muste and Roger Straus to have the proceeds from my pamphlet go to Muste's peace movement. Long conversation with Muste. When he makes a public speech, he is able to charge it with an intense and not grandiloquent emotion; but in private conversation he is extremely shrewd and not at all sanguine. His attitude is that of the intelligent churchman who has resigned himself to hoping to accomplish very little or perhaps nothing perceptible at all. He gave me an entirely realistic analysis of what was going on in the country. He agreed that the peace movement did not have the same leverage as the desegregation movement. When the Negroes should have achieved a few of their objectives, they could not be expected to go on making efforts for more general ends; and in the meantime there were so many people whose jobs depended on the war industries that they couldn't be expected to oppose them. The only hopeful possibility was that in the long run the unemployment caused by increasing automation might

1996: In the end it has, to some small extent, withered away.

swell the number of protesters. The enemy was the war establishment with the industries dependent on it, and it would be a very long time before any impression could be made; he couldn't see that it could be got rid of by anything short of revolution. In some Middle Western city, he had talked with a security agent who had been sent out to watch their rally. This man had said in substance, "I agree with you, but I can't do anything about it, because my whole career has consisted of this work I am doing, and I couldn't bring myself to let down the other men I am working with."

Elena came Tuesday and left Friday.

Back in Talcottville, Mary met me at the airport. She had a drink with me at the house and was evidently prepared to stay out to dinner, so we ate the little supper of spaghetti that Mabel Hutchins had left for me. I played for her the whole of the Hungarian recording of Kodály's *Háry János,* which has all the Hungarian dialogue. With her usual capability and deftness, she got the old phonograph running smoothly, and she translated the dialogue fluently. When she relayed to me the angry speeches of the abandoned peasant fiancée, she would make the appropriate gestures. Of the triumphant march of the interlude, she said truly that though it was meant to sound rousing, it had also a strain of melancholy. She was much interested in the whole thing.

I had given her a record of Bartók's *Concerto for Orchestra,* telling her to note the sudden alternations between somber brooding and ecstatic high spirits. George said, "I'm used to that. It's what I get all the time."

Lincoln White, the Mohawk Iroquois who was superintendent of the school at West Leyden, has now a simi-

lar job in a bigger town, Marcella outside Syracuse. He
dropped in to see me one morning—very cheerful and
evidently enjoying himself. He said that in his academic
career he had so far encountered hardly any prejudice on
account of his being an Indian. St. Regis, the Mohawk
reservation which is likely to be much disturbed on account of straddling the St. Lawrence, so is partly in the
United States and partly in Canada, as well as on account
of the conflict between the Catholic priest and the present
nationalist revival of the aboriginal Longhouse religion,
is now, he says, relatively quiet.

The Fentons spent a night with me, July 26. They
talked about their European trip. Bill said he found the
scientists in Prague, if you did not talk to them about
politics or get into the problem of the genesis of races,
exactly like the scientists anywhere else. He is going to
an anthropological conference in Moscow and is screening
the U. S. delegates.—He says that the "borshch belt" in
New York is moving up almost to Binghamton—these
are the third generation of well-to-do Jews who spend part
of the week in the country. Also, that in this part of
New York the old civilization is on the decline. Many
farms are being abandoned, and this is perhaps the reason
why the wild animals are coming back.—He made my
blood run cold by his account of what was happening
to the Seneca Indians as a result of the Kinzua Dam.
The Indians or the Quakers who were working for them
had consulted a housing expert, who had referred them
to some Madison Avenue publicity man. This man had
advised them that the only advantageous thing for them
was to create an Indian Williamsburg, a replica of an
old Indian village. It would become a tourist attraction,
would bring trade to Salamanca. Some of the Senecas

were quite interested in this idea, and Fenton thought he might even coöperate in some advisory capacity.

I have lately, it would seem, been suffering from a mild form of auditory hallucination. I seem to hear the telephone ringing just before I am completely awake in the morning. At first, I would go to answer it, but find that it was not really ringing. Now I simply lie in bed, and if the sound is not repeated, I know that it is imaginary and don't get up. When I first came up here this summer, after Rosalind had gone away, I once thought that I heard her calling me.

The weather has been hotter this summer than anything I remember up here. This house is cooler than anywhere else; but even here it has been sometimes stifling, and even at night. In the morning, I have occasionally waked up sweating. One day I had to have a towel while working, and it reminded me of the days long ago in Red Bank when I was writing *I Thought Daisy* in the summer with a towel around my head.

Elena came in August and spent almost two weeks. Everything went well. I understand now that one of the factors that made things difficult before was her worrying about and trying to keep tabs on Helen, who was constantly out with the village children. They were in the habit, as I learned much later, of hanging their washed condoms out to dry. The boys are now adolescent, and I had been growing apprehensive myself.

We had a party soon after Elena arrived: Gauses, O'Donnells from Utica, Langs from Syracuse, Walter Edmonds and his wife and his son, Bette Mele and her husband, the Marcelins, the Morley Callaghans from Toronto with their boy Michael, the Tharett Bests with their daughter, the Crostens and the Howlands. We were pretty well steamrollered by this. I think that it is a better idea to dilute these annual affairs with some local and less intellectual people. The Callaghans and the Marcelins stayed on, and the next morning there was reëstablished something more like the leisurely atmosphere of prolonged and reflective conversation of the Callaghan household in Toronto. I catechized Morley and Michael, and they gave me exact information about politics and education and the judiciary in Canada. Then, in the morning, there arrived unexpectedly a liberal Scottish lawyer whom I had known at the time I was visiting the Six Nations Reservations in Canada in connection with defence of the claims of the Iroquois. He was accompanied by his son and his new South African wife, who had one of those colonial semi-cockney-sounding accents. I had asked them to look me up when they came to the States. We had planned a picnic at Independence River, but everything seemed to go wrong. We drove there in two cars, and I made the mistake of not going with Elena to make sure that she would know how to find the way— with the result that she overshot the turn-off, and I waited with my party at the river so long that I began to get worried and had Michael drive us back to the house. No one there; we returned to the River, where the other party appeared, having just eaten part of the picnic. By the time they had found the right road, we had made our trip back to Talcottville. But now there appeared to be something amiss that neither Elena nor I was able to put our finger on. When we were finishing the picnic on the river bank, I was sitting between Phito Marcelin and the South African wife of the lawyer. I was aware that I was finding it impossible to involve them in a general conversation, and that the lady was always facing away from us. The same kind of thing occurred when we had driven back to the house; and I noticed that when they were leaving she did not shake hands with Phito at the time her husband did. It was only sometime after all the guests were gone that it dawned on Elena and me that this South African lady had been practicing *apartheid*. I had made the mistake when they first arrived of presenting Phito to her as "the most distinguished writer of Haiti."

(Phito has since told me that he had had no awareness of this, but had found the lady sympathetic. Could this all have been on our part imaginary?)

XVIII

1964

Spring. As always happens at this time of year when my departure for Talcottville approaches, Elena has been getting annoyed with me. In spite of our differing tendencies, which sometimes put us at cross-purposes, we do not really like to part from one another.

The income tax people have refused to accept a part of my settlement, some $1200 that they confiscated through their lien on the Red Bank trust fund, and I am now going to have to mortgage the Talcottville house in order to pay this. With 6% interest, it amounts to some $1500.

Bad dream last night, June 7. Elena and I were in a room in which the ceiling fell, and then, one by one, two or three gray bricks came down; but Elena was standing against the wall beyond where the ceiling was falling.

Early June till late August. Have neglected this diary

on account of being occupied with *O Canada* and *Bit Between My Teeth.*

When I gave Mary P. the embroidered table set that I had bought for her in Budapest, she said at once, "I can do that kind of embroidery." I have learned from Sándor Rado that the Hungarians have the word *ezermester, master of a thousand (arts),* which perfectly applies to Mary.

I have done a lot of writing at Talcottville, but otherwise my summer has been melancholy and also rather annoying. I was here seven weeks alone, with only two overnight visits from friends. Gertrude Loomis is quite dotty, didn't remember Rosalind when she came to see her; Huldah is suffering from arteriosclerosis. Jessie Howland, who thought last summer that an operation had cured her, is now back on crutches again. She is noble in never complaining or in making any show of her infirmity. Everett Hutchins suddenly died of a cerebral hemorrhage the evening he had come back from a trip with his truck to New York. He had just changed a tire for Rosalind, then gone off to the Boonville Fair. When I went to see Mabel after the funeral, she said something like "Well, we have to go on, though we don't know why we should." It reminded me of Edna Millay's poem about the death of the father: "Life must go on—I forget just why." It seemed all wrong that Everett should have had to die like this when he was not yet old. I think the truck company worked him to death. These twenty-four-hour spells to New York and back must be too heavy for anybody. He was a highstrung wiry man, and when he got back he had said to Mabel that he would never make that trip again. Even the young men go to sleep and run off the road. They keep themselves awake with "pep pills," and they are compelled by the income-tax people to produce receipts for the many cups of coffee that they take along the road. Of course Mabel had great difficulty in collecting any compensation. Old Albert Grubel is so feeble now that he has even sold his car. Fred Reber died during the winter at the age of eighty-eight, but was still able to do a little work last summer. I cannot remember a time when he was not active in Boonville. In my childhood, he was a photographer. Lately, with wonderful ingenuity and skill, he did all kinds of odd jobs for me—framed pictures, refinished the bar chairs, repaired other pieces of furniture. He was entirely in business for himself, did not have to work for anything like a truck company; and he loved being able to do all the things he did. I bought from him for $2 the well-known picture of the authors of America, which he had got from the effects of some local judge. I have hung it in the hall with my other curiosities. The likenesses are terrible, and it is somewhat comic—obviously a New York job, because Cooper and Washington Irving are holding the center of the stage while the New Englanders are pushed to one side. Poe moodily prowls alone, not associating with any of the others.

The side wall of the stone barn has fallen out, as Fred Berger, the builder, has warned me it would do, and I could not bear to sit outdoors with those ruins near me. I have had Bob Stabb rebuild it, and it is costing me quite a lot. The Stabbs are old natives of the village, and Bob's father built me bookcases when I first came back. He is an old-fashioned stone mason, whose craft probably goes as far back as the original building of the barn, and he has done a good deal of the work in helping Bob to rebuild it. The roof of the house, also, has to be repaired and painted. My relations are good with these old-timer families. Even when I don't remember them, it is as if I had always known them.

The Crostens were less jolly than usual because they have left both the children in California to work at summer jobs. Leslie was waiting on table in some restaurant and wrote her parents that she was rather homesick for Boonville. On account of their moving around so much, they had given the big police dog away. Leslie missed him terribly, and I missed him, too. His great idea was to have you throw things into the pond so that he could plunge in and retrieve them. Once when the Crostens were away, he kept Rosalind and me doing this endlessly. The beavers, however, are back after mysteriously having disappeared last summer, and late in the afternoon you can see them swimming from their lodge, trailing silver streaks in the water behind them. One day intruders tried to climb on the lodge and made the inmates furious so that they slapped their tails to get rid of them. I met Mary Crosten one day in the post office, and she said she had something to tell me but didn't want to be overheard. She would wait till we had gone out in the street. I expected some local scandal and was all agog to hear it, but it turned out to be simply that otters have been seen in their pond. They didn't want it known for fear that somebody would shoot them.

Malcolm and Dorothy finally arrived. She seems much better than the summer before last. She can walk, though only slowly, and she seems to be perfectly clear in her mind, though she does not talk very much. I said to Malcolm that he was wonderfully patient with her. "Too much so, perhaps," he characteristically snapped. Why? "Because she mustn't get to be too dependent." He gave me a copy of an address he had delivered called [*The Conservative Fellow Traveller.*] He was evidently making an effort to formulate a declaration of his opinions about everything; but, as I told him, what with his ambiguities, his habitual indirectness, I couldn't tell what he thought about anything. He replied, "That was why I wrote it"; but when I quoted this later to him, he denied it: "I didn't say that: you did."

Dorothy Mendenhall died during the summer. She had been in the nursing home, and hadn't really been functioning for several years, and nobody, I think, could have felt real grief. Dorothy expressed no sorrow, and yet her aunt's death must have affected her quite deeply. One felt that something was gone from us—even when not actually present, a presence. She had been there in the background so long—always a "tower of strength," though domineering and difficult to cope with—to her sons, I suppose, somewhat crushing.

Dawn Powell

[Dawn Powell, my dear old pal] came up for almost a week while Rosalind was here. She is in and out of the hospital and seems, for her, rather emaciated, rather yellow and haggard. I was alarmed about her when I saw her in the mornings. She would collapse on her bed or the couch. But she never complained, and in the later afternoon, after a couple of drinks at the Towpath, she always came to life again—sometimes forcing her wisecracks a little. She is unique among my visitors in her natural feeling for smalltown life. She remembers and identifies the local characters. She understands sitting on the front porch and watching the people go by.

Dos Passos, who is now a big Goldwater man, has written for the *National Review* a preposterous hysterical

piece about the San Francisco Republican convention,
at which Goldwater was nominated for the presidency.
It sounds, as I have said to him, as if it had been written
by a teenager squealing about the Beatles. Dawn thinks,
probably rightly, that this present state of mind is inspired, not only by getting back his patrimony, his
property in Virginia, but also, along with this and his
second wife and having a daughter, with a belatedly
developed family sense which is bound to produce conservatism—as Dawn says, the desire to "belong." He had
his daughter christened, though I doubt whether he is
any more a believer than I am. He seems to want to become now very much the kind of man who once aroused
his indignation, a member of the comfortable propertied
class, an upstanding American citizen. He used to like
to shock people by his radicalism, now he tries the same
thing with his conservatism—but the latter seems as
puerile as the former. The enemy, the person to be
shocked is, in either case, always what he calls "the
liberal," who is mainly a creation of his own, a rejected
state of mind inside himself. I tell him that the trouble
is that he was born a liberal and has always been ashamed
of it. He began to become difficult to talk to when he
went all out for Robert Taft. Then he seemed immensely
proud of having lunched with Hoover and Landon. (I
can remember his shuddering, at the election of Hoover,
at a prospect of his "steamrollering" the country in the
interest of the Big Business he represented.) He now
takes the same attitude about the Russians as, at the
time of the first war, he ridiculed people for taking about
the Germans. He cannot quite denounce the peace movement, but his attitude about it, as publicly expressed,
seems to me absurdly patronizing and reminds me of
Oscar Wilde's "Those Christs that die upon the barri-
cades,/God knows that I am with them in some ways."

The author of *Three Soldiers* is now apparently not unwilling to advocate war as a defence against the menace
of Russia, and he talks seriously about taking refuge in
shelters and so pulling through an atomic war.

Elmer Roch of the general store has been on a trip to
the West and feels ashamed of the backwardness of our
part of the world. Out west they have highways that run
above whole cities!

It was also depressing in Talcottville to find that the
John Birch Society and juvenile delinquency had made
their inroads here. The Birchers have put up posters—
"Save the Republic. Impeach Earl Warren"—one on a
tree on my vacant lot across the road, which I tore down,
and one on the gas station in front of Elmer Roch's
store, which was torn down—not, it turned out, by somebody with anti-Birch opinions but by some of the delinquent youth. It then appeared in front of a miserable
house across the street from where the Sharps live. A
farmer neighbor on whom Carrie Trennam has depended
for getting certain things done for her, appeared before
Carrie and, pointing at the poster, at that time in front
of her house, demanded, "What do you think of that?"
Carrie said, "I don't like it." "Then I won't work for you
any more!" He has announced that he won't work for
anybody who doesn't go along with the Birchers, but he
mowed my back field for the hay as usual, undoubtedly
not knowing what my attitude was. The Catholic priest
in a neighboring town is said to be an ardent Bircher—I
suppose on account of the Supreme Court's action
in eliminating opening prayers from the schools. I am
told that all this emanates from somebody in Port Leyden,
who sends out the John Birch literature and has tried,

unsuccessfully, to persuade the principal of the regional school in that part of the world to give each of the graduating seniors a copy of some Birch propaganda book. The Birchers have created in Talcottville a certain amount of bad feeling of a kind that I have not been aware of here before.

As for the juvenile delinquents, there is now quite a gang that, when the boys have motorcycles, as they all seem to aim to do, travels from town to town. I found them all congregated one night on this corner and on my lawn. After the Crostens, who had been there, were gone, they slipped in the back door and stole what was left of a pint of Scotch. Later on, I found three boys drinking beer and drunk in the chairs on the front porch. I appeared to them with a roar and the ancient gun that the Civil War collector in Boonville had offered to buy as a relic, and they immediately took to their heels. After that, when they gathered, I bawled them out and succeeded in breaking up the group. Of course, there is nothing for them to do here—the movie house in Boonville has burned down—and no place for them to go, except this corner with its street-lamp, and the general store. At one time, later on, they swarmed around the store and seemed to have Elmer Roch terrorized. He made friends with them, but they robbed him. I don't know what means he took finally to get rid of them. Three boys were arrested for robbing garages and put on parole at Lowville. One boy got a job, and the sheriff asked Fern if she thought he might be let off parole. Fern advised him not to but he did. Then, not long after my difficulties with them, he ran into one of the Jacksons' cows while racing a car on his motorcycle. The cow was killed, and the boy was taken to the hospital. Things were quieter for a while, but they have done a lot of thieving and wrecking. Why break, as they have been doing, old ladies' windows?—the Loomises' and Carrie Trennam's. Mrs. Clark Lang says that in Boonville they pull up her flowers and throw them around the lawn. Early in the summer, one of Walter Edmonds's cows was shot by someone with a truck to take it away, evidently to sell it for beef. But Walter came out, and they fled. The poor cow was running around the field bleeding and very soon died. A recreation center is planned for Boonville.

When I saw John Gaus at the Crostens', I thought that he behaved rather oddly. He seemed to avoid speaking to me, and in the middle of dinner, he made some remark about not having read my tax pamphlet. He gave the impression of not having been able to bring himself to read it. He had only seen some reviews and, on the basis of these, he disapproved. He made some crack about supposing that I was all for Goldwater, because Goldwater was campaigning to reduce taxation. This annoyed me since I am not in principle against taxation, and I sent him a copy of the pamphlet, which he later made excuses for still not having read. He is so much infatuated with his notion of the soundness of the democratic American community which accommodates itself to a variety of different kinds of people—derived from his early recollections of what he imagines life was like up here—that he doesn't want to pay attention to the unpleasant things going on now. You really can't get him to talk about them. Malcolm tells me that, during the McCarthy era, John would quickly shut him up if he tried to discuss the subject.
I think this was also in evidence the evening that I read *The Duke of Palermo* to the Crostens. I had not expected to find the Gauses there, and I was a little shy before John of reading an academic satire that was partly derived from Harvard. I know now that I have made a mistake in ridiculing the academic world as freely as

I have in the presence of academics. I of course always made the assumption that the people I was speaking to were intelligent and must feel about these absurdities as I do—in fact, that they are different from the average professors. But after all it is the way they make their living, and if they are serious people at all, they must take their profession seriously. And John Gaus is an intensely "dedicated" teacher who gives more personal attention to his students than is nowadays usual at Harvard. Making fun of the competition for academic status is a practice in bad taste on my part.

Mary Pcolar's mother died last winter, and it is plain that this has upset her equilibrium. She either seems worried or, as one evening when she came late from the store, rather unnaturally merry. She told me later about the projects of her boss in the drug store at Rome. He wants to buy out a brother who has another drug store in Oneida, combine the two under one management and altogether make a bigger thing of his business. Mary would be a partner, and he would give her a more important position. He later put her in charge of his department of "surgical appliances," and she made some trips to New York to get some special instruction in this. He talked about buying the place next door and turning it over to her department. I think he seemed to hold before her eyes a vision of a little empire of which she would be the queen. She seems already to have her clientèle—customers who count on seeing her. And yet she did not seem to be altogether happy about the arrangement. She must have much depended on her mother to keep her on an even keel. If it weren't for her family, she said, she could devote herself to business or education. I said that her children depended on her. "They won't do anything without me. They say that picnics and things are no fun without me."

I hardly ever think about the past, my ties with the old life hardly exist any more, and my relations with the current community are now something of a nuisance and annoyance.

XIX

1965

My visit at the end of March to see about getting repairs made on the house and the stone barn. Since it was already fairly warm in Boston, I foolishly failed to inquire what the weather was like here. I found snowdrifts around the house, and it has been snowing off and on since I have been here—so repairs are out of the question. I can't even see what has already been done. But I am glad to have a glimpse of the place under heavy winter conditions, and I enjoy seeing the people here, although there has been some very bad news. Poor Mabel Hutchins has had an operation—a tumor removed from her spine and is in the hospital now. In January, George and Lou Munn had a horrible accident in their car. George was driving Lou to her job in Boonville at 7 in the morning when it was still pitch-dark. The road on the Lewis County side had been sanded up to the county line; but after that, beyond Boonville, the Oneida County people had allowed it to become glazed with ice. The Munns drove over the hill without being able to see what was going to be on the other side. A car had slipped off the road and was caught on the protective fence. A tow truck had come to haul it out, and this had held up a lumber truck. No flares had been placed as a warning, and George ran into the lumber truck. Lou was nearly killed —it was doubtful whether she would live. She had broken innumerable bones, and will have to spend months in a cast—she also had concussion of the skull. George was less seriously hurt, and is now back on his job.

Mary P. drove me up from the airport. She horrified me by having peroxided her hair. I told her that this was all wrong for her, it did not fit her clothes and color, and she said that other people had said the same thing, and she was going to dye it back. She has had a kind of breakdown, had been to our Boonville doctor, who said that she was anemic and gave her vitamins. He told her that she must stop overworking, that she would have to "cut corners," give up either her job or work at the college— so she had dropped her two courses at Utica. What had definitely made her realize that she could not go on at Utica were a professor who had talked for three hours about the romantic poets without her being able to get hold of anything—I have heard or read just such lectures, for Mary a sheer waste of her precious time—and having been assigned for immediate homework both *Nostromo* and *Pickwick Papers*. It seems to me that *Nostromo* is one of the most labored and tedious novels ever written and that it should never be assigned at all. She would only, if she had lasted till spring, have achieved the credits equivalent to a freshman year. When I saw the Costas, Dick told me that Mary had been becoming quite maternal with the other students in the class, who were all so much younger than she. We had dinner at the Towpath that night, and she told me on the way back that she felt as if I were her uncle. I said I was complimented that she hadn't said her grandfather.

I had stopped in Utica to go to Planter's. I wanted to

get some Beluga caviare, which used to last me in Talcottville for three or four days when I made it into luncheon
sandwiches. I was appalled to find that Planter's had
gone out of business. The liquor store next door was still
open, and the old proprietor was there. He said that he
couldn't keep the business up. The neighborhood was
run down, and there was no longer much demand for
such delicacies. He said that I shouldn't be able to find
any Beluga caviare in Utica. This is typical of the decline
of the well-to-do classes who were able to afford such
luxuries. At about the same time, a grocery store in Hyannis which had catered to the same kind of clientèle has
also gone out of business.

When I woke up the first morning here, I realized that
it was delightful to find myself in one of my own houses,
instead of, as in Boston, at a hotel or, as in Wesleyan, in
someone else's house.

The silence here is punctuated by the dropping of
icicles and the thudding of snow from the roof.

Dinner with Glyn and Gladys Morris. He feels that
he is making progress, was quite satisfied, I thought, with
his projects. They have started a vocational school, which
is supposed to train backward boys for a trade, and he has
made improvements in his house, and set up a projection
room in the basement, where he is able to show films
from his library for schools. All the schools, he says, have
one now, and they can get a great variety of films, docu-
mentaries, scientific films and old Hollywood pictures.
I very much enjoy watching these, with a glass or two
of wine after dinner: *Force of Gravity, Wild Life in
Canada, A Legend of the Micmac Indians,* which last
showed nothing of this dying tribe but mostly Canadian

scenery. The "background music" is amusing: the people
who provided it must be often hard put to it to find something appropriate to their subjects. My favorite film is
one that shows the life-cycle of the bee. You see them
doing the dances described by Fritsch by means of which
the scout, on his return to the hive, shows the rest where
to find the honey. They are very cruel to the drones—
throw them out to die when they are done with their
services.

Cocktail party at the Towpath. They told me to bring
Mary, so she came with George. I had never before seen
it when the skiers were there. I talked to some middle-
aged couples. I hadn't realized that such people came to
the mountains to ski. Some from Rochester who had
known Ed Mulligan told me he had died since I saw him.
There were a scientist and his wife from New Jersey.
He had been studying the mechanism of lightning bugs
and other such luminous organisms. Mary wanted to
stay on for dinner, but I couldn't face any more conversation, which, with strangers, fatigues me terribly nowadays, so George drove me back to the house. We talked
about Mary. He knows she is remarkable. When I had
complimented him once on the behavior of the children,
he had said it was all due to her. Now he said that he
had neither encouraged nor discouraged her in regard to
her courses in Utica—so he couldn't be blamed for anything. He is sensitive and very likeable.

I woke the morning I was leaving to find it snowing
again, and heavily. I called up Mary to ask whether she
thought she could make it and was told she had already
left. We found, by the time we started for Utica, that we
were plunging into a blinding blizzard: we couldn't even

see where the road was and followed a car ahead or the bald spots in the middle of the road. But Mary handled it with her usual skill, never tried to go too fast or got stuck. She thought it was exciting and so did I—a dramatic aspect of the life up there of which I had had no experience. In Utica, however, it was absolutely vile, cold, snowing or raining, and windy; streets ankle deep in water and snow. I went to see Mabel Hutchins in the hospital. She had lost a good deal of weight, and her face looked very much younger, almost youthfully pretty like Beverly's. She had been through horrible weeks, had been under morphine for days. But she could walk now and felt much more comfortable, and was due to leave the hospital that day unless the snow prevented.

I spent the night at the Club, and Cecil Lang drove me over to Syracuse at 11 the next morning. I admire his sharp independence, his refusal to subject himself to some of the worst nuisances of the academic life. I think it was much later, during his first year at the University of Virginia, that he told me he had prefaced his lectures by announcing to his students that he was there to give a course in the English Romantic poets and that he was going to confine his activities to that. He was not interested in what they might write outside of their papers for the course, or in what they thought about anything else. He was not interested in their personal problems and did not want to hear about them. He is obviously quite set up about his well-paid new job in Chicago. It amused me that Dick Costa, who does not even know Lang, was able to tell me exactly the figure of his new salary. All this kind of thing is known to one's colleagues all over in the academic world, and it establishes a hidden hierarchy, invisible to the man from outside. I thought Cecil's French wife very bright, and remarkably flexible for a French woman; but she had lived many years in Brazil and, unlike most transplanted Frenchwomen, spoke English extremely well. She had been reading Huysmans all winter, an interesting taste in a woman; and was doing what Elena is doing at Wesleyan: teaching little colored children to read. She gave us a perfect light lunch, which exemplified the best of French cooking: some consommé-type fish soup, but richer than consommé, something attractive made of cheese which I don't know how to describe, watercress salad and mixed fruit dessert.

I never leave Talcottville nowadays without an uncomfortable feeling of never being able to do justice to my relation to Mary Pcolar. I am almost twice her age, and, as she says, she is to me like a favorite niece. Elena was later to reproach me for taking more interest in her than I do in my own daughters. But the sole function I can have with young people seems to come down to instructing them, and neither Rosalind nor Helen has ever shown any signs of caring to be instructed by me. I can only in a small way teach Mary, and I cannot really educate her, as she ought to and wants to be educated. She always asks probing questions about whatever she does not understand: What is philosophy? What caused the French Revolution? I do not always find these questions easy to answer, and sometimes my difficulty in answering them makes me aware of to what extent educated people are in the habit of taking it for granted that they all understand a great many things that actually they have only just heard of. In explaining the French Revolution, I told Mary about Marie-Antoinette's asking, "Why don't they eat cake?" when told that the people had no bread. She said that her mother had told her this story, but had attributed it to the Empress Elizabeth. This shows how legends spread, so that the very same stories are accepted as authentic at wide distances all over the world.

Middle of June. I have settled down to very quiet habits: working during the day, reading *Middlemarch* in the evenings, playing phonograph records that I've brought up here but have never yet listened to seriously. Specially impressed by Ives's Second Symphony, which seems to me one of his most successful things: semi-sacred music originally composed for the organ, alternating the comic and the rowdy with quotations from Beethoven and Brahms, and snatches of old hymns and Stephen Foster, and ending with *Columbia the Gem of the Ocean.* *Middlemarch* is tranquillizing—that slow and solid chronicle of an English country community in a story that goes on and on. My life is so very subdued that an evening out is wildly exciting. An evening of talking and drinking with the Edmondses, though I left at 10 o'clock, went to my head to such an extent that I came home and had the worst attack of angina since three years ago in Cambridge. It kept me more or less awake all night.

The place is greatly improved by the trimming Bob Weiler gave it last autumn. He cleaned out the peonies and the gooseberries and tulips. It gives all the good things a better chance. The yellow lilies in the choked-up back garden have come out as never before, and the lilacs have been much more in evidence.

I had a dream in which I thought I was talking with Elena and saying that I didn't want Helen to get completely out of touch with this place, when somebody came to the door. It was three or four newspaper men. They said there had been a newspaper story in which it was asserted that I had no right to this property. I replied that the family had been living here since the end of the eighteenth century. They said there was some question about the title. I said that I couldn't comment, not having seen the story.

Bob Stabb is doing some work on the place. He has found that the front porch and its pillars are now partly rotten. It is depressing to see how much ought to be done; I can't have the whole floor of the porch rebuilt. But I enjoy having people work around the place: it gives me a vicarious feeling of accomplishment.

Discovery of the Showy Ladyslipper. Walter Edmonds told me last year that his son had found these orchids on the Black River and transplanted them to his place. I asked him to call me up when they bloomed, which he says is in the middle of June, always on almost exactly the same date. I went over to see them this year, and they are really amazingly beautiful. They are well shown on the bank of his brook. The bulbous part is bright pink—rounder, less elongated than Cypripedium—and the streamers above are white. The inside of the *orchis,* the testicle, is striped with pink dotted lines, and there is a thing like a small petal that folds down into this bulb, the upper part of which is white and the lower part a pink-speckled yolk yellow. I had just learned from the Loomises that they had one. Huldah competitively asked me how hers compared with Walter's, and I told her that it was somewhat paler but had three blossoms instead of two. She did not want to tell me where she had got it from, but Mary Pcolar, who was driving me, extorted from her that Mrs. Weiler had brought it. I then found out that Mrs. Weiler had known the place from childhood. I called up the name on the mailbox there and found that the lady of the house was reluctant to have a stranger come on the place. How had I known about the orchids, etc.? They had moved out there to live because they didn't want people around. She would have to consult her husband and call me back. But she identified me as the person who lived "in that stone house," and told me that she had been in Beverly's class in high school. Later, she phoned me that she would be glad to have me come Saturday, so, Elena and Helen being with me by then, we called on them, and they couldn't have been more cordial. The orchids were growing in a bog, and they let us take away two plants, which we transplanted to Wellfleet, but they didn't last. These people have also had, they told me, besides the common pink ladyslipper, the yellow kind, which is very much rarer.—I have only seen it once, in the country outside Detroit, when I was in camp there during the first war.

The husband's father lives with the young couple, and though both the men have jobs, their principal interest seems to be hunting. They have a wire-enclosed kennel of three or four black and tan dogs with which they hunt the bobcats that are killing the deer. The dogs put up a great baying and were trying to leap out of their enclosure. The bitch, named Molly, with a sensitive gentle face, was not allowed to be outside because they found she could leap out of anything. The young husband took me around the place and enthusiastically told me his plans for it. It had been formerly owned by people who lived in New York and only came there for the summer. When the present owners had bought it, they had had some trouble with the caretaker, who seemed more or less to have made it his residence, and that was why they were being so careful about letting other people come there. Some people, said the present owner, only acquired such a place when they retired from their life in a city and

had only a few years to live; but he had been lucky
enough to buy this when he was young enough to enjoy
it. They have four hundred acres. There is a delightful
little lake in front of the house, with a shelter for wild
ducks; and on the lawn there was a picnic table in
process of production. His father had taken color photographs of the Showy Ladyslippers. I promised not to tell
where they were.

Have just read Lampedusa's *Racconti,* which delighted
me—especially *Lighea,* the story about the Greek scholar
who had an affair with a siren. He says the sensations
must have been a little like those of the Sicilian goatherds
who had intercourse with their goats. Also, the memoirs
of his childhood in the "mastedon" family mansion at
Santa Margharita. My tastes would run to this kind of
magnificence—having a private theater, etc.; but I do
very well with Talcottville. I wish that this place and
the Wellfleet house were not on much-travelled highways,
but had grounds all around them like the Edmondses' or
were surrounded by a forest like the Chavchavadzes' or
like Margaret De Silver's place in the woods at Stamford.

I am trying to run down, at Lowville, the history of
this house. It would appear that Thomas Baker bought
the place from Jesse Talcott as early as 1832, and that
the Talcotts lasted here only two generations. I am told
that there are still two or three Talcotts in Port Leyden,
but I have never met them. The only Talcott left in
Boonville is the curator of the town dump. In a book that
Tom O'Donnell lent me, I found a horrible story about
a Talcott in some not very far-away town who, after his
wife's death, had intercourse with his two little daughters.
I noticed, when I asked the Loomises, usually so proud
of their Talcott blood, about the fallen fortunes of the

surviving Talcotts, that they did not seem eager to talk about them. Huldah answered that they had always regarded the Collinses as the top family of that locality. They are related to the Collinses, too.

All the family, Reuel and Marcia, Henry and Daphne and their little girls, Elena's German cousin Freya and her Russian cousin Marina with her children were converging on Wellfleet this summer, so I went back with Elena and Helen after the 4th of July. The Sharps had not been able to come here on account of Dorothy's illness and the Crostens had been in Europe.

September 29. I flew up from New York, and Mary met me—she had bad news about herself. She had thought she had solved her employment problems by getting a job training stewardesses on the Mohawk line and had written me a jubilant letter; but she had had to give it up— the first time I have ever known her to confess that something was too much for her. They had had a rapid turn-over in men doing this work—three in five years—and this was apparently the first time they had tried a woman. She had been led to believe that it was merely a question of supervising the stewardesses' appearance—which was thought to be unsatisfactory—and telling them how to behave, and she had at first had a man who worked with her. But then the man had gone away, and she found that she was stuck with the technical side, which she had not had time to master. There are five kinds of planes used, and they are all constructed differently. You have to know how they all work and teach the girls how to jump from the wings onto mattresses. They made her wear slacks, which she didn't like. And in all the two months that she spent there, she was never off the ground once, so she had to be teaching the girls pure

theory—which turned out to be particularly difficult at
1 or 2 in the morning when they were tired from their
day's work. She said she spent a good deal of her time
simply sitting in the office and studying manuals. When
she was left without anyone to work with her, she found
that she couldn't face either the work or the responsibility,
so she finally threw up the job.

She tells me that the air people now insist on calling
the safety belts "seat belts" and the emergency exits "not
normal" exits.

The Jenckses from Wellfleet came to see me, bringing
Charlotte Kretzoi, whom I knew in Budapest and who is
over here studying American Lit. Mabel Hutchins was
unavailable on account of a brother-in-law in the hospital
in Utica and an aunt in a nursing home in the opposite
direction, and Mary, when I mentioned this, engaged to
provide a dinner. She produced a huge and rich Hungarian repast: soup with many ingredients, chopped meat
in cabbage leaves, pork chops and mashed potatoes, and,
for dessert, little pastries with a variety of fillings, prune,
chopped walnuts, etc. She had brought for the middle
of the table a small wicker cornucopia, with large grapes
and other fruit spilling out of it. Charlotte, before dinner,
had a long conversation with her in Hungarian.

Charlotte told me that she and László Országh, my
scholar friend, whose dictionaries I use, regarding me as
an honorary Hungarian, were in the habit of referring to
me as Ödön Bácsi, Uncle Edmund. Bácsi seems to be
something like the equivalent of Russian *batushka*; an
uncle by blood is *nagybácsi*. I told Mary to call me this;
she had been mistering me all this time.

After dinner, we went to the Morrises' to see a very
chichi avant garde picture, called *Dreams for Sale*, which
I had borrowed from Renata Adler. I had Glyn show

also my favorite documentary, *The Life of the Honey Bee*.

The next day we started out about 10, Gardiner Jencks driving, and—rather to everybody's surprise—made Wellfleet by 1 o'clock in the morning, taking in the Oneida Community and Cooperstown on the way. It was an admirable piece of driving by Gardiner, who had evidently been enjoying himself, writing music in the Talcottville dining room. I did not need to point out to the Jenckses the beauties of the upstate scenery. They were constantly exclaiming about it, and both reproached me for not paying enough attention to it.

XX

From May 21. This has so far been my most depressing visit. The weather has been mostly horrible: overcast, rainy and misty. I have finished my academic play and the new sections for *Europe without Baedeker,* and as always when I come to the end of something and have not started anything new, I find myself in a let-down state—sit drinking and playing solitaire and listening to the phonograph. Fern has had another of her awful accidents. A cow stepped on her foot. It is badly bruised, red and purple; the blood vessels are still bursting. Albert Grubel is dead.

Mary P. met me and brought me up here, but I have not been able to get her to do anything for me since. She has really gone into business with her boss: she plugs the pharmacy on TV and evidently shares in the profits of the store. She has also sidelines of her own, which, however, are advertized in the drug store: a charm school, in which she teaches the girls of Rome how to hold themselves and make up and dress, and a series of conversation classes for the older ladies of Rome. I asked her how she handled these last. The first problem, she said, was

to get them off the weather. And their children? And
then their children. How did she go about that? Why,
she would say that she'd just been reading a book that
had some interesting ideas about child psychology. She
has also joined a literary society, but has so far got to
know only one woman—who turns out to be Jewish, of
course—who has any cultural interests. She also attends
PTA meetings; and is tomorrow to be mistress of ceremonies at some sort of tap-dancing contest.

I am depressed about the local delinquents' having
smashed up the stone bowl and one of the stone posts
in front of the house. It must have cost them some effort.
They have also broken into Aunt Addie's old house,
where the Sharps have been spending the summer,
smashed things, poured something sticky over the stove,
and stolen all the electric light bulbs.

When I called up the Loomises, I got Gertrude, who
said, "Huldah's gone out with a boyfriend—I don't know
where." In going into town, I saw her in front of Aunt
Addie's house. The "boyfriend" turned out to be a young
boy who was working at fixing the iron fence. Two of
the town kids had been racing in cars and had gone off
the road and wrecked the fence. I have never seen
Huldah look so gray and *abattue*.

I have come to realize nowadays that I cannot really
live without Elena. Aside from my difficulties at the
present time when neither the Hutchinses nor Mary can
take care of me, Elena and I have now been together
nearly twenty years and, in spite of communications that
are rather oblique in certain ways, we have become quite
dependent on one another.

> You fade, old presences, and leave me here
>   In dismal trickle of a dimming May;

I play old records and lay solitaire
   Through aimless hours of Memorial Day.

Cities I'll never visit, books that I'll never read,
   Magic I'll never master. In a cage,
I stalk from room to room, lose heat and speed,
   Now entering the dark defile of age.

I cleared up yesterday (May 22) from my depression
and feel quite cheerful and normal again. The weather
is warm and fine. The narcissuses in the back garden
have all suddenly bloomed, and the dandelions are out
on the lawn. I had a very pleasant dinner with the
Utica O'Donnells last night. They are recent enough
friends to be appreciative, or pretend to be, of all my
old anecdotes—the kind of thing that, when I begin
telling them to guests, makes Elena find something to do
in the kitchen. It has also rather raised my morale to read
Anaïs Nin's diary. It is certainly her magnum opus, and
it has made me feel, though it is so long since I have
seen her, that I have had in her, since she also keeps a
diary, a kind of steady companion.

I was given on May 11, in Boston, a medal together
with a thousand dollars by the American Academy of
Arts and Sciences. This was founded in 1780 and once
presided over by the first two Adamses. It also gives an
admirable prize, named after a Francis Amory, for "out-
standing work addressed to the alleviation or cure of
diseases affecting the human reproductive organs," as
well as the twin medals in gold and silver, struck from
the same die, established by Count Rumford for "the most
important discovery or useful improvement" tending "to
promote the good of mankind" made during the preceding
two years. It seems now to be a more or less phantom

organization. I had already had a medal from the Institute of Arts and Letters, one of Kennedy's Freedom
Medals, and this summer a $5000 National Book Award.
On the occasion of the last of these awards, I wrote that
my age and infirmities made it impossible for me to go
down to New York, but that I'd be glad to give them
lunch in Utica. This turned out to be an excellent arrangement, for it enabled me to curb the publicity and
keep down the size of the lunch. We had lunch in a
downstairs room at the Club. Rosalind very ably played
hostess. Roger Straus came up and was the life of the
party. The Fentons came on from Albany. Mary was
present, well-dressed in blue, and behaved with perfect
dignity—though she insisted on taking pictures with a
newly-acquired Polaroid camera that produces instanta-
neous prints. She had bought it to take pictures of her
teen-agers before and after her charm treatment. These
pictures are on show in the pharmacy. When someone
at the lunch asked her what it was that she taught her
charm pupils, she told him as a joke that she taught
them to drink gracefully out of drinking fountains. Roger
said that her snapshot of me reading a speech of thanks
looked as if I were singing "God Bless America." Brett-
Smith from the Oxford Press, as my other publisher, also
came up, and I talked to him about his father's edition
of Etherege, which I had lately been reading. I don't
think he was entirely at home: the English cannot adapt
themselves to our loud-laughing conviviality, which is
often too much for *me*. We also talked, apropos of my
academic play, about Thomas J. Wise, the literary forger.
He said that Wise sometimes came to see his father at
Oxford. He always wore the same kind of suit and little
bow tie—by which Brett-Smith seemed to imply that Wise
was rather "jumped-up." Although Brett-Smith's father
would occasionally go upstairs to get some book to show

a visitor, he was always careful, when Wise was there, to send his son instead, so that Wise would not have a chance to slip anything into his pocket.

One of the men from the Book Committee told a good computer story. A gigantic computer is constructed, designed to surpass anything hitherto contrived. It required a special building in which to be lodged. They begin by feeding it a difficult question, to which, after long waiting, they do not get any reply. They try again with something slightly easier, but again there is no response. On a third try, a slip comes and the operator reads: "It says we'll have to sacrifice a goat." Charley Walker had told me about seeing some men, in the course of his labor research, who were working with a computer. They would say: "Let's put it to him this way"; "No: let's put it to him like this." But someone else at the luncheon said he had always heard them referred to as "she." When I discussed this at Helen's commencement with a lady I met there, she suggested that they called the machine "she" only when it let them down: "She's broken down again."

These awards are in some ways deflating me instead of puffing me up. They make me feel that I am now perhaps finished, stamped with some sort of approval and filed away, that I am what Stephen Potter would call an "OK figure." Longevity in itself would seem to bring some kind of recognition. Roger Straus tells about a sculptor he knew who began to get awards when he was past seventy. When Roger congratulated him, he said, "The thing is to outlive the sons-of-bitches."

The cultural explosion in this "area." Something of the kind, I suppose, is going on all over the country—*pari passu* with delinquency and crime—partly due to federal handouts and foundation grants. Glyn Morris says he has more federal money than he really knows what to do

with. Loren Crosten tells me that there is a great vogue
for "art centers" now, where music, ballet and theater, for
example, are supposed to be somehow combined. He regards this idea as futile: each of these arts, he says truly,
has to be learned by itself. And there is a tendency for
such projects to duplicate one another. I am told by
Evgenia Lehovich, the director of the School of American
Ballet, who goes out on tours of inspection, that there
have been founded now, subsidized by the fund made
available under the Kennedy administration, ballet
schools all over the country that are quite often at a loss
for either instructors or dancers. Two boys came to see me
the other day—one an English teacher at Utica College,
the other a painter who admires Soutine—to talk to me
about a project, which seems to me vague and impossible,
of setting up a summer school at Leonardsville, where
the painter has inherited some property. They say they
want people in the different arts to be able to talk to one
another; some more or less distinguished person to come
on once a week to read a paper or speak—to be followed,
of course, by discussion. I think I shocked them by saying
that for a painter or a writer to talk to a musician—unless
they happen to be special friends or to have other interests
in common—was like a carpenter talking to a plumber.
What a person practising one art can get from someone
practising another must come from experiencing the
other's work. But shouldn't they ask "why" they practise
their art? I said that anyone with a real artistic vocation
rarely asks "why" he practises his art.

The Boonville library has recently been much improved: all reorganized, and more space between the
shelves, more new books, modern lighting installed—and
Jessie Howland says that there has never been in Boonville such demands on it. The big square old house beside
the library that belonged to the millionaire miser Pratt—

who lived in the kitchen with his housekeeper and never let anyone else into the house—has been left by his heir to the Library and will be used for its books and perhaps a museum. Pratt, in his miserliness, had not made a will, and the next of kin was a woman who ran an undertaking business in Brooklyn and had not known what to do with the money or the house.

Utica College, a branch of Syracuse University, seems to me already, in a few years, to have done a good deal for Utica—as have the Munson-Proctor museums. I have been thinking up a project to be carried out with Tom O'Donnell: a series of readings of papers, or perhaps merely a volume of papers, intended to inform the people of this part of New York about what there is of their local culture they seem to know nothing about it: Harold Frederic; Lewis Morgan; Samantha and the Widow Bedott; Tom O'Donnell's recent discovery, the early short story writer, Philander Deming, who was published by Howells in the *Atlantic Monthly;* Arthur Davies and William Palmer and Henry Di Spirito and Palmer and the Utica art school, our neo-classical architecture, the Oneida Community.

I flew back to Wellfleet June 10, for Helen's commencement at the Cambridge School.

Interlude. Reading the newspapers, and even the world's literature, I find that I more and more feel a boredom with and even scorn for the human race. We have come a long way, yes, but we still have a long way to go, so many baffling problems to deal with. Wars are such impediments and setbacks: [sex gets to seem rather silly.] When I read even a love story that might once have moved me—instead of thinking that, except on the very lowest level, a principle of selection is at work: they are trying to improve the human breed—I think, Oh, it's just a man trying to get his penis into some woman. And the books that describe these things, no matter how well —with a lot of effort to formulate some conception of the point at which we have arrived. The policies of the lying governments; the inevitable standardization of what we assume to be "exotic" and "backward" peoples; the stupidity of applied ideologies; the competition for "success" and "status"—and with all this, the inferiority, mental as well as physical, of the specimens of the human race that I see all around me in America.

Morley Callaghan refuses to entertain such ideas. He once said to me that what men have accomplished "has really been very remarkable." This is, of course, a more encouraging point of view. It is true that he is several years younger than I am, but I doubt if his point of view will change.

Returned to Talcottville, August 6. The house looks somewhat better with the new screens in the windows, and the roof and the back bedroom painted.

Mabel Hutchins seems in very good shape and now has more free time to look after me. She has just dyed her hair and has a new red-flowered dress. Kay, her daughter, is now working as assistant to Dr. Vela, the Boonville dentist, and seems to be delighted with her job.

Mary has dyed her hair again, a pale yellow which is more becoming to her. She has lost weight and seems to have, for her, an almost lilylike fragility. She met me as usual at the airport, and we had dinner in Constableville. It was the day of the firemen's fair and parade. Both Mary's daughters were in the parade, which went by just after we had finished dinner. Susie was playing the clarinet and Janet, I think, just marching in the contingent from West Leyden. The whole thing was touching and cheering. Each town had sent its delegation, and they competed with one another in music and display, the stick-twirling of high-stepping majorettes and other parade specialties. In one delegation, there was a girl who did flips; in another, all the girls, at a signal, would suddenly sink to the ground, then quickly start up again.

Young Hungarian from Syracuse, sent me by Charles Mihály. Good-looking, intelligent, with versatile interests. Had studied engineering and history of art at Columbia; had wanted to study medicine, but then decided he wanted to write. He brought not only a bottle of Tokay and a Beatle record for me, but boxes of chocolates for Elena and Helen, who had not come up yet. Since he arrived at 5 o'clock, I invited the Pcolars to help entertain him. He and Mary talked Hungarian—he told me that her pronunciation was good but her vocabulary rather limited—while I talked with George and Ed. But after the Pcolars left, I sat up with him drinking and talking about Hungary. I suffered the next day from what I have come to call Hungarian fatigue—but I think that I really invite this by stirring them up about Hungary, which always makes them emotional and loquacious. I found that this was even true of Istvan Deák, who teaches European history at Columbia. I had come to regard him as the perfect type of the sober and reasonable Hungarian of the younger generation, who has outlived the old romantic panache, and so he usually is. But when I got him started on Hungary one evening in my study at Wellfleet, he became quite demonstrative and vehement—a touch of the old nationalist frenzy that still smoulders in every Hungarian. It turned out that what the young

man from Syracuse really wanted was to talk about Scott
Fitzgerald.

August 9. A cracking thunderstorm—they are a feature
of this part of the country. It blew out the bulb
at my writing table, and when I moved the table to the
middle of the room, it blew out the center light, too. I
established myself at the other end, and the thunder and
lightning moved off. It turned out that both the telephone
and the phonograph had been put out of commission, too.
A ball of fire had been seen in the road.

Walter Edmonds had written me that a moose had
been shot at Malone—getting the man who shot it into
trouble: they are protected because on the way to become
extinct; and that a black panther had been reported. I
now learn that somebody is sure that he has seen the foot-
prints of a mountain lion, and Mrs. Hutchins later told
me that, visiting a hill cemetery at nightfull, she saw
something that could only have been one.

Mary drove me, with her daughter Susan, over to Blue
Mountain Lake, where the Heusers of the Towpath are
now operating for the summer at Crane Point Lodge.

We looked at the Museum, which has now more exhibits and is more interesting than when I last saw it.
The art collection is quite attractive. It mostly consists of
paintings of Adirondack lakes by visiting artists from elsewhere.

The Lodge which the Heusers are managing is itself a
kind of curious relic. It is a comfortable and quiet place
in the woods and on the lake. It was originally a summer
residence shared by two well-to-do families, one from
Rochester and one from Cleveland; but now for the last

nine years it has been rented by them for a kind of old-
fashioned hotel, to which families from farther west have
been in the habit of coming in the summer. One sometimes sees three generations. There is a very long living
room, the kind of thing that I like, which I had in the
De Silver house outside Stamford, but on an immensely
larger scale. Mignonne first told me, with a nuance of
irony, that life there was "very healthful," and explained
that they had constantly to observe "tradition." The
clientèle would not tolerate changes. There was consequently no bar—"Isn't it terrible!" said Klaus; but the
Heusers gave us highballs from their private stock, instructing us not to take them into the dining room, where
we were curiously eyed by the old Cleveland "squares."
They have to have their meals on the dot, and Mignonne
has to wake them up at 8 by ringing a dinner bell. She
sits doing jigsaw puzzles—I understand she is a crack
bridge player—at the end of the long room near the
entrance. I had a strange experience when I first arrived
and happened to be alone in this room. There is a formidable bear rug in front of the fireplace—an immense
Kodiak grizzly. I was, I suppose, in a rather dim state, still
suffering from Hungarian fatigue and no doubt made
sleepier by the higher altitude. I thought I heard this
bear growl. I waited and heard it again. I looked out the
window for a large dog, but there was no such thing to
be seen. When Mignonne came back, I said that they
had evidently put a mechanism in the head of the bear,
like the phonographic voices in dolls; but she laughed and
said that this was not the case. She thought that I was
joking; but it must have been another of my auditory
hallucinations—the first one I had had by day.

August 10. Mary drove me to Utica. It was her day

off from the drug store. She had arranged an "international week" to attract trade to the lunch counter. Monday they had had French onion soup; Tuesday, Mexican beans with chili. Both of these had been made by herself; but now, Wednesday, it was Polish stuffed cabbage by a Polish girl who worked in the store. The Polish girl had said that she wished that Mary were going to be there, so that she could give publicity to the dish of the day. Mary had this on her mind and stopped off on the way back to see how the Polish cabbage was going over with the customers.

We called on Henry Di Spirito. I thought he was perceptibly changed. I think it has meant a lot to him to have been given an appointment at Utica College and a studio in which to work. He has at last been able to lay off from his brick-laying, which he has hung on to all these years, since he could not depend on his art to keep up the standard of living of his extremely well-appointed and well-mannered household. He is having two exhibitions this summer and has won a prize at Cooperstown. He does not have to pretend to be humble, has been authenticated as an artist. His face now seems even more remarkable, under his shock of snow-white hair—more expressive in its enthusiasm and humor. It is as if his physique, which before seemed as strong as one of his carved boulders, had become, with greater freedom, more flexible. His wife says that he has lately had a great burst of working; he is, past sixty, prodigiously productive. I have seen only once a clay model of any of the animals he carves, and he tells me that, with his training as a stone mason, he is the only American sculptor except Zorach who does all his own carving with a chisel. He apparently sees the animal in the stone and brings it out—I don't know whether he makes pencillings first. It seems that even Rodin and Maillol first molded clay models, then had the statues cut by artisans.

Elena arrived by plane, still ill from the flu—she didn't even feel able to drive a hired car, though later she recovered, and we got one. Very gloomy days at first. She said she was afraid of the old house, always had been, had to steel herself.

We had an unfortunate dinner at the Gauses'. I had an amiable talk before dinner with John in his study, explaining about the project that Tom O'Donnell and I are working on to celebrate the cultural achievements of this region, and he responded to it rather favorably, suggesting that he might do a more or less "personal" talk about Marietta Holley, the author of the once well-known Samantha books, whose place in Jefferson County he had once taken the trouble to visit; Thomas Jones, Jr., the Boonville poet, whom he had known; and Franklin B. Hough of Lowville, the distinguished county historian, who, he tells me, was the original creator of the United States Forestry Bureau—also, possibly, Allen Upward, a writer I know little about. They would illustrate, John said, the "variety" of American life, a favorite subject of his. We had three fairly stiff drinks, which may partly account for what followed. *stupid to say*

At dinner, I set John off by asking whether he didn't think a law should be passed making it impossible for a Texan to be President of the United States. He resented this extremely. He had recently been in Texas and had had himself photographed against the background of the Johnson ranch. I had never seen before—though I had felt, despite our friendly relations, a certain lack of sympathy behind them—John's aggressive and rather oafish side. The truth is, I told him, that he has idealized

interesting stuff on Vietnam.

America too long, seeing it all in terms of upstate New York as he had known it in his youth. He had bored me eulogizing the modern motels as successors of the old-fashioned country inns where travellers made interesting acquaintances. He will not listen to criticism of anything and never seems to read anything critical. Tonight he really tore into us. He declared that we were "pathological" about Viet Nam and were merely following "the line"—which especially irritated me because I took him to mean the Communist line. He said he had talked with school friends of Lyndon Johnson who had said he was a splendid fellow, and that they were better men than I was. To explain Elena's attitude, he fell back on her European background: they were against the war in Europe because they didn't like our spending so much money on it—they wanted the money themselves. My own point of view, he said, was entirely derived from my Princeton-New York Eastern background—I didn't know the rest of the country. I told him that I thought I had seen as much of the U.S. as he had, and that I had seen a damn sight more of the rest of the world. He said he had reports from all over—I suppose from former students abroad—that confirmed his approval of our policies; and, gesturing toward his bookshelves, that he was justified by having read a good many books, as if implying that I couldn't be so well informed. All the ordinary people supported the war. I retorted that a local man who worked for me did not appear to support it. "Isolated cases!" he said. Elena reminded him that while the war went on a great many American boys were getting killed. "Not so many!" "Two are too many." "More young people are killed every year on the roads." He greatly applauded Dean Rusk, the idiotic Secretary of State, for having told them so frankly in South America that he knew how "to understand the have-nots" because

he himself, at his birth, had been delivered by a veteri-
nary—seeming to mean that we had no right to speak since
we had not enjoyed that privilege. The opposition to the
war was all due to the Communists and the Catholics—
the latter turned out to be Bobby Kennedy. I had slapped
my hand on the table when he seemed to be accusing us
of the Communist line, and he now said we were "emotionally disturbed." I told him he was emotionally disturbed himself. It got to the point that to all our arguments he would simply reply, "Forget it!" "I can't forget
it." "You will!" At one point, he made the ringing announcement, "I love my wife best of anything in the
world, but next to her I love my country!" Jane took no
part in this conversation except to say something tactful
and noncommittal. After we had left the table, we
changed the subject, but we did not stay very long. John
saw us into the car, but did not shake hands or say
goodby.

I decided that his belligerent opinions were due to the
German coming out in him, that in Germany he could
easily have been a Nazi. I believe that his minute and
accurate knowledge of everything connected with this
region may also be a German trait. He also has always
to some extent the tone of having a social chip on his
shoulder which seems to me central European rather than
characteristic of the earlier American life that he glori-
fies. Yet, as Elena says, this disagreeable evening was a
valuable revelation, because we "liberals," as they call us,
tend to forget that there must be a great many people of
John Gaus's way of thinking. I heard later from the
Strauses of another dinner that came to an even more
violent end. Fred Dupee, who now lives on the Hudson,
had invited a new neighbor, an IBM tycoon. The subject
of Viet Nam arose, and the tycoon asked Dorothea Straus
for her opinion on the subject. Dorothea made the tactful

reply that she took the war question so seriously that she would rather not talk about it. The tycoon said something invidious about her being Jewish. Dwight Macdonald became inflamed, and the tycoon offered to sock him in the jaw, but this was somehow prevented. Fred Dupree got his visitor out of the house, and wrote an apology to the other guests.

We had lunch with Grace Root at Clinton. She is very arthritic now and has a specially made footstool with cleats to keep her feet from slipping. She gets around but only with difficulty. Yet she is still going very strong in her role of salon hostess. She handles her guests well, but has a rather abrupt way of ending a conversation, when the person she had been talking to is in the middle of saying something, by starting a conversation with someone else. I had been writing about Kelly Prentice and talked to her about the special characteristics of the people who came from Albany, of whom she seems to me a typical representative. I have a feeling that the Albany James family must have looked and talked rather like her: clever intellectual conversation, rather old-fashioned formality. She said that the conflict between the English and the Dutch might have made the Albanians peculiar, that the Dutch resistance to the English might have set them off from other people. She herself was William Bradford (one of her ancestors) till 5 o'clock in the afternoon: conscientious, sober, practical, answering all her letters and attending to household matters; but then, after that, the Dutch blood reasserted itself: she was lazy then and rather heedless.

XXI

1967

July 20. Mary drove me up from the airport, and I found her in a very bad mood. She had just had a row with her boss, and their relations seem to have suffered a fundamental change. She had been compelled to drop her charm school and other non-pharmaceutical activities. She says she has to work too hard and does not get enough time off. Next week it will be her turn to cook the lunch. It seems to be the same story as Utica College. She subjects herself to too heavy a strain, then breaks down and is disappointed—the disappointment this time is particularly bitter because she had been looking forward to making herself a career in the development of the Rome pharmacy. She has come to a decision to quit, but is obviously enraged and reluctant, yet one gets the impression that, on his side, her boss is reluctant to have her go, that she has made herself indispensable. She talks about it constantly, too much, the only time she has really ever bored me. She says that her children say to her, "Well, Mom, you've decided to quit. Don't talk about it all the time."

In the spring, she took Susie and a girlfriend to Spain and Portugal on a week's trip that for Mary and Susie

cost $1200. She says that now she has once been to
Europe, it will be easy for her to go again.

I found Rosalind and the house in better shape than I
had expected. Talcottville is rather fading out on me,
but it makes it less lonely to have Rosalind here. I have
had, as I always do when I first come up, a wonderful
sense of quiet and freedom, all my time to dispose of
myself. The traffic past the house is not so bad now that
the parallel road has been finished, and the delinquents,
as I am told, are mostly either working or married.

I am reading a biography of Cole Porter. I first heard
of him and saw him perform when I was at Princeton
and he came on for a concert with the Yale Glee Club.
A Yale friend used to sing songs from his Yale smokers.
I can hardly believe, at my age now and so far away from
that period, that I really lived through all that and did
all the things that I did: Mary Blair, Frances, Margaret;
Vanity Fair, the *New Republic.* Some wonderful things
to look back on, but also naïve and nasty things that I
hate to have to remember.

The Crostens came in for drinks. They told me about
the jobs to which they had to resort in New York when
they were first married and very hard up. Mary worked
as a detective for a law firm till she got too sympathetic
with one of her clients that she was supposed to be hired
to spy on, so she gave this work up. Loren worked as a
gigolo escort and was warned not, under any circumstances, to go to bed with the ladies he escorted. At night
they would entertain one another by telling about their
day's adventures.

Expedition to Sodom. I had always been curious about

this place, which I only knew from its name on the map
—how it came to be called Sodom and how the inhabitants
feel about that. I assumed that, like the other names in
this region, Carthage, Rome, Utica and Ithaca, Tyre,
Poland, Denmark, Copenhagen, Russia, Peru, etc., it had
simply been picked at random by the early ignorant
settlers, who ran through atlases, classical dictionaries and
Bibles. They thought that Sodom must be all right because it occurred in the Bible. These names I have always
found irritating—the Indian names, if you know what
they mean, have always some geographical appropriate-
ness.

I decided to explore Sodom and got the Pcolars to run
me over there one Sunday. It proved to be quite a long
way—to the east of Speculator—in a wild and primitive
part of the Adirondacks. From the glimpses of human
life there, I began to think that the people could never
have read the Bible at all. A few scattered camps; a few
human beings—we wondered what they did for a living.
We had lunch at a rather crude restaurant. After this,
the road was no longer surfaced. Someone from whom we
asked for directions said of Sodom that it was "down the
road: you just wink your eye"—by which he meant that
it was insignificant, and actually we passed through it
without noticing it. Then we inquired of a man who was
evidently a summer visitor. I asked why the town had
been named that: "I don't know—they missed out on
Gomorrah." When we succeeded in identifying the place,
we found a motel there called the Black Mountain Ski
Lodge and Motel, which was run by a German Jewish
couple who had come there from New York four years
ago. There were a few Jewish camps in the neighborhood.
Mrs. Kappler was fully aware of the implications of the
name. "God was kept busy," she said, "knockin' off the
horns of the people." "Horns?" She stuck two fingers up

from her head. "When He decided to wipe it out, He
certainly made a good job of it. What I call Gomorrah
is down the road. If it was cleaned away, it would be
beautiful." I thought this must be some sort of eyesore,
but Mary thought it was "a house of ill repute"—which
I had difficulty in imagining in that hardly populated
spot. The motel-keeper's wife told us that a man who,
I gathered, had recently bought property there wanted
to have the postal address changed to Peaceful Valley.
She referred me to the Methodist minister, who she said
was a fine man.

But the minister, when I called on him, explained that
he had only just come to the church there and referred
me to the minister of the Pentecostal Church, who happened to be a woman. He said that this was one of "the
more emotional sects." I found out later from Glyn Morris that the members of the Pentecostal Church are
known elsewhere as the Holy Rollers. They have religious orgies, at which they babble in strange tongues;
and, after driving over washed-out and rocky roads, we
found the minister and her family preparing for a camp
meeting and picnic. A tent had been pitched in the yard.
She was a sturdy and pleasant woman. She said she had
been born in Sodom and had lived there all her life; that
she had taken the name for granted, and that it had only
been very recently that people had been asking about it;
she had not given any thought to the matter. She explained that there had been a lady belonging to a well-
known rich family whose papers, which had been given
to the Blue Mountain Lake museum, might throw some
light on the subject. When I left her, she said "God
bless you."

Morris Bishop at Cornell later told me that Ithaca used
to be known as Sodom when there was an army post near
there and this was where the soldiers went for their

drinking and whoring. I met a man at Glyn Morris's one night who told me that he came from near Sodom, and that it had a bad reputation for incest and the habits suggested by the name. He said that if I wanted the low-down, I ought to talk to the local policeman. I don't expect to go so far as this.

Expedition to Clinton. I called on Grace Root, who is now almost completely immobilized, but who is able to carry it off with her incomparable authority and ability to put people at ease. She explained her account of herself that had puzzled me last summer when she said she was a New Englander all day, busily writing letters, etc., but that at the end of this practical stint, the Dutch side of her heritage took over. She had meant simply that at the end of the day she began to drink like a Dutchman. "I will now illustrate it," she said, and had a bottle of wine brought in. We talked about Albany, a neighbor who was a grandson of U. S. Grant and much occupied with the American Legion, her elaborate garden behind the house—she said that she had come to prefer plants to people. Her son and his wife came in. We talked about the Middle East, where he had gone for the State Department but had remained as an agent of Standard Oil.

The Austin Briggses picked me up. I had just read his dissertation on Harold Frederic and thought it the best thing I had seen on the subject. He is in the English department, but has no academic attitudes; Margaret Briggs is extremely pretty; she comes from North Carolina but went to Radcliffe and is quite bright. I took them out to dinner at the antiquated Alexander Hamilton Inn, where I was staying: television, a small refrigerator with facilities for making ice-cubes, but no telephones in the rooms even for calling downstairs. Whisky in my rooms after dinner.

I stayed in bed all through the next morning, then went to the Briggses' for lunch. An atmosphere of domestic adjustments: they have just adopted a baby, and the cat has just had kittens. They had invited only "Lafe" Todd and his wife. He occupies an old-fashioned chair of Rhetoric and Oratory, and is the man who has just discovered and is engaged in making a big hullabaloo about A. B. Johnson (1783-1867), the Utica universal genius, a Jewish banker, who wrote on economics and was a precursor of the modern semanticists. He also wrote some fiction and an autobiography which has never been published—Grace Root has been reading it and says it is dull. Johnson had married an Adams, and his wife's family tried to suppress the first chapters, in which he tells about his Jewish origins. Todd is going to celebrate an anniversary of Johnson's birth or death by two days of tributes and festivities at the Munson-Proctor Institute, upon which he has been working for a year and for which he is bringing from all over the country—and even one from Sweden—various scholars, especially semanticists, who have a special interest in Johnson. The culmination of these proceedings will be the laying of a wreath on Johnson's grave, followed by a bang-up cocktail party. Todd is mostly interested in literature, used to know Edward Marsh and has read a lot in Marsh's period. He is entertaining to talk to except that, in his present mood, the conversation always gets back to A. B. Johnson. The Briggses and Todd's wife kid him about this, and I said that I expected that the next step would be a theory that Johnson wrote Shakespeare. Tom O'Donnell and I are arranging—also for the autumn—a celebration for Harold Frederic, and we can't help feeling, in a spirit of competition, that we are running Harold Frederic, as most

Mrs. Edward Root (*Judy Tomkins*)

distinguished Utica intellectual, against A. B. Johnson. Tom has been assigned the function of speaking on Johnson's fiction and says that it is so mediocre that, in the canonization of Johnson, he will be playing the role of Advocatus Diaboli: "If Johnson was ahead of his time in Semantics, he was far behind it in fiction." Todd was rather miffed when I told him that Grace Root was finding the autobiography boring: "There are beautiful descriptions of an autopsy and a hanging, and Grace wouldn't like those." When we talked about having our celebration the week after he had had his, he protested, "I don't know whether Utica could stand having two great men sprung on it one after the other." I told him I had the suspicion that he himself had invented Johnson, and he said that Lewis Jones, the head of the Cooperstown Historical Association, had also accused him of this. Altogether a very gay Sunday lunch that lasted till late in the afternoon.

The Tharett Bests gave what was for Boonville a prodigious all-inconclusive party in honor of their daughter and her husband, who have been living in South America. I have never seen anything like it here. Tharett had a policeman in front of the house to check on invited guests and guide them to where to park. A little grandson opened the door, greatly enjoying himself, and the family received at the entrance. Inside was all the local buzzwuzzie of Boonville, Alder Creek, Utica, etc. A bar with a bartender. A few people I knew or with whom I could establish connections. I took Penberthy out to the iron benches on the lawn behind the house and had some more interesting conversation with three business men from Utica whom he knew. We were all wearing party jackets of a different color from our trousers. This seemed to be a kind of "status symbol." One of these men was

the head of a company which had managed to function
in Utica after all the other "knitting mills" had been
driven south by the New York State social legislation.
This company specializes in the kind of clothes required
for Arctic and Antarctic expeditions—made to order for
any degree of cold and any velocity of wind. This equipment is complicated and costly. Now they also make
costumes for aeronauts. His account was rather grisly of
what the aeronauts have to go through. They cannot take
along water because this would increase the weight, and
they have to drink their own urine, which is made potable
by some process. They defecate into a capsule in their
rectums, and the capsule then goes down into their pants.

I had to go back to Wellfleet in midsummer—and was
rather glad of the pretext—to supervise the enlargement
of my part of the house. Having been lately in so short
a time in so many places I already knew—Rome, Paris,
Israel, Jordan, Boston, Wellfleet and Talcottville—it seems
to me almost now that I can be in them all simultaneously. I can feel myself with equal vividness at the
American School in Jordanian Jerusalem, the King David
Hotel in Israeli Jerusalem, the Paris Hôtel Castille, the
Boston Ritz, the Hulburt House in Boonville and the
Blacksmith Shop in Truro, and I can see at any moment
all the books in the bookcases in both of my houses.

October 12. Elena drove me to Talcottville on account
of the Frederic celebration. This was described as a great
success—Tom says that it was far better attended than
the Johnson celebration, with which we felt ourselves
competing. In spite of the terribly bad weather, snow,
rain and very strong wind—the moment you got out of
the car, you found yourself walking in water—the big hall
at the college was nearly filled. The program was papers

read by O'Donnell and Stanton Garner in the afternoon,
the first on Frederic in Utica, the second on Frederic in
England; in the evening, by me on his writings, and
Austin Briggs on Frederic and Howells. Party at the
Schuyler Club afterwards. This, I think, was a success,
too; but almost everybody, as the stupid habit is, stayed
in the ladies' lounge, where the bar had been set up,
with the inevitable result that no one had elbow room
to move around and it was impossible to hear what other
people were saying—though the whole ladies' dining room
had been cleared for the occasion. I finally went in there
and sat down and brought in some other people, and
managed to have some genuine conversations. Mary
found a Hungarian, who had left Hungary in '56 and
was at Hamilton teaching American Lit. They talked
Hungarian while the professor's French wife talked
French to Phito Thoby-Marcelin.

The Gauses had come to the afternoon session, and
they had dined, as we did, at the Club. When I left the
table for a moment, Jane came over and talked to Elena,
whom she was obviously glad to see. When I came back,
I sat down with John, and we talked about Thomas
Jones, Jr. Any awkwardness was thus got over, our old
friendly relations seemed to be restored. He was to die of a
heart attack not very much later.

Dinner with the Howlands. When I found how much
they suffer from the long and confining Boonville winters
and that John amuses himself with a variety of hobbies
—fixing clocks, astronomy, providing food and houses for
birds, I gave him Al Baker's books on magic and sent
him a set of linking rings, and he is now quite accomplished with cards, and performed a routine that I didn't
know. He entertains his customers with card tricks, when
they sit around the Clark Layng furniture store more or

less as if it were a club. Someone has said that he never knew a furniture store where the furniture was so much used. This is due to old Clark Layng's genial and sociable spirit.

XXII

1968

I flew up on May 9. Mary met me, somewhat upset by a car accident her boy had just had. Another car ran into him. He wasn't hurt, but his car was badly smashed up.

Annoyances. Hearing, in the old schoolhouse, on the new four-lane highway that they contemplate putting through. I shall have to intervene in order to save my front steps. It is true that something ought to be done about the old bridge, where several accidents have occurred, but there is already a wide new road that runs parallel to this. Why do they need another one here? Otis Munn, after the hearing, came in and we had a long talk. He, too, is discouraged by what he calls the "riffraff" who are making Talcottville look so tumbledown and which inflict on us the plague of these delinquent children. Three of them have just been arrested, and Mabel Hutchins thinks that they may now be a little quieter. Otis says that he has thought of moving away, but I doubt if he ever will. One of my Talcottville neighbors complained to me that last winter they ran over everything with their snow machines. They have ridden through my currant bushes and partially killed them.

I have had a wire fence put around them. I stopped in
at one of the houses where one of the fatherless families
lives, to complain about the breaking of the windows of
the barn and to tell them not to cut my corner with their
motorcycles, by which they make great gashes in the
grass. I asked them why they didn't go for real trips on
these cycles but only did a constant buzzing back and
forth past my house and the store and riding up the little
blind alley toward the schoolhouse. I asked them whether
it were true that they couldn't go along the main roads
because they couldn't afford to get licenses. They said
that the problem wasn't money for the licenses but the
$140 for compulsory motor insurance. I felt rather sorry
for them. The house seemed perfectly bare: a table, a
few chairs—no decorations or comforts, no signs of "a
woman's touch." Their mother is evidently away all day.
They tell me that the boys get the snow machines and
motorcycles by paying a first instalment, then, when
they haven't made good on the second, allowing the company's agent to come and take them away. Then they get
one from another company.

Trip to Chicago to see Reuel and Marcia's baby. This
city, which used to have a kind of grandeur and which,
before I spent a summer at the University there, and
realized that it was rather oppressive, once seemed to me
quite romantic, is extremely unattractive now. The high
buildings here and there, the products of a desire to
compete with New York upset the proportions of Michi-
gan Avenue; and the Art Institute, seen from a distance,
is now almost unidentifiable. Some very ugly structures
are going up—a monstrous black towerlike thing—insur-
ance, I think—that is truncated at the top. The people
seem less tough and dynamic, pale and measly city-
dwellers, quite joyless. On the South Side, the Negro

slum is squeezing against the University, and the University people live in fear of further riots. Reuel tells me there are rumors that, at some point this summer, they are going to begin taking potshots at whites. The Negro streets are full of damage: broken panes and boarded-up shops, with sometimes "SOUL BROTHER" painted on them in order to ward off attack. The whole effect is claustrophobic. You find yourself in the middle of the *Chicago* Middle West, and, sitting in the hotel and reading the papers, you feel that all the horrors of a hateful, convulsive and chaotic civilization are closing in on you from every side. Reuel and Marcia, after three years of it here, will be very glad to get away.

It was a relief to come back to Talcottville, with its clear air and cool weather, to escape from that heavy Chicago heat, which was beginning to set in when I left.

Trip to New York, June 10-16. America has changed so much that when I visit New York or Chicago, I almost feel that I am seeing a foreign city. Airplanes give travel such a different aspect. Going so quickly from place to place—I got back to Utica in forty-six minutes—has the result that on arriving somewhere you can still see quite clearly the place you just left, as if they were interchangeable. The airports have a special character—they are quite unlike railroad stations: not smoky, better-managed, streamlined. My impression of New York was sinister— especially on Broadway and the streets in the Forties, which run across the avenues: women in skirts so high that they make them look like little girls—one of them had yellow stockings on her thin unattractive legs; Negroes much more in evidence than I remember ever seeing them before; young people as to whom you couldn't tell whether they were pimps and prostitutes or simply hipsters and swingers. In one of the cross-streets an elderly woman was sitting on something and crying, "Look out for your bags and wallets! They'll frisk you here!"

My Showy Ladyslippers, brought me and expertly planted by the Weilers, are almost all blooming now, and I am extremely proud of them. Five are in flower or bud—though the one that has flowered is as yet rather measly. It is as if the plants themselves had contrived with much taste the combination of deep-pink pouches and white ribbonlike streamers, of smooth surfaces and speckled interiors, with the piquancy of the single dots of yellow and red. I feel that they are exquisite independent beings who are, nevertheless, willing to live here.

This summer has so far, I think, been the pleasantest I have spent up here. Old age has its compensations. I feel that I can loaf in the mornings, be less anxious about what I am going to write and not suffer afterwards so much about the gaffes and errors I have made. My regrets mostly nowadays are about the things that I can't any longer do; but I dwell on old love affairs, and this does not impose upon me any further responsibility for them. Mabel Hutchins has more time to devote to me; and Rosalind keeps me company. All kinds of people write me, and I get a lot of papers, books and magazines. I probably waste time, however, with the papers and magazines, and a good deal of the mail is a bore: requests to read manuscripts or teach or speak, advertizements, petitions to sign, school children asking questions which their teachers should have prevented instead of, as they sometimes do, encouraging them, letters from lunatics and crackpots. People have asked me out a lot, and sometimes I have had to refuse in order to get an evening to myself.

The weather has been mostly delightful. I am becoming more involved in the community, discussing the local problems with the Munns, Chet Rice and the Talcottville O'Donnells. John Howland has made me a present of a bluebird house and a bird-feeder. Bob Weiler's gardening has very much improved the whole place. The white rose by the front porch, which my mother always called "Aunt Lin's," has begun blooming again, and the gooseberries are now abundant. Both had seemed to be dying out.

June 23. The Heusers came in for dinner: a giddy evening. They no longer keep the Towpath open in summer —we miss the dinners there—but manage a Utica country club. They come up here every Sunday for a rest—Monday is their day off. They didn't arrive till after 8, because it had been such a beautiful day that people had lingered on the golf course. Then Klaus had cut his finger on a knife, just coming short of cutting a muscle. There had luckily been a surgeon there playing golf, and he had taken Klaus to the hospital. They must have had a drink for relaxation from the strain of work and Klaus's accident. I had never seen them entirely off duty before. Mignonne was wearing a red bobbed wig, which I told her made her look *polissonne*. She recited a little bawdy rhyme, and when I asked her where she had learned it, Klaus replied, "In the convent." In the middle of dinner, he suddenly announced, "I am the Baron Gasthaus-Heuser!"—his father was a German chemist. They left very soon after dinner, on account of their daughter Monique, who was spending the weekend at the Towpath. Klaus showed off the new trailer for two in which they were planning a trip to Mexico. It is equipped with all kinds of electric light and an electric toilet that is flushed with some chemical. They have a new young

spaniel named Alfie, who spent his first six months in a
kennel and is neurotically shy of people. Mignonne took
him for a walk on a leash. She unleashed him when she
got into the trailer, but afterwards stood in the door, and
he slipped out past her. He was intoxicated with freedom
and would not allow himself to be lured back. She finally
gave it up, and they had to go home without him. Rosalind and I sat on the back porch in the hope that we
might catch him. He sat on the lawn and barked, com-
municating with the other dogs in Talcottville in the
howling way that dogs have. In the morning, he was
still around, and Mignonne came over and got him. Eventually, they had to give him back to the kennel.

The enforced decorum and discipline of the Heusers'
regular routine must put them under something of a
strain; but Klaus told me that they really "liked people,"
liked to deal with them and observe them: they were all
different. This accounts for their popularity. When you
go to dinner at the Towpath, Mignonne always receives
you, standing as it were at attention, looking very neat
and appetizing, in blond dresses that always seem fresh.
They like to laugh between themselves about their customers. Elena quoted someone as saying that one of the
great pleasures of marriage was the husband's and wife's
laughing together about things that they would not be
able to laugh about with anyone else. Mignonne says she
wants to write about her experiences as an "innkeeper,"
that she loves to write letters. I have had with her quite
a little correspondence more entertaining and friendly
than was needed for our practical purposes.

Lunch in Cazenovia at the Marcelins'. He and Pierre
have finished their new novel, *Tous les Hommes Sont
Fous,* but Phito is still working on it, revising it. Pierre
is back in Haiti. Phito says, *"Il est inexportable."* Phito

and Eva live on the top of a high windswept hill. It enables Eva to be near her family, who are Sicilians in this wine-making part of the country, but I wonder that Phito is able to stand the winters. They say they live like recluses.

Dinner with Arthur Einhorn and his family. He is a young man from New York, who is getting a degree in anthropology at Buffalo University. He is married to a wife who has Micmac blood and they have bought a house and settled in Lowville, from which he commutes to his college. He knows a lot about the Iroquois, and has given me an excellent False Face mask, carved by a Cayuga out of the regulation basswood, but not yet blessed to give it its magic power, so that, from their point of view, it is not yet necessary to keep it covered all the time for fear of its bringing a curse. They told me a curious story about a Seneca girl who worked for them. She began having something like fits, and couldn't perform her duties. They sent her back to her reservation, where the False Faces and the Husk Faces both performed their curative rituals, and after this she completely recovered.

July 7. Picnic with the Crostens at Independence River. I stayed behind below while they climbed up to the falls. Strange to think that only a few years ago I was able to scramble up by the rocks or at least to walk up by the path. I drank the rest of a gallon of white wine, played with a little pale coffee-colored kitten that a friend of Stephen Crosten's had brought and read in a paperback of Yeats's plays that this friend had also brought. Yeats's poetry still moves me. The friend is in our State Department—from which he says he is going to resign—and in the consul's office in Montreal. He says that in Canada he finds that it is impossible to be, as he wanted to be, a foreigner. They either think you are pro-English or an American who wants to get something out of them.

Back in the house, I played for Loren the first side of Ginastero's opera *Bomarzo*, and he thought it quite good, as I did. It exploits all the possibilities of the twelve-tone system for the macabre and the sinister—and these possibilities are considerable. I have never heard this done before: ballet of Monsters, ballet of Mummies. The composer's idea is that the life of the young Orsini duke has been spoiled by his deformity, which has made him so neurotic that he is sexually impotent, and there is a scene with a Venterian courtesan with whom he has been hoping to cure himself that couldn't be more frustrating and grimmer. Loren had said to me just before that Britten was the English Meyerbeer, and I told him I supposed he would say that Ginastero was the twelve-tone Meyerbeer. "No," he said. "The twelve-tone Verdi."

Elena came Friday the 12th.

We had supper with the Mihálys on a horribly hot day. He took us to see Deerlick Rock, a local landmark which I had never known about and of which not even the Loomises had ever heard. It is a very high brownish boulder that covers five acres. An Indian couple of lovers are supposed to have thrown themselves down from it. The lover had stolen the woman from the man with whom she was living, and in order to escape his vengeance they had taken refuge on the rock, which was supposed to be a sanctuary. Eventually hunger and thirst drove them to kill themselves. At the time of the French and Indian wars, a company of French soldiers are supposed to have left a cache of money buried at its bottom. Mihály bought it some years ago and turned it into a "park." He has planted sixty-five thousand trees there, and one of his sons and his family are living in a house on the premises. The mosquitoes and the heat were too much for me, and I did not attempt to climb the rock.

At supper, Mihály told us about his life. He comes from the middle class, he says, but his grandfather was a landowner with quite a lot of serfs. His father had been a radical, a follower of Kossuth, in politics. He had written a number of books. Mihály says that he was surprised to find, in one of my books, such names as Liebknecht and Karl Marx, authors he had read in his youth. His father had brought him here at the age of thirteen. He had tried to import the Hungarian *ásvanyi viz,* the mineral water one still drinks in Hungary. The son sold real estate to Hungarians and is now the principal dealer in this part of the Adirondacks. His real interest, however, is numismatics: he has now the most complete collection of Hungarian coins that exists outside of Hungary. He has just received from Hungary a Széchény medal, of which he is very proud.

July 18. We had a big mopping-up party such as we haven't had for years: Crostens, Howlands, Perry Williamses, Morrises, Einhorns, Talcottville O'Donnells. Elena and Rosalind and Mabel Hutchins worked hard over it every day, and people seemed to enjoy it. Discussed the delinquents and the new road.

On one of our last nights, the motorcycle brigade, as Elena calls them, came back, more or less drunk, from some sort of "field day," and made such a racket in the road in front of the house that they woke up Rosalind and me. They were standing out in the road trying to stop cars and make them swerve. I called the sheriff in Lowville, and they sent over a part-time deputy, but he failed to catch anybody. They hid in our shrubbery and behind the store.

We came back to Wellfleet on July 23, then I went back to Talcottville for September 27-October 20, to take part in our second demonstration for New York State culture at Utica College.

Mary met me. She is reconciled with her boss and beaming. She is getting more money, and I think more time off. We stopped at the gas station near the store, and the proprietor came out also beaming. He talks as if he were going to proceed with the enlargement of their little empire by buying the building next door.

Rosalind tells me that Mabel Hutchins said of the Di Spirito stone animals, which are out on the lawn when I am here but otherwise kept in the house: "I guess those monsters will be glad when Mr. Wilson gets back."

General letdown perceptible following the nomination of the presidential candidates. Even Fern, though a Republican office-holder, is evidently not enthusiastic about Nixon—says that she and Otis had sat up late the night before talking about the elections. An interview with Humphrey in the *Saturday Evening Post* made me think he was a little more intelligent and a little better informed than I had thought but I can't feel very much confidence in him. I suppose that I'll have to vote for him, simply to keep out Nixon. This and the Russian invasion and suppression of Czechoslovakia and the interminable New York school strike make the world seem very discouraging.

I paid a visit to Palmyra, the home of Joseph Smith,

where he fabricated the Book of Mormon, in order to include a description of it in my book about the Dead Sea scrolls. It is not hard to see how, with the vistas of that countryside, from the high steep ridge of the "Hill Cumorah," an imaginative unscrupulous boy, who had had access to little reading but the Bible, could have imagined himself as a Moses, the recipient of revelation. At the Mormon Bureau of Information, a Mormon woman missionary, full of friendliness and solicitude to see that we were properly informed, supplied us with brochures and folders and ran for us a colored film in which a very much idealized young Joseph Smith was shown being visited by his angel. I asked what had happened to the Book of Mormon, and she said that the angel had taken it back to Heaven. We went into town for lunch and saw that all the other churches were flourishing— though the old lady who ran the inn said that the Mormons were making progress.

Mrs. Hutchins came down with a cold, and I could see that she could hardly get around, so I decided to spend two nights at the Schuyler Club and had a very comfortable spree. The new manager is unexpectedly a cultivated and very agreeable man, part Russian and part Swedish, very much, I think, a Baltic type, who has lived a good deal in France and to whom I can talk about books.

Across the side street from the club is a new little triple movie house called Cinema, 1, 2 and 3. I took Jo Costa to one of the shows, a respectable but uninteresting picture, *The Bride Wore Black,* with Jeanne Moreau not at her best; and then later, alone, I tried another called *Campus Confidential.* It proved to be one of the new smut movies that are known in New York as "flesh flicks," which it rather horrified me to find just around the

corner from the principal street of Utica. The characters
did not speak, and the thing was commented on in one
of those cheerful nauseating voices that are trying to sell
the public something: "Young people like to have good
times. We were all young once." You see the students of
a college, which is presented as a clean and well-ordered
place. A couple of nude Lesbian girls are about to go
into action, but are checked by a roommate who arrives.
Then we are shown an orgy, which begins Friday night
and lasts till Monday morning. "Fred's parties are always
groovy. We're only young once, and Saturday night is
coming." Then we are shown the party, which consists
of drug-taking and necking presented in an amateurish
way. You see the doped stupefied students writhing
around on couches. Two nude male homosexuals are
shown beginning their caresses. Some of the drugged
young people are becoming delirious and have to be put
away in a padded room. At the end, the clear-eyed healthy
young boys and girls are shown, on Monday morning, on
their way to their classes with their books. No evil consequences have been suffered. Boys and girls will be boys
and girls. Another such picture followed, of which I saw
only the first few minutes. Later on, when I was in New
York, I saw a double bill of supposedly reputable pictures
—though shown among the shops for pornographic books
—on West Forty-second Street. Both had the quite un-
necessary but now obligatory love scenes, of the lovers,
entirely nude, rolling around on a bed. This, together
with what Hollywood mistakes, attempting to emulate
Europe, for far-out avant-garde fantasy, has come to be a
common accepted genre. But when I had bought a Sunday *Times,* I found that I could not carry it, on account
of my bad heart, and that I could hardly get back to the
Princeton Club. I dumped the bulk of the paper in a
trash can, and went into the nearest movie in order to

go to the men's room. I did not notice the signs in front, which in any case were not explicit; but when I was coming out and saw what was on the screen, I sat down and watched the performance. It was an enormous human vagina which an actress in various ways was showing off. She manipulated from time to time an unconvincing dildo. Her genitals, close up and magnified, had the thoroughly repellent appearance of the pieces of raw meat in a butcher's shop. This film was followed by another of the same routine kind; but the second girl smiled at the audience, though the first one had looked rather sulky and as if she thoroughly disliked what she was doing. After this, there was a talking picture, which made some attempts to be dramatic. I was too far away from the screen to understand what was being said, but one of the main themes was the operations of a rapist. He was made an unpleasant character, and in the end the law caught up with him. But in the meantime, he had committed three successful rapes. In the case of the last of the girls he killed, he slung her nude body over his shoulder and dumped it on a rubbish heap.

I do not think that such films should be allowed. College students should not be encouraged to go in for drug-taking orgies, and the film about the rapist could be taken as demonstrating how easy it is to commit a rape: just follow the woman up a dark alley and give her a clout with a club.

Elena arrived on Thursday. Lunch with the Briggses Sunday. An afternoon of rousing shop talk, which I seem to need from time to time. Edwin Barrett and his wife were also there. He does Shakespeare, and we talked about the Elizabethans. Many wisecracks and much laughter. Grace Root had asked us to her house after lunch, where we found some of the students of the new girls' college, Kirkland, which has been started in association with Hamilton. The curriculum did not seem as yet very highly developed: no languages and all the sciences lumped under one course called Science. The girls, who had been to lunch, very soon left, and we had some more shop. Grace is really quite wonderful: she manages to give everybody attention, yet dominates and leads the conversation.

The most beautiful fall here I have ever seen. We drive out into the country and take little walks along some uninhabited unfrequented road. Foliage so wonderful that, at this time of life, having already done so much describing, I hardly try to describe it: rose orange, blood orange, pale lemon or deeper copper. One road ran uphill through a wood toward a tunnel completely yellow, a little falling stream below. There has been almost no frost, and this produces different effects from the sudden blasting blazes of red. Sometimes a gold-soaked mist.

I told Elena how very much I had been enjoying that week, and that the only flaw in my enjoyment had been her not enjoying it as I did. She answered that there was something chemical about one's enjoyment of places.

It all ended in rain on Saturday, and the trees were now partly denuded.

We arranged a conference with the Talcottville O'Donnells and two of the local sheriffs about what was to be done to contend with the delinquents. The sheriffs complain that it has rarely been possible to catch one of these boys in the act of committing any mischief, so that it has not been possible to arrest them, and on the occasions when they do arrest them, the judges are likely to let them off.

The Lyons Falls sheriff has been keeping as a pet one

of the large type of weasels called fishers, which are rather rare in this part of the world. He had found her in the middle of a road. She had been dropped as a cub by her mother, and John Harris brought her up on a bottle. She was brownish black and, counting the tail, forty inches long. He kept her in the barn and let her out twice a day. Sometimes she would climb to the roof of the house and jump down onto his shoulders. His hands and arms are much scratched and bitten. He always wore gloves when he fed her. Once she was playing with the lobe of his ear and bit through it. Like all weasels, the fishers are fierce. She bit several strange people. Harris once saw her catch a rabbit, and when he came near her, she uttered weird screeches. A game farm offered to buy her, but he didn't want her imprisoned and let her go.

Our session on the Iroquois on October 16 was not so well attended as the one on Harold Frederic last year: we had to compete with a concert by the Utica Symphony Orchestra. Bill Fenton read an admirable paper on Lewis Morgan and the Six Nations, Tom O'Donnell one on Robert W. Chambers, who, it seems, as I hadn't known, wrote some rather ambitious novels on the Iroquois, and I read the chapter from my Iroquois book on the Little Water Ceremony.

XXIII

1969

I first spent a night with Elena in Cambridge. My Boston dentist at last gave up on the bridge he had made for my lower jaw and suggested my trying another dentist. The night of May 10, we were both under a nervous strain: Elena woke up in the middle of the night for her usual worrying spell, and this woke me up to worry, too; when I went to sleep, my sleep was horribly tense. Worry about teeth, Rosalind, Svetlana. Svetlana had just been to see us at Wellfleet: her book was about to come out, and she had evidently been apprehensive about the possible consequences.

Mary met me at the airport. Rather to my surprise, she did not talk about the pharmacy. The doctor had told her to take six weeks off—she told me later that she had been overworked: she had had to keep the accounts as well as attend to her surgical devices and do a lot of other things. She looked quite pretty and rested, was wearing a becoming brown dress that went with her coloring, her hair having been restored to more or less its natural tint. She had been offered a job at the West Leyden school

as supervisor in the study room. As a result of the short-
age of teachers, a policy has been adopted of "para-profes-
sionalism" (*para* has now become the fashionable prefix)
to make it possible for people without academic degrees
to qualify now as teachers. This of course opens to Mary
an opportunity that she didn't have before. The job won't
begin till fall, but in the meantime she may go back to
the pharmacy for one or two days a week. I took her to
the Parquet for dinner and, in spite of my extreme weari-
ness, I drank a cocktail and a good part of a bottle of
Piesporter in order to be able to talk. It was a relief to
talk about Svetlana and explain about Tolstoy and the
Russian Revolution—she had imagined that Tolstoy had
had some connection with the Revolution. She and George
had been reading a recent book about Nicholas II and
Alexandra. I told her that, in spite of the heroic feat of
Svetlana in informing herself on Russian history, we had
sometimes been surprised at noticing gaps. Mary said
regretfully, "And in mine, too."

When I was back in the house alone, I unwisely went
on drinking—quite a lot of a bottle of Old Bushmill's
Irish whisky, which seems weaker than Scotch, but is,
I believe, more powerful. The next day I had another
of those attacks of the malady—some form of malaria
perhaps—that I seem to have picked up in Jamaica: chills
that made my teeth chatter ended in violent vomiting
and on this occasion ran my temperature up to 103. I
could hardly, on account of my shivering, get to the
phone to call up the doctor. Mrs. Hutchins came to get
me supper and found me still on the couch. I finally got
myself to bed, and Mrs. Hutchins spent the night in the
house with me. Still wobbly Thursday and Friday. Only
today, Saturday, do I begin to feel pleasantly normal. Yet
I find it enjoyable to be here: quiet, a thin subdued
spring. Rather than attack Mrs. Ginzburg's chronicle of

Soviet horrors, which I have engaged to write about, I
went on with the new biography of Firbank—though it
turns out to be only another of those arid Ph.D. products
—with no pretension, as the woman who wrote it says,
an American who teaches at Skidmore College—to being
"a critical biography," and not quite so bad as the similar
one of Barham that I have just written about, but made
up to a great extent of more or less uninteresting facts
that give merely the exact addresses at which Firbank was
living at different dates, exactly how he arrived at Oxford
when he was travelling down from London, with no
evocation of the atmosphere of the period or appreciation of the humor of Firbank's eccentricities.

On Sunday, Mary drove me over to have lunch with
the Marcelins. It turns out that she and Di Spirito have
been having quite a rapprochement. She had been out
with him on a painting expedition—he has offered to
give her instruction, and she had brought in the car to
show me a little landscape she had done—a very Hungarian palette, as in her other picture, brown with a note
of purplish blue. She had also a clay bust of herself by
Di Spirito, which did not resemble her and which I did
not like. When she brought it out at the Marcelins',
Phito and I had immediately the same idea that, with
its essentially masculine head and sly one-sided smile, it
gave the impression, as Phito said, of "Voltaire jeune."
I had not known how good Eva's translation would be of
the Marcelin novel, *Tous les Hommes Sont Fous,* and
was relieved to find that she had a sound instinct for
writing literary English and was fully aware of the danger
of translating French expressions literally. I had with
Phito an unusually interesting and almost entirely intelligible conversation about Haiti, Marx, Phito's brothers,
etc. I talked, in connection with Jamaica, about the

snobbish mulatto élite in both places; but "no more!" he
exclaimed about Haiti. He would say of certain people
that they were of good or fairly good family; then he
threw out his hands and declared that there was really
not so very much difference between the various repre-
sentatives of this upper mulatto class in Haiti. I told Eva,
as we came in from the kitchen, where he and I had been
sitting after lunch, that we had had an unusually satisfactory talk. She said that she could suggest an explanation: she meant that we had not had so much whisky as
usual. It is true that, under these conditions, his soft
French becomes more inaudible and his English less easy
to handle, so that we miss communication. I told him
that I was getting old—(terrible thundercrack in the
middle of this conversation—I thought at first the house
had been hit—all the lights went off)—and he said that
he was, too. I said that I was ten years older than he, that
he had the advantage of me. He answered, and I felt the
poignant force of this: *"Mais moi, je suis en exil!"* He is
not at all a type of complainer, but he had told me before
how hard it was for him never to have Haitians to talk to.
After lunch, we sat out on the lawn among the apple and
pear blossoms and looked out at the wonderful view. He
is lucky in having Eva, who has character, good looks,
brains and an appreciation of him as an artist.

When Mary and I left, we didn't want to have dinner
yet, and bought a paper to look up the movies. We decided to go to *Mayerling* in Utica—which turned out to
be a rich heavy repulsive load of Hollywood grandeur and
elegance, with no possible human appeal. Catherine
Deneuve, always beautiful, showed no sign whatever of
emotion; Omar Sharif, as the Austrian crown prince, was
as usual Arabian and wooden. But it did not bore Mary
so much as me. I asked her whether she could fall for a

grandduke like Sharif, and after a moment of puzzling
about how to reply, she gave a little smile and said yes.
All this summer, I have been going with the Pcolars to
the Rome and Utica movies more or less as they come.
One is able to get in this way a somewhat different per-
spective on them. One sees them among the people for
whom they are made. A picture called *Funny Girl* on the
career of Fanny Brice, which features a dreadful woman
with a horrible blaring voice who is now getting a big
reputation but who makes no attempt to reproduce the
comic personality of Fanny Brice, and with Sharif very
polished in evening clothes as Nicky Arnstein, the underworld character with whom Fanny Brice was in love,
seemed to me one of the very worst pictures I had ever
had the endurance to sit through. But the Pcolars said
that if I had seen the picture based on the career of
Gertrude Lawrence, this one would have seemed rather
good. Sidney Poitier, the Negro actor—we saw him in
two films—scores heavily in pictures which are perfectly
aimed to please this provincial audience. The Negro hero
has to struggle against race prejudice and injustice, but
of course is made to come out on top as a brave man and
good fellow acceptable to suburban whites. In *Guess
Who's Coming to Dinner,* the young dedicated Negro
doctor marries a devoted white girl; but what we are not
allowed to ask—as O'Neill does in *All God's Chillun*—is
how this marriage is going to turn out.

Glyn Morris ties up the general disquietude with the
much talked-of "identity" problem. I got something out
of this conversation, which led me to formulate the theory
that the big power units now do not give people personal
identity except as assigned bureaucrats in units assigned
to be governed by bureaucrats, and that this drives them
to the fanatical, though sometimes tiny, nationalisms: Scot-

tish, Welsh, French Canadian, Czech, Polish, Swiss French, Swiss German, Swiss Romansh, etc., which provide them with a national identity. There have always been prejudices and rivalries between different local groups and groups of different derivations, but never, it seems to me, so many embittered and passionate groups declaring war on one another.—To get down to the individual, I can sometimes see that other people do have "identity" difficulties; but I myself am well aware that although I embody different tendencies and remember that, in my early life, I was sometimes in doubt as to what kind of role I wanted to play, I have never had much real doubt about who or what I was.

The Boonville dentist, when I went to him, implied that the Boston ones had made a botch of my lower jaw bridge, and said that it ought to be possible to find a way of fastening the bridge better by putting pegs, as I had already suggested in Boston, in the remaining roots of the lower teeth. He has sent me to a Lowville dentist. This has made me feel more cheerful, since it has been a constant source of annoyance not to be able to chew and to have to live on wheatena and such pallid fare.

It sometimes seems to me strange that I am still alive and writing this diary. When I look into old books of mine, it is almost as if they had been written by someone else, and I cannot take very much pride in them because they seem to me now dated.

At moments, especially when reading in bed, I have a brief comfortable reassuring feeling of the renewal of some such sensation as I have sometimes enjoyed in the past—a natural echo of organic vitality cropping up in my now infirm self.

Dr. Edgar Miller in Lowville turned out to be a great success. I was astonished to find dentists there so well equipped and staffed as he and his brother are. He did a lot of arduous work on my lower jaw, even drilling a hole in the jawbone, and has provided me with a bridge which stays in and with which I can effectively chew. He is enormously skilful with his hands and amuses himself with all kinds of hobbies, such as feats of ingenuity in contriving decorations and masks out of railroad nails and old bits of iron. Is also well informed and intelligent. I have got to know him and his family, as well as his brother, who lives in the old house of Franklin Hough. The family came originally from Talcottville, and there are Millers in the cemetery on the hill.

Since the two or three days of pouring rain, the country has been flooded as I have never seen it: the pastures turned into lakes, the Black River all over its bordering fields, Sugar River a turbulent muddy torrent, a pond in our back lot.

New York June 2-10.

June 13. An almost two-hour session with Dr. Miller. I am impressed by his careful expertness, the close attention he gives to everything, commenting constantly to the nurse, who seems to have been well trained to understand these procedures.

But it may have been something of a strain. I had had little sleep the night before. Next morning, the bad chills, high temperature and convulsive vomiting of my confounded tropical malady. I was knocked out for three days. Dr. Smith attended me, and Mrs. Hutchins nursed me, spending the night in the house. Asleep, unconscious most of the time. When I came to, I read snatches of the Hemingway biography by Carlos Baker. The book has a certain monotony from Hemingway's always turning nasty and picking a quarrel with anyone who has ever done anything for him—I see I am not spared; and his repeated self-injuries through clumsiness which give somewhat the impression of self-inflicted wounds. He had a high sense of honor, which he was always violating; and this evidently gave him a permanent bad conscience, which I suppose contributed to his drinking. It is altogether a depressing story, because his work, as he knew, was deteriorating. Then his constant competitiveness could become so disagreeable. I learn from Mr. Baker that both Henry Strater and Archibald MacLeish refused to go with him to Africa because they could foresee what they would have to endure if they shot a bigger lion than Ernest.—A copy of my book on the Dead Sea scrolls arrived in the first stages of my attack, and I didn't at the time have the energy to look at it. When I did, I found a horrible *and which* sentence on page 130—not only an *and which* but otherwise the statement didn't make sense.

Glyn faithfully came in to see me and helped keep me going by making me talk, as he had after my first attack. I may very well have bored him with my old stuffy anecdotes, which were all I was able to muster.—The Morrises left for Maryland on the 18th. Last winter had been very hard on Gladys, and she has relatives that she can be near in Washington. I hate to have them go.

Mabel Hutchins, at dinnertime, wanted to know whether I minded if she asked me a question. She had heard that there was a group in Lowville who gave parties at which all the wives threw the keys to their houses in a pile. The men wore a loop in one ear and the women a single blue earring, which contained a contraception pill. Each of the men would pick up a key and go to the house of the lady to whom the key belonged. "But suppose it turns out that the man has drawn a woman he doesn't like." "Well, I guess he'd have to lose the key." Did I know whether this was true? I asked Fern about it, and she answered, "Oh, that was at the _____ Hall, and they don't do it any more."

I went to Clinton and had lunch with the Briggses. Ezra Pound, as I had heard in New York, had been visiting Hamilton without publicity. He had been to college here, and had already returned once some years ago. He had stayed with the Roots and, according to Grace, had behaved with considerable rudeness, demanding to have a shirt laundered at once when he had sweated in it at tennis. There had been an unpleasant scene when he had been heckled, in the course of a speech, by another commencement guest. But they told me that, on this occasion, he had been rather surprisingly subdued. His policy, now that he is eighty-four, is not to speak but to maintain a polite silence—he says that people can read his writings if they want to know what he thinks. I have, however, been told that an economist who came to see him has shaken his faith in Social Credit, and I suppose that it might be embarrassing if he were challenged about this. Margaret Briggs had been asked to have him brought there to lunch on short notice, only that morning, and she had had to make a special effort. They had dressed him in a gown for the Hamilton Commencement, and he was given a tremendous ovation. Margaret said he was still handsome, as when I saw him the only time I met him, in the twenties, on the street in Paris when I was walking with Djuna Barnes. He was tall and lithe, with his trimmed red beard, and behaved to her with the gallantry of the medieval troubadours with whom he liked to identify himself. But at the Briggses' that day he had said almost nothing. He had been escorted by a woman companion who helped him in his contacts with the world. When asked by Margaret whether he would have light meat or dark meat, he answered, "Just as it comes," and, as he left he made some apology for giving Margaret so much trouble. The only opinion elicited was when she asked how he found New York, and he answered, "Too many people."

A fit of coughing after dinner intensified into another attack of that damned Jamaica malady, which turned me inside out and left me feeble for nearly a week. Tried to read *La Marge* by André Pieyre de Mandiargues, incredibly slow and boring. At a certain point, I merely skipped through to the end to see what was being withheld. I think the whole thing is a swindle.

An artist from Thailand whom I met at the Morrises. We were talking about the present boom in sex, and I asked him whether they were giving this aspect of life any special publicity in Thailand. He answered, "We live in a different culture. We think that it is something private between two people."—When I asked him to repeat something, I told him that I was somewhat deaf. He explained that he talked in a low voice because in his country it was considered bad manners to talk loudly.

The departure of the Morrises has left a gap, a blank. I feel that I am now much more out of touch with what is going on in the local community.

4th of July. Hardly a firecracker, we had no evidence

of any celebration at all. I've never known so tame a 4th. Rosalind and I tried to create some excitement by driving to Cape Vincent. No traffic to speak of, the town itself dull and mostly denuded now of all that once made it interesting. The old summer hotel where we used to stay, with its gardens to walk in and its elegant stuffed fish, has been torn down—it was no longer profitable. No amusing shops, no place to get a halfway decent meal. I didn't see anything of the shop that sold hunting and fishing gear and had something of a museum of wild life —run by a man who claimed that his father had been one of Napoleon's soldiers.

Later, I read in the Watertown *Times* that the experimentation in fish conducted in the old Cape Vincent custom house by the State Conservation department had been horribly vandalized. The windows and doors were smashed, and "hard to obtain fish such as sturgeon earmarked for public display have been removed from tanks in a burglarized building and bashed to death and left to die on the floor. Small-mouth bass being studied in an extremely important survival experiment were mutilated or killed." The director of the station is quoted as saying that, "The damage caused to this experiment [to determine the effect of netting on the fish] cannot be undone. The loss of such information can have a real effect on future bass fishing in the area. Also, the money for such research comes from taxes and fishing licenses." "The destruction makes the expense a complete waste.... Vandals, presumed to be children, bombarded the fish with rocks.... The seriousness of the problem has been stressed at the local branch of the Thousand Island Central School." The police, of course, have been appealed to. But what can school or police accomplish when confronted with an impulse to wreck any constructive achievement which illiterates cannot understand and to

get away with wanton destruction which establishes for
them a claim to audacity?

Highmarket—so bleak and deserted now—though Elena
especially enjoys it, because, in its stark way, it *is* very
picturesque. But there is even more ruin and decay here
than in the places which are still inhabited: a well-
patterned old white door on a background of peeling
asbestos shingles that imitated pale brownish bricks; the
vast gray capsizing barns and the smaller ones settling
askew; huge carcases of prostrate buildings, with mixed
bones sticking out of a heavy hide; squalor of a little
asbestos-shingled house, with the front porches fallen
through.

I visited the old Collins house, where we used to stay
in my childhood. The excellent old red bricks have recently been painted an unpleasant chocolate. It is inhabited by the family of a farmer, who now owns the old
Munn farm. Though I had spent so many summers
there, I could hardly recognize the rooms, which had
been completely gutted of all the amenities of life, the
furniture reduced to the bare necessities. The farmer's
wife a heavy plain-talking woman, entirely a product of
the farm life and with no ambition to be anything else.
Perfectly affable. On account of a baby asleep upstairs, I
couldn't go up to see the room where my cousin Sandy
and I used to sleep or the room where, later on, I used
to read Thomas Hardy in bed, while the large upcountry
moths roasted themselves on the oil lamp with a perceptible smell of cooking. Her married son and his family
lived up there. Her daughter-in-law made hookrugs,
which I had seen displayed on a clothesline. The
daughter-in-law was summoned, and I bought two for
$20. This wiped off completely that pleasant old past.

The front lawn where we used to sit presents the only touch of gaiety with its varicolored just-washed clothes also hung out on the clotheslines.

I thought I ought to have my physical condition looked into. I could see that in upstate New York they didn't know much about tropical diseases, so I went for five days to a Boston hospital. I concluded that in New England they were not in this field much better equipped than in northern New York. I was afterwards told that for this kind of thing I should have gone to a veterans' hospital. I had two further and much milder attacks, then whatever it was disappeared.

While I was in Wellfleet, Helen Augur wired me to call her in California: "dying of cancer." When I talked to her on the phone, she told me about having many tumors, and I could see that she was relishing it rather, boasting as she had always done about her peculiar ailments. I wondered whether this were really as serious as she said and asked her if the doctors had told her she was dying. She said no, but she knew that she was. I said that I had been in Talcottville, and she began at once to tell me about some illness that she had contracted when she was living in the Stone House—hadn't found out what it was till afterwards, something you got from living in caves—she gave me the scientific name, which she always loves doing. She said that she thought some very sweet things about me as she imagined I did about her. She is in a sanitarium. There is a niece out there who looks after her.

Talcottville again, September 24. Mary met me and told me on the way about her four-weeks' experience of presiding over the study hall at the West Leyden school.

She is still a little uncertain about how she likes it, it is something of a strain to keep order all day among the children of the different grades; but it is evident that she is also enjoying it. She has developed, I suppose, a technique of charming them and at the same time maintaining discipline. She told me about one boy who had punched another and thus started trouble. She had reprimanded him, and this aroused his sister to come to his defence and threaten her: "You'll be sorry for this!" She sent them both to the principal, and when the girl came back, she apologized, and Mary talked to her sympathetically. She made a point of being reasonable, allowing for their points of view. She could read when she sat at the desk, then at intervals would walk down the aisle and see what was going on. It reminded me of Mr. Turner, who presided over study hour at the Hill School and who preserved such an effective discipline without ever getting on bad terms with the students. I imagine that she is going to be a success, and I hope she will get promoted, when the new regional school is opened, to something more interesting.

Helen Augur's sister called me up to tell me that Helen had died. Her doctor, on account of her hypochondria, had been inclined to treat her illness lightly, but it turned out that she did actually have cancer of the lung. Her body was cremated, and her sister Dorothy—named, she tells me, after Dorothy Mendenhall—brought the ashes on to have them buried in the Adams family plot in the Lowville cemetery (their grandfather William Adams had been the head of the Lowville Academy). I used to discount Helen's statements about the conventionality of her sisters and brothers, but I could see that it was true that they were more or less "square" and that she must have been always at odds with them. Her brother told me anecdotes about Helen's misfortunes as a girl—such as riding downhill on her bicycle and shooting on right into a lake: "She was always rather different from the rest of us, you know." After the ceremony in the cemetery, I took them all to lunch at the Hulburt House, where we had a much-needed drink. Strange to find that these Middle Westerners tie up with old Lowville and the Stone House.

October 1. Lunch with Dr. Miller and his wife, a brisk bright little brown brunette. She has had four children, was married at twenty, but still looks almost as if she might be one of them. I was surprised to find them Democrats and "liberals," something almost unheard-of in Lowville. They had not been able to bring themselves, in the last election, to vote for either of the presidential candidates. We went, after lunch, to his brother's house, in which Hough the county historian and "the Father of American Forestry" used to live. There is a plaque about him at the door. The Millers know quite a lot about local history and lent me two books on the subject. You are really in old Lowville here: the bathroom has old-fashioned washstands in elegant mahogany cases; handsome old turning staircase. Mrs. John Miller, a finelooking woman, very dignified, with graying hair. Some wine and much conversation.

I went to bed early, then woke up between 2 and 3 and finished Macaulay's history. Though he was dying, he more or less rounded it out by doing the deaths of James and William in fragments detached from the run of the narrative. Quite fortifying to find him thus sustaining the work, with the same high morality and thorough research, through all those parliamentary develop-

ments in connection with the Irish forfeitures—same
patience and eager interest.

On Saturday night, September 27, the Browns were
having a birthday celebration, and the boys were racing
in their cars up and down Water Street and along the
main road. The racket was so annoying that people
thought of calling up the State Troopers. One of these
boys, a Young and another, a distant cousin of mine who
has shown signs of becoming a black sheep, having got
in with the local gang and run away from home once or
twice, did not arrive at the Talcottville church, where
the other team was waiting for them. Someone went back
to find out what had happened and when he came back,
he said to the boys who were waiting, "If you can pray,
you'd better start now." The car with the two other boys
had run off the road and straight into a tree. The Young
boy was dead, his neck broken. The other boy was badly
injured and taken at once to a hospital. When I asked
about him later, I was told that he was still unconscious
—he hadn't recovered yet from the concussion. It was
impossible to tell who had been driving.

I talked to Barbara Erwin about this boy, whom she
had had in one of her classes. She said that he was not a
bad boy, she had found him sympathetic; but he didn't
fit into farm life. He would come to school in the morning, after getting up early and attending to the cows, and
drop his head on the desk and go to sleep.

The panes with the quatrain by Stephen Spender and
the poem by Louise Bogan have been broken by these
local mischief makers and were repaired when I was not
here, and the pieces thrown away.

XXIV

Arrived in Talcottville on May 11. I had a heart attack
in New York in the early spring and have had to be
careful of making any effort, but Elena drove me to the
airport, and a porter with a wheeled chair took me down
in an elevator to the lower level and got me on the plane.
Mary met me at the other end. I thought she was rather
discouraged. Her job disappears with the reorganization
resulting from the new regional school, and she says that
the kids are impossible to control—though, talking about
it later, she spoke of particular children in her relations
with whom she had become rather interested. In one
case, she had walked down the aisle weeping, and she
thought that had made some impression. She has decided
to spend $2000 she has saved on a two weeks' trip to
Europe which will involve a week in Hungary and stopovers in London and Paris. She had promised her younger
daughter a graduation present and thinks that this will
be appropriate.

Mary on the Women's Liberation movement: she
thinks that the women who are agitating are "not as

351

feminine as they ought to be," that women and men are different and have to perform different functions. One of the differences is that sometimes women "have to play dumb like a fox."

I have had a bed moved downstairs to the back of the big room. I live as I did at Wellfleet, working, sleeping and eating in the same room, with the bathroom adjoining, and I find it pleasant enough. Mabel Hutchins stayed nights during the first week, but now (May 26), I'm not afraid of an emergency any more. I can get around with little difficulty—go upstairs only once a day and space my excursions and guests.

This summer I visited Henderson House, which I have described in an earlier chapter, Hyde Hall, which I shall tell about later, and the Campbell House in Cherry Valley. All these old places were owned by people—Robertsons, Campbells, Clarkes—who did not live far apart and composed a kind of country gentry who had a social life of their own, paying visits back and forth, in the fashion of the early days, that sometimes lasted for weeks. All these houses became white elephants that have been or are about to be turned into museums or other institutions. In the last of these I visited, the Campbell place at Cherry Valley, in which the same family have lived since the eighteenth century, I found that the present owner, Mr. A. P. Whitehead, a New York lawyer, who is connected with the Historical Association, has also decided to sell it. He has kept up the house and has still two farms here, but only comes up in the summer. There is nothing for him to do except hunt and entertain guests. The second floor, as in the case of our house, is not properly heated for winter, and it would not be worth the expense for him to get it insulated. He is unmarried, the active outdoor type, Princeton '31—he seems to have gone in for athletics there.

It is a very fine old frame house, now painted yellow, with the inevitable solid stone doorstep. The older part was built by 1796, the later part added between 1853 and 1863. In the older part, a good white carved mantelpiece like ours, with the familiar oval motif; in the new part, a big fireplace with decorative plaster molding that is less handsome and rather out of keeping. In this living room, long guns on the wall from the Revolution and subsequent wars, and framed letters, among them one to some ancestor from James Fenimore Cooper, who was living not far away at the bottom of Otsego Lake. A large marble bust of Eliphalet Nott, at one time the pastor of the Presbyterian Church in Cherry Valley, and later for many years the President of Union College, Schenectady, which he established on a sound financial basis and at which he made a considerable reputation. We were given an excellent lunch. Attractive portraits of women in the dining room—the character brought out in the faces more interesting than in most old American portraits—and a very large steel engraving of a banquet in celebration of Waterloo, with Wellington standing up at the center of the table. Though I had had a highball before lunch, Mr. Whitehead seemed to feel we were not drinking enough. He asked us at lunch whether we would have champagne or "still wine," and when I had asked for still wine, he said, "You can just as well have champagne," and champagne was what we had. Our glasses were assiduously replenished, and the champagne was very good. "It's just like drinking water," he said.

My distant cousin in Talcottville, who had the bad car accident in which another boy was killed, has been sued by the family of this boy on the assumption that it was he

who was driving. He was brought to court while I was
there this summer, and the case was settled out of court
for a sum that will have to be paid mainly by the insur-
ance company. After the accident, the boy had gone out
to the Coast. He had a dip in Haight-Asbury, which
horrified him: filth and every kind of degradation, boys
so drugged they could only mumble, promiscuous girls
getting pregnant. He came back to New York so dis-
gusted that the family had hoped it would sober him up;
but soon he got arrested again for breaking the windows
of the Township of Leyden building, which somehow
involved the breaking of the windshield of a town car.
—These boys here have what they call "drag races," which
consist of seeing who can beat the other turning corners
with the brakes on.

Rosalind and I have the problem of finding a decent
place for dinner. We usually have to fall back on the
principal Boonville restaurant, where the menu is the
same as elsewhere: same rubbery frozen turkey, of which
I only eat the dressing, same South African lobster tails.
We heard about a place with a big-animal name that was
supposed to be very popular. Mabel Hutchins said that
she thought it was so much in demand that we should
have to engage a table. When we got there, it was not
inviting and proved to be the very worst of the restaurants
we had tried. It had the look of one of those Adirondack
places where the bears come in to eat the garbage, and the
fancy occurred to me that these bears had taken over the
restaurant and were running it according to their own
ideas. Bears do not eat meat on a large scale, but the
cuisine consisted mainly of huge hunks of pork and beef
—no soup, uninteresting vegetables. I became so depressed
by the place that I drank the whole of a bottle of very

sour white wine. The customers—big rural-type men and women—also resembled bears.

Mable Hutchins drove me to Hyde Hall. Alternations of sun with soaking rain. The characteristic skies up here, which have always impressed me since my youth, seem to correspond to the country in covering more space than is appropriate to our little human beings, with their beetle-like cars, and their knocked-together dwellings, barns and silos. These skies seem more in keeping with the life and conceptions of the Indians. A bank of cloud above a long green hill, forested a darker green on top; and gray rain-clouds which seem the emanations in vapor of remote invisible beings that move them slowly and, as it were, waveringly. Shreds of mist dripping here and there on the hills around Cooperstown.—Glyn Morris believes that the peculiar effect of the sky is due to the elevation which enables us to command greater distances.

In the morning of June 12, I went with Anne Miller to the chasm on Sugar River below the old railroad bridge, which I don't seem to have described before and wanted to see again. Anne, in tennis shoes and white tennis skirt helped me through the broken stones—I could never have got there without her—which was rather humiliating. When we got to the swimming hole and cataract, she went up to the falls, where she found a rope that the boys had evidently swung out on to drop into the deeper water. Her slim brown figure—she tells me she has Indian blood—looked very pretty in the dark water. I sat on a ledge—it is some years since I have seen this place. When you get beyond the stony descent, where the flowers of the season are blooming in the long grasses—wood anemones, buttercups, blue bugloss, with a sprinkling of forget-me-nots and violets, and with charred marks of picnic fires, the inevitable sprinkling of beer cans and spearmint gum wrappers, you find yourself suddenly in a high-walled ravine of stratified limestone rock, which is feathered with green fern and lined in the cracks with green moss. The river runs shallow here, fractured with moderate rapids. Birds flit back and forth between the walls. The cliffs where they overhang are dripping with the streams from springs, and the farther one goes toward the cataract, the more densely they are plumed with trees: ash, hemlock and elm, sumach bushes. A dead tree droops down over the stream. The cascade shows white, rather crooked and ragged; and below it floats a brownish froth. This froth and what she thought was a stagnancy of the water in a kind of inlet made Anne, with all the talk of pollution, afraid that the river might be polluted, and hesitant about bringing her children here. This is a relic of primitive landscape just off the traffic of the motor road but invisible from it and frequented by few. Above the ravine, against the blue, the coverlet of small dappling clouds crawls slowly below the sky.

The place is given a kind of sinister quality by two tragedies that occurred here. A boy was found drowned in the water—he is thought to have commited suicide; and two girls, crossing on the trestle, were once overtaken by a train: one lay down on the ties and was unhurt when the train passed over her, the other tried to hang on with her hands, but let go and fell and was killed.—One summer, several years ago, I liked to come here and watch a brood of hell-divers. They would shoot along like aquaplanes, then disappear under the surface and swim for a long distance, then suddenly reappear.

Loren Crosten has bought a place across from their camp on a back road. The children there used to annoy

them. They found behind the house a horrible dump of
garbage, scrapped cars and other junk. The inside of
the house seemed more horrible still: there was an upstairs room where the children apparently peed and
shitted on the floor. Loren is going to raze the house and
hopes to have established there a biological laboratory
where the hormones of insects will be studied.—They
have had a bad winter at Leland Stanford: the bombing
of the Music School was threatened, the windows of
their house were broken, and they were wakened to sleep-
less nights when the police would call them up and tell
them to look out for attacks.

I went back to Wellfleet on June 23 and stayed till
August 16. Reuel and his wife and his little boy have
come on from the Coast for his new job at the University at London, Ontario. The humid sticky stifling
American summer, with all of its messy arrangements of
getting meals and going to the beach. It was so hot that
it was a real ordeal for me to crawl to my writing table
and get a little work done every day. I don't remember
suffering so from the heat even during the summers in
New Jersey, but I suppose, being younger then, I was
better able to stand it. Past our house the flood of holiday
traffic poured slowly in a crowded flow. When we had
to go to Hyannis one day, we inched along at a rate of
about five miles an hour. Life in Wellfleet became very
complicated, with children and grandchildren and
friends, and Elena was quite exhausted and looked rather
haggard by the end of it. I brought Mabel Hutchins on
to help her, but Elena always wants to do everything
herself, and Mabel is made to play more or less the role
of a guest, whose only occupations are getting me breakfast and killing time by polishing the silver.

Tania Ledkovsky served as my secretary and, after

Reuel and Marcia left to spend a month in France, she
acted as nursemaid for two-and-a-half-year-old Jay. I had
wanted her to help me with my Russian book, and she
had brought up her father's Russian typewriter and filled
in the Russian quotations. Though she was born in
Europe and has never been in Russia, she has seriously
studied Russian in a way that few Russians have and
can answer all questions about grammar and the forms
of Russian words. I have been reading Russian plays and
having difficulty with the extremely colloquial dialogue.
In spite of all the time I have spent on the language,
I still often have to look up words. In Talcottville I got
through the trilogy of Sukhovo-Kobylin, but, after I went
back north, I got stuck in the second act of Fonvizin's
Nedorosl. I find I have been suffering lately from a
general antipathy to Russia and the Russians. Just how
deep do the differences go that the Revolution has made?
I found in Talcottville Marie Scheikévitch's *Souvenirs
d'un Temps Disparu* and read it through for the first time.
She was brought as a child from Moscow to Paris and
was astonished to find that the French talked constantly
about politics and current events. She tells of hearing a
woman who sold fruit say, "Que voulez-vous, madame,
avec leur sale politique ils font monter les prix." "In
Russia," she notes, "the ignorant frightened masses would
never, through the mouth of such a woman, have dared to
criticize the government in this way. I was surprised to
find that the political problems of France could be discussed by any citizen. They were dealt with by means of
actions that he could influence, approve or blame, that
were not veiled by anything mysterious. It had been forbidden, in school in Russia, to express the least opinion
on a public event." This seems to be equally true today.

I was glad to get to Talcottville again. It was cool

there; the weather had cleared. Mary told me about her
trip. She had "had a ball" in Budapest. She was pleased
that, on account of her Hungarian, she should have been
asked when she had left Hungary, though she was born
in the United States. I feel that since her return she is
somewhat let down. She not only spent her $2000 but
has run to some extent into debt. I believe that her husband is annoyed at having been left—with her and Janet
gone and Susie away with a job at Old Forge—with nobody to get him meals. I told her that this would infuriate
me, but she hotly defended herself: I lived a different
kind of life from the kind of life that they lived nowadays; she had left the larder provided with everything
that George would need for the two weeks she would be
away. She has gone back, under the pressure for money,
to her old job in the Rome pharmacy, and is gratified that
people who meet her on the street are glad to see her
back. In her spare time, she plants her flowers, and she
has thrown herself energetically into building a new
porch for their house.

I had been looking forward to making, with "Lafe"
Todd and Austin Briggs, a trip to Lily Dale in Chautauqua County, the spiritualistic community, near which,
at Dunkirk, the former was born. "Lafe" stands for Lafay-
ette. He tells me that his great-grandmother had been
present at a reception for La Fayette and had named her
son Marquis de La Fayette, not knowing that Marquis
was a title. When this was explained to her, she changed
it to Marcus.

The trip lasted three days, August 28-29-30. The
country west of Syracuse is monotonous and dreary, perfectly flat. Thick fields of corn and goldenrod, both of
which have been abundant this summer, and beyond
this the miles of vineyards draped on their posts and wire.

Welch's grape juice is made out here; but other grapes
are sent to California, and the wines are exported from
there. But the wine we were given in the restaurants here,
extremely sour and coarse, seemed to me the very worst
that I had ever had anywhere. The food on the way was
equally bad. I had thought that the chain of restaurants
on the Thruway farther east was even considerably worse
than the chain along the Massachusetts Turnpike, but
in the west there is a chain even worse: cafeterias with
no trays to carry the food and not even paper plates to
eat it on. We decided that the people who went there
had no idea how bad it was. These inhabitants seemed
very low grade. Not even pretty girls, but pale gray-eyed
lean ill-built Polish women and the usual thick loutish
men. One wonders how these men and women can feel
enough mutual attraction even to breed more of their
unattractive kind. The shadow of the Alleghenies looms
on the sky near Fredonia—this is the furthest western
corner of New York State. Lake Erie is so polluted that
swimming in it has been forbidden, and the fish from
it are dangerous to eat. The huge bulk of a Niagara-
Mohawk Power Company building, squatting in the
water at the edge of the lake, looks menacing in the half-
darkness.

Lily Dale, named for the water lilies in the little lake
on which it is located, is certainly a very curious place—a
last remnant of one of the cults that were planted in this
part of the country. The mean little house of the Fox
sisters, the first inspirers of the Spiritualist religion,
though they eventually confessed they were frauds, a
statement not accepted by their followers, was moved to
this settlement from near Rochester. The house burned
down, but its site is still sacred and commemorated by a
plaque. The town is protected on one side by the lake
and on the other by a tall primeval forest. You have to

pay seventy-five cents to get in. There is a gate with, above it, the announcement, "The World's Largest Center for the Religion of Spiritualism," and, behind it, a shabby imitation bronze fountain of a woman pouring water out of an urn. Todd says that Lily Dale was always disliked by the outside inhabitants, who regarded it as "a sore" and tried to disregard it. One of the factors which had given them a bad reputation was their having had open sewers that directly drained into the lake. As a boy, he had sometimes had to go there selling waterlilies—charging extra for the rarer pink kind—and had some disagreeable experiences with the male mediums, whose peculiar character seems not to have changed. He obviously loathes the place, though he has sometimes taken visitors to see it. He once brought Carl Carmer, the New York State writer, who insisted on introducing a magician, the late John Mulholland, the distinguished scholar of magic and the author of *Beware Familiar Spirits,* which has a chapter devoted to the Fox sisters. In those days there were regular darkened séances of a kind that has since, we were told, been forbidden, in which the participants sat around a table holding the hands of their neighbors on either side. Mulholland dropped out, joining the hands of the people who sat beside him, and slipped away at the moment when a glowing bunch of "ectoplasm" was floating about the ceiling. He illuminated the room with a flashlight and revealed the shoeless medium carrying a broomstick on which was fastened a large wad of cotton saturated with phosphorus. Mulholland and Carmer were made to leave, and the medium was had up by the corporation which owns and runs Lily Dale. She, too, was expelled; this seems very unjust but the gravest offence possible was for a medium to be found out. The corporation has no hesitation in suing irreverent visitors on such charges as interrupting a séance and endangering the medium's life.

These old-fashioned séances have, as I say, been discontinued—no more "trances and trumpets," as they refer to them—whether as a result of exposure or of incompetence in trickery on the part of the mediums. At the center of the town stands a billboard, which tabulates the names and addresses of three categories of ministrants: clairvoyants, mediums and healers. Eighty percent of these wonder-workers are women. No one is allowed to recommend another. One can imagine how such recommendations might cause trouble by setting up factions and bosses. The place has a strange appearance, as if nothing had ever been planned, as if the town had grown up like a mushroom clump. Huddled houses with steep sharply peaked roofs; a few with the white fringes of wooden lace and spindle-ribbed porch railings characteristic of upper New York; a few desultory flowers—geraniums, gladiolas, begonias. There is a curious exotic motif of clumsy and ugly pagodas—one in the center sells ice cream cones and pop and brochures that explain the community. There is a very old-fashioned library with a lean and white-haired librarian: shelves of torn and dark-covered books which, except for a few works of reference, all seem to deal with the history of Spiritualism. A small white office building that sells postcards has a sign behind the counter that announces "Phenomenon: Reincarnation. This may be observed in many offices 5 p.m. when all the dead people come to life." This the woman in charge explained to me was "a jest." These women, including the mediums seem all to look very much alike: fattish waistless elderly persons with glasses. No children. A few squint-eyed girls look as if they were training to be witches. Briggs and I both had the feeling that the place, so cut off from the outside world and occupied with pursuits quite alien to it, seemed unreal and was decidedly uncomfortable. Briggs said that he had the impression that he was everywhere surrounded by a conspiracy. I was reminded of those stories of the supernatural by Algernon Blackwood in which someone visits an actual or convincingly described place to find that he is in the midst of something extremely queer—in one case, I think, a city inhabited entirely by sinister cats.

Briggs and I wanted to ask for a private séance, and a medium with a Polish name said, smiling with her little white rodent teeth, that she would "try to squeeze us in." We went there the next morning at the time she had said, but nobody answered the door, and when we came back, later, there were several ladies on the porch who were evidently also waiting. We finally gave it up, assuming that whatever she did for us would not be essentially different from what we had already seen and heard at two public séances. Todd thought this medium had been apprised that a writer had come among them, and that she had not been anxious to see us. I thought there were certain signs that we were kept under observation. One can rent a house in Lily Dale, but one cannot buy property there unless one subscribes to the faith.

With the regular old séances no longer practised, the whole stock and trade of Lily Dale seems to have been reduced to simple fortune-telling. The first public exhibition we attended in a large Assembly Hall was conducted by a chinless man in spectacles and a respectable dark suit, who had the piercing nasal voice and the unctuous pronunciation of the old-fashioned Methodist or Baptist preacher, and who constantly rubbed his hands, even when he was not on the platform. He fished for questions in the scant attendance, and did his best to supply the questioners with reassuring answers, supposedly dictated by spirits: yes, they could go on that

trip that they had been looking forward to; yes, their
beloved aunt or sister would recover from her menacing
illness. The meeting was concluded by a blast from the
organ. We went on to "the Temple in the Woods," a
little building open at the front like a Punch and Judy
booth, with a sign that said "In Memory of Mother."
The visitors sat on benches among the tall naked stems
of maples. Here another of their short groundhog women
in the usual flowered dress was groping for leads from
the audience. Before replying, she would bend her head
as if listening to the messages of the spirits. Was there
somebody named Ed present? One of the men in the
audience answered to this name. "Ed is crazy about fishing." The real Ed said he was not. "Oh, this Ed loves
fishing. I can see him fishing!" She went through the
pantomime of gleefully reeling in a fish. She had developed a repertoire of cues—common names and common events, dead relatives—which she relied on to elicit
recognition. Was there anybody there, she asked, who
had had something dropped on his toe? This has never
happened to me, but I am told it is a common occur-
rence. If any of her fumbling guesses was corroborated
by the one questioned, she would thank him or more
often her with great cordiality. On one occasion, she said
that a little girl spirit beside her was clapping her hands
for joy. One lady seemed to be a "plant": after corrobora-
ting everything suggested, she left as if she had discharged
her duty. This medium's clientele consisted mostly of old
ladies. She presently relinquished her platform to a male
medium of dubious appearance. I thought that his accent
was Central European, but Todd thought that it sounded
Irish. One wonders where they get these male mediums.
He identified one of the men as a truck driver and told
him that he was soon to drive a "box car"—which is a
vehicle equipped with wheels that can either be carried

on a truck or hitched onto the cars of a train. When this interchange was over, we left.

One of the lures that draw people to these mediums is that they often give predictions on the stock market. If a customer turns out to make money by following one of these tips, it is a fine recommendation for the medium. In winter, they migrate to Florida, where they have another Lily Dale, a town called Cassadaga. Todd believes that they numbered in his youth something like five thousand, but a local lawyer friend of his says that they are now probably not more than a thousand.

We visited "the Temple in the Woods." Here the bare trunks of very tall old trees, below which grows much yellow jewel-weed, had leaves only at their distant tops. A little sign directed one to a pets' cemetery. The "temple," just beyond which a barbed wire fence is implanted among the bushes to keep out intruders, had a floor of stone blocks on each of which was inscribed the name of some famous medium. There was a broad "Inspiration Stump" which was used as a pedestal for the speakers. One gathers that Lily Dale was formerly much more frequented and had much more serious pretensions. Todd says that its presence there had encouraged in all that neighborhood many other manifestations of the spirit forces.

We had dinner the last night at what Todd said was the best restaurant and which was actually comparatively pretty good. Instead of the radioed Hammond organ which seemed to be standard in these places, a real man was playing a real one; a young waitress who, with a smear of rouge, was at least making an effort to be pretty; a dish of whitefish retrieved from some unpolluted part of Lake Erie; but more of their horrible wine of a vintage called Emerald Dry.

Todd's lawyer friend had invited us to a party for an old lady, a friend of Todd's family, who was celebrating her hundred and second birthday. I begged off because it now costs me too much effort to meet and talk to new people, with the drinking that that involves. I stayed in the dreary motel, where I found a huge spider in the bathtub. I covered current events with *Time*, *Newsweek* and *Life*, and the local Sunday paper; and read Kingsley Amis's latest novel, *The Green Man*, which was peculiarly suited to the spirit of Lily Dale. It combines the erotic with the supernatural and has evidently been very much influenced by the ghost stories of M. R. James: antiquarian documents and an unconvincing fiendish agent made apparently of bushes and branches. God comes in at the end in the guise of a disarmingly friendly and slightly apologetic young man. The erotic part is quite funny, but the book is unsuccessful. Sad to see Amis, who has already been rooting for the Viet Nam war, going in for religion, too. The next evening Todd told me that I had been wise not to come to that party. It had consisted mainly of very old ladies, schoolteachers, and Austin Briggs, when he first arrived, was made to wonder which was a hundred and two. Then it turned out that the old lady in whose honor the party had been given was indisposed and unable to attend. It reminded me of Ronald Firbank's *Valmouth*. Todd and Briggs had drunk too much Bourbon in order to get through the evening and seemed to feel somewhat the worse for it.

On the way back, we visited the town of Chautauqua, which was different from anything I could have imagined. The ridicule of Mencken and others has led one to expect something sleazy and vulgar. It is an enclosure like Lily Dale, but on an infinitely bigger, cleaner and more prosperous scale. You are checked at the entrance,

and there are certain places to which you are not allowed
to go. Todd says it is pervaded by policemen. The familiar type of New York house: fancy woodwork, neo-
classical fronts. It is extremely puritanical. There is a
big palatial hotel of the period of those of Saratoga and
San Diego; but it has not been permitted to achieve their
splendor. The lounges have a certain bleakness. No bar because the whole town is strictly teetotal, and consequently
no atmosphere of festivity. Todd says there is a small
core of people who live there and enjoy the good music
and other cultural advantages, but who pay no attention
to the religious activities in which the town is otherwise
steeped.

On the highway driving home, we found ourselves
just behind an accident. I was half-asleep in the back seat
and did not know what was going on; but they told me
that the car ahead had seemed to rise up in the air as if
in slow motion and land beside the road upside down.
It was driven by an East Indian, with his wife and boy
in the back. The woman and the boy were both hurt.

I was glad to get back to Lewis County, with its mountains and its wild animals.

Dinner at the Edmondses'. Walter says that several
people, including himself, have seen a black panther on
the place. He even tried to shoot it. He has also seen a
large animal that looks like a timber wolf.

Tug Hill is a great shaggy beast lying down with its
head between its paws.

The old set of Charles Reade is here that my grandfather gave my mother when she was married—also, a

two-volume edition of *The Cloister and the Hearth* that belonged to my Uncle Paul. This was a favorite book of my grandfather's, and I set out to find out what it was, reading it in bed late at night. I finished it on September 4. It is hard to understand the raptures of Swinburne even on the part of one so given to raptures. John Hearne, the Jamaican novelist, smiled when I said I was reading the book. He said he had read it at twelve, implying that it was appropriate for twelve-year-olds. I agreed with him and agreed that it was terribly dragged out. A kind of improvised adventure melodrama, which one is always conscious that the author is making up and not taking quite seriously himself: "Gerard caught Margaret, but was carried down by her weight and impetus; and behold, the soil was strewn with dramatis personae." The picaresque first half is more or less amusing, with its elements of historical authenticity; but the second part becomes exasperating. The author, in the fashion of those days, has continually to invent obstacles to prevent the lovers being reunited. Then the very tedious pathos of the inevitable Victorian deaths. The catchwords that get on one's nerves: the dashing Frenchman's "The Devil is dead!," the heroine's, "I am but a woman." The reiterated humility of this last almost makes one sympathize with the Women's Liberation movement.

I have started George Borrow's *The Bible in Spain*. I need some long nineteenth-century book to supplement my nembutal tablet. After that, I shall go on to Byron's *Letters and Journals*. I was born in the nineteenth century, can remember the death of Queen Victoria, and it somehow consoles me to revisit it in literature. I have even bought a paperback reprint of Trollope's *The Eustace Diamonds*. At college I read *The Warden* and *Barchester Towers*, which an admirer of Trollope had given me, and swore that, although these books were mildly

amusing, I should never waste any more time reading
Trollope—a resolution I have kept to up till now. ⌝

In driving at night from Mary's house, I found that the
road to Rome took much longer than I remembered—
forty-five minutes, she says. In commuting to the drug
store where she works, she has to do this twice a day. I
commiserated with her about it; but she says she doesn't
mind it. She goes by a back country road that has very
little traffic, and it gives her—she explained with a certain
eloquence—between her business life and her family, an
interim to live in her real self, to be free of other people.

When I told Dr. Smith I was sorry that I hadn't been
able to go to the dinner in honor of him and Clark
Laying, he said that it had really been more for Clark,
that Clark was "way up there, too." This is the way he
always speaks of old age.

Glyn Morris took me to see the new "vocational
school," called the Area Educational Center, now in its
first year. I was astonished by its size and equipment. It
represents a new form of education—a training in different kinds of skills for young people not qualified to
graduate from high school. In its many light ground-floor
rooms, they are taught carpentry—a house is being built,
which eventually will be sold; car-repairing; the construc-
tion of farm machines; electronics; conservation, with
stuffed exhibits of birds and animals; the preparation of
food—here are a restaurant and a soda fountain for the
students to practice on. The women are trained as practical nurses and in beauty parlor work, in which they
now work on each other and are about to take on real
customers. There are all kinds of prints and instructive

films—the contents of Glyn's "gadget factory" at Lyons Falls has now been turned over to the school. There is one of those one-way mirrors, which on one side is opaque but transparent and on the other allows observers to look in on the students without the latter knowing they are being watched. There are devices which I did not know existed. Reading is taught by tape recordings and pictures. The girls who are studying advanced business methods work with typewriters which can reproduce letters that have been dictated on tapes, and a computer can reproduce a document punched on a card. There are two rooms for subnormal children: one for those to a certain degree educable and another for those barely trainable. These departments depressed me horribly—the open mouths, malformed faces, overswollen hyperthyroid types. Some of them volunteered to shake hands with me.

We also stopped in at the new modern high school, very different from the older kind: plenty of space and plenty of light. Large auditorium and library. The librarian was related to the Mrs. Johnson who took care of my father during that awful summer at Red Bank. We found Barbara Erwin in the Home-Making department, giving instruction in the making of layettes. In another room they were learning cooking.

These schools, which I had not before visited, do something to offset the miseries of the abandoned farms, collapsed barns. The new schools and the new roads are the principal forms of improvement. Mary tells me, however, that in Rome there is a prejudice against this vocational schooling. Some parents do not want their children to be trained to work with their hands, they want them to study for a profession. In the Glenfield vocational school about twenty percent drop out. The completeness of the plant and staff are said to be unique in the state. I under-

stand that Glyn himself had a good deal to do with pushing it.

The road-building is, however, being overdone.

Glyn took me for a drive on Tug Hill to investigate
a country road that was being enlarged and improved
but did not have any intelligible purpose. The only
buildings along it were two or three ruined farmhouses;
the only object it led to—by way of a road that branched
out of it—was a firetower, to which it would not seem to
be useful since the messages from it were signalled. On
another afternoon, Mabel Hutchins took me and her
three little grandchildren for a ride, in the course of which
we explored an unknown road through a woodland. This
was also being widened and surfaced and seemed to be
equally pointless. We drove for what seemed to be miles
without seeing any signs of life except the paths to two
or three camps. I finally told the children that it eventually led to a ferocious animal that one had to be careful
about, and they were rather disappointed when we never
encountered this animal. There was nothing of interest
whatever. At moments we thought of turning back, but
persisted and came out on a road to a town that could
have been reached without the road through the woods.

Surveying has been begun on a four-way highway
running past my house that seems to us more or less
superfluous, since a parallel highway a few miles away
has only just been completed. It is true that drunken
drivers have come to grief by not turning promptly at
a kink just before the Sugar River bridge, and further
on there is another kink where George and Lou Munn
had their horrible accident. But does this demand a four-
lane highway? They are taking a large section of my lot
across the road and a corner from my other lot across
what used to be called Water Street, and they offer to

pay me only $500 for them. The value of land here is
for some reason going up—people are even buying lots
on Tug Hill—and these lots of mine on a state highway
must certainly be more valuable than that. Penberthy is
working on the problem of trying to get me better paid.

I asked John Howland to take me to the mess that is
being made of Dry Sugar River, our old fossil-studded
and bird-haunted picnic spot that I always continued to
revisit, where the river goes underground. This land has
been bought and turned into a quarry for the "black top"
and crushed stone that are used for the making of these
roads. One suspects that the crushed-stone interests and
the road-building interests and no doubt the oil interests,
too, are working closely together. (It turned out later
that the man who has been operating this quarry has the
contract for the four-lane highway that is going to be
such a nuisance to me.) Crosten has told me that, when
the quarry is working, an unpleasant cloud of brown
dust rises among the green hills, but on the morning
when we visited this industrial desolation there was not
much being done, and no one interfered with our movements. You thread your way among the skeletons of stone-
crushers and the mountain ranges of black powdered
surfacing material. There is nothing left of Dry Sugar
River but a gaping rectangular excavation: gray walls of
gutted striated rock, with feeble streams trickling down
the sides. I couldn't see whether the strange creviced
woodland survived through which one passed to the
romantic spot, with its old mill and huge prostrate millstone, where the river emerged again, gushing out of the
side of a hill. I should think that the blasting out of this
quarry must have wrecked its underground course.

I attended a celebration of the Mihályis' Golden Wedding. Since it was held in the Methodist Church, there was neither drinking nor dancing, only fruit punch and an enormous wedding cake. I told Mrs. Mihályi that I had been looking forward to seeing her and her husband dance the czardas; but "there's no music," she said. I had an interesting talk with their grandchildren. There is a boy who is very New Left-minded and who is the leader of the movement at his state college. I was told he wanted to talk to me, but there was nothing illuminating I could tell him. He claims that the pressure of his group has resulted in some interesting lectures on subjects not included in the courses, and they are trying to get a course in Marxism. I do not see how Marxism can help them much in dealing with our present problems. They talk about opposing "capitalism," but do not seem to understand what this means. They are up against an almost all-controlling government identified with the industrial and commercial interests. This in a sense is socialistic like that of the Soviet Union, but like it a tyranny of bureaucrats. This boy is evidently intelligent and did foresee the danger that any kind of reformed institutions might fall into the hands of bureaucrats.

Just before I was going to the dentist, I found a boy I did not recognize sitting on the front steps. He got up and went away, but presently came to the door. He told me that he had hitchhiked to see me all the way from Atlantic City, and I gathered from his references to them that he had really read some of my books. I told him to come back at half past four, but did not know that my session with the dentist would last three hours and that I should be fatigued at the end. I could not advise or inspire him any more than I had been able to do the Mihályi boy. He did not seem to want to write. He much admired Norman Mailer, as a good many young people do. I don't know precisely what he wanted. He had

$3,000, he said, and was going to Austria without any idea of what he was going to do there. His family had originally been German, and he has studied and read some German. He said he was uncomfortable in the United States, and I think that what he really wanted was to get somewhere—though not Germany—where German was spoken and which would be in that respect somehow native to him. He said that on the way he had wondered what he would say to me when he met me. I didn't know what to say to him. I was so worn out with my dentistry that I turned him over to Rosalind for dinner at the Hulbert House. She said that he talked volubly all through dinner. With me he had been reticent and shy, and so low-voiced that I had difficulty hearing him.

Gertrude Loomis, now that her mind is nearly gone, is evidently a more serious problem than Florence was. She is always hiding things and wandering out for walks alone. The other day, in her nightgown and dressing gown, she walked to Talcottville down the middle of the road and called on the people, whom she did not know, now living in Carrie Trennam's house. She seems to have developed an antagonism to Huldah, but when Gertrude broke her leg last winter and had to be away in the hospital, Huldah says she was lonely without her. Huldah herself, although now rather deaf and although her eyes are failing, is still quite clear in her head and able to cope with the situation.

I sometimes feel that nowadays—eating, sleeping, and working in the same room—I am living like an animal in a den.

Bob Weiler has a badly mangled hand which was

caught in a machine at the mill, and a rib or two were broken in a car accident. But he is able to push a lawn-mower, and has now at last, at the end of the summer, managed beautifully to weed out my place, as to which up to now this year I have been rather inattentive. He has bunched the Showy Ladyslippers in front of the house. The ones behind were not doing well.

Elena has told me over the phone that Helen had a bad car accident in Maine, where she has been going to a Skowhegan art school. A car in front of her stopped suddenly without giving a signal, and she was thrown through the windshield cutting a great gash in her head that almost went through the skull. Twenty-three stitches were taken. Her car was completely smashed; the one in front merely dented. The stitches were eventually taken out, but the gash can only be concealed by doing her hair so as to cover it.

The pretty old rounded maple across the road in front of the house is beginning to turn with autumn. A reddish orange patch has appeared in the middle and will spread to the rest of the tree. It is going to be cut down to make room for the road, and this may be the last time I shall see it.

Mary's older daughter has married a boy who is mainly Cherokee Indian. His seventeen-year-old brother was arrested and put in jail for "reckless driving, speeding, being an unlicensed driver and failing to comply." The family says he was driving the car for the owner, who was drunk and incapable at the time. He hanged himself in prison with a sheet.

XXV

Epilogue, 1970

What I have written above shows the gradual but steady expiration of the world of New York State as I knew it in my childhood and the modifications that its life has undergone. It is true that Lowville and Boonville have changed less—unless perhaps Charlottesville, Virginia—than any other part of this country that I knew when I was a child. But, as has been seen, it has reflected all the changes that, to a greater degree, have been taking place in the life of the country as a whole. I do not mean to deplore all these changes. Anyone who still takes seriously the American democratic ideal of opportunity for everybody to prosper according to his best abilities and to enjoy such advantages as he can understand ought not to complain of the many cars, the "mobile homes," of the movies and television sets, of the grills for outdoor cooking. None of these things seems to me attractive, but I probably have no right to be contemptuous about them or to blame them entirely on the people who manufacture and advertize them. If people want them, why should they not have them? Don't young people live better in trailers than they did in old-fashioned frame houses, which were often so ill-built and dreary. I remember that in Red Bank, New Jersey, a typical bourgeois suburb, the general possession of motor cars and of comfortable modern houses immensely cheered and brightened that suburban life. We were only four miles from the ocean, but nobody could get there to swim unless the family had a carriage or, later, an automobile, which at that time was expensive and required a driver. Few people habitually rode bicycles. But presently a trolley was installed, which ran between Red Bank and Seabright. And now everybody owns a car, and in summer one can go to the beach every day. Our old house in Red Bank stood not far from a kind of suburban slum, unsightly and supposed to be something of a den of immorality. My mother's new house that she bought after my father's death, more convenient and much lighter than our gloomy old place, stood in a new street called Buena Vista, and all along it were a class of people that in the past could never have lived so well. On the opposite side of the street from us was the family of a bank clerk, whose wife was pretty and well dressed and whose equally attractive daughter was a great friend of my daughter's. It is true that, when I walked along this street, the radio could be heard from every house and all were playing the same program, so that, no matter how far one walked, the continuity was never interrupted. The implications of this uniformity did not at that time escape me; but I generally approved of what was going on. This, for the people of the United States, was an improvement in their condition. Today in upstate Lewis County there is a whole community of trailers among the trees of a little woodland behind and across the road from the great mansion and mowed grounds of Constable Hall. Constable Hall is now a museum, and the big houses of the well-to-do professional men and dairy owners and merchants have now either been turned into funeral homes or are inhabited by several families. To what other uses could these places be put? And the people who ride in cars, though they are frequently killed or injured in accidents, have no longer such constricted lives. The old way of living up here threw them back on their own capacity for instructing and amusing themselves: reading, playing the piano, sentimental songs, charades, as well as making pies, jams and breadstuffs and quilting and embroidery and the other household arts. But they often, even in the bigger towns, did not see very much of the world. Our old trips in carriages to Carthage and Rome now seem so slow as almost to be comic. I am able to go to Rome now as often as I like to have dinner and see a movie. I have described the quality of the dinners—though Rome has still, dating from 1908, an excellent Italian restaurant; but at worst they are better than the savorless meat and the vegetables in what we called "birds' bathtubs" of the local hotels where we used to have to eat in the course of our longer journeys. And even the worst of the movies are better than the rare melodramas that occasionally made us laugh in Boonville.

Of course there used to be a much greater difference between the "educated" and the "uneducated." Lowville Academy was once a great local center of schooling to which students came from miles around. The "Ivy League" colleges were places of training for what were called "the learned professions": law, medicine, the pulpit, certain kinds of science and the academic career. Today every young American enjoys the inalienable right to enroll at a state university and, as soon as he pleases, drop out. Negro and white children both may go all the way through primary school without ever learning to read. An "education guidance" man I know, who can certainly not in his work or his life be accused of being undemocratic, has told me that he has come to the conclusion that it is useless to try to educate a good many of the children beyond a necessary minimum. The problem of preventing the abler and more brilliant students from being retarded by the incapacity of the duller ones has sometimes been dealt with in the colleges by having special courses and classes for the former. I do not know enough about the present system to offer predictions or suggestions. I suppose that such vocational schools as the one I have described above must represent a new attempt to deal with the partially educable. It is a kind of successor to and substitute for the old apprentice system. There are in any case now relatively few examples of young people ambitious of meeting, outside the fields of technology, the higher standards of competence and culture.

My reaction to all the things that I disapprove and dislike is that of a member of a once privileged class which is being eliminated all over the world and has very little means any longer of asserting its superior "values." In this, the situation in the United States is not now very different from that in many other parts of the world—including the Soviet Union, except that in the latter the old educated and travelled and comfortable groups were less numerous and more quickly and completely suppressed. But our groups of well-to-do landowners and merchants and able professional men who made the American Revolution have now largely been reduced to the Nixons and Agnews of the present administration, who are hardly superior to the mediocrities that preside over the Soviet Union. It was thought by Veblen and others, that the technocrats would take over as a ruling

class, and this to some extent has taken place. I cannot foresee the future, but can only go on with my old occupations.

The fading-out in New York within such a brief period
of the ideal of feudal grandeur is of course only a special
case of the swift transience of everything in the United
States. These mansions mostly date from the early years
of the nineteenth century, and the family estates were
acquired in the later years of the eighteenth. Their ideal
was represented at its most pretentious by the great building called Hyde-Clarke Hall, which stands at the northeast of Otsego Lake, on the waters of which it looks out.
This imposing "pile," as the old writers would have
called it, was first built in 1817—the façade was added
in 1834. The first of the family in this country was an
Englishman, George W. Clarke, who came over in 1703
and was Lieutenant-Governor of the Province of New
York. He had been at Eton with Wellington, after whom
he named a hill on Otsego Lake, now usually known,
however, as the Sleeping Lion. He married the daughter
of Edward Hyde, the royal governor of North Carolina,
and became, by the law of coverture, the owner of the
Hyde estate in England. His great-grandson, who had
inherited the Clarke estate in America, came over here
after the Revolution and built for himself Hyde-Clarke
Hall out of the limestone available in this region. The
architect was also an Englishman, and he seems to have
aimed to reproduce the design of Elizabethan houses—
the house is built around a court—though it is masked
by the neo-classic portico which was eventually added.
The Hyde-Clarkes lived with great magnificence; and
they kept up the feudal tradition by resisting the demands of their many tenants at the time that the "rent
war" was causing trouble. But the son of the Clarke who
built the house had a mania for buying land—it was as

if he wanted to own the old province. He would buy and then mortgage, and went bankrupt, leaving nothing, as he said, but his clothes. The family sold the land in 1888. But in the meantime, in vying with the English great houses, they had succeeded in creating a legend. They were even supposed to have a ghost, and there was a saying that no woman could be happy there: all the ladies suffered from afflictions and disasters.

The state bought the house in 1964 for $500,000; it was then in such bad condition that it was proposed to demolish it and make tennis-courts for the state park in which it is now enclosed. But a Friends of Hyde Hall was organized in order to rescue and restore it. It was estimated that this could be done for a minimum of half a million, but it looks as if a million would be nearer the mark. The plan has been to bring back the original furniture, now in storage, and to turn it into a museum.

The old place is still a dominating presence. It is much larger than either Henderson House or Constable Hall —190 by 90 feet—but less attractive than either. Four high pillars, composed of round segments of stone, which would hardly seem out of place in Karnac, support an ironwork balcony, rather fancy but of the utmost dignity, and an entablature with a classical pediment. An oval window under the peak of the triangle and four square windows below. The walls are built of two kinds of stonework, both smoother and more tightly fitted than ours. There are palatial reception and living rooms, all with big marble mantels, mottled in white and black; a library and a chapel. But inside it is now all a dark desolation. The wallpaper is peeling in sheets, and the plaster is falling from the ceilings, leaving naked the narrow slats. The shuttered light is too dim to make out the ornamental cornices. On certain rooms are placards: UNSAFE. The floors have become rather flimsy, and

Hyde-Clarke Hall

Dining room of Hyde-Clarke Hall

one hesitates to climb the stairway—which, like ours, has brown banisters and a curlicue fringe along the steps. Old mattresses lying in piles. Even the rooms to which the family resorted when the place became otherwise uninhabitable could never be lived in now. Here there are a few old photographs lying on floors and tables; a copy of the Tauchnitz edition of *Lord Ormont and His Aminta,* which was considered very naughty in its day. The Clarkes seem to have been strangely careless of their property, as the Clarke who bought land was reckless. The "office" of one of the masters of the house who died in 1835 was locked up after his death and never opened till 1890, by which time the floor had collapsed and the furniture had fallen into the basement. In a barn that is going to pieces, there are the gruesome remains of a grand piano, which was never unpacked from its case but left out on a porch to rot. The story is that it had been ordered from London to be played on some special occasion but, when it came too late, was simply scrapped. In one of the downstairs rooms, there are toilet seats and other bathroom fixtures of comparatively recent date, which do not ever seem to have been installed. In proportion as the family abandoned the house, the wild life about invaded it, and when people slept there they took care to stop up the cracks under the doors in order to keep out the snakes. Hyde Hall, with its grand view, set among its ancient trees, is now a boarded-up slab of masonry, with a ragged screen of brush behind it, above which is vulgarly flourishing the pink wild flower called Bouncing Bet. When I last saw the house, there were boys on the balcony investigating the bats in the attic. They were going to get in an exterminator.

But this passing of such splendors as New York State could pretend to has made me feel not only the transience of all forms of life in America, but at my age the constant flow and perishable character, rather than the constant renewal and hope, of everything on the earth. Greece and Rome and classical France left behind them much more durable monuments than our old mansions gone to ruin and our broken-off fragments of old canals; but the aeons of time required for the mammalian plantigrades of the human race to achieve what we can now see to be a very moderate and partial degree of civilization has been coming to discourage and bore me. I look at the creatures on the street and think, well, we have begun to walk upright and our toes, now more or less impractical, are shrinking like the toes of elephants' feet. We have now arrived at a skill of uttering and writing sounds that can convey rather special meanings. But our problems of future development are still absolutely appalling. I do not have any chance, and feel that I should not have the patience, to wait through the countless millennia that would get us past our ages of blind quarreling and of our blindness in sexual selection that makes so much trouble for the children we breed. How much longer must it be before the inhabitants of Russia, ignorant and easily led, spread over such enormous spaces and with so little hunger for information that at the time of the last war there were people to be found in Siberia who not only did not know that there was a war or even that there had been a revolution—how long will it be before such people can organize a modern democracy and cease to attempt to exterminate their original and creative countrymen? I speak of a modern democracy, but how long will it be, for that matter, before the United States can organize a livable society which is free from the even more modern tyranny of bureaucracy? Democracy is actually one of those vague words which are supposed to command approval without giving us a chance to take stock of what our "democracy" consists of. Can I even be sure that, in the language I use, I am formulating these issues correctly? Will these terms not seem very crude to a remotely distant future? —that future I cannot wait for. And where do we get the standards by which we judge our earthly conditions and which are bound to be subject to continual change? When I think of these struggles and transformations to come, I am almost ready to call it a day, at this time of my waning powers, for my own more or less well-meaning efforts. After all, are not my literary activities, like new roads and vocational schools, clumsy gestures in the interest of ends that can only be reached—and what then?—in the course of innumerable centuries that are now entirely unimaginable? As one grows weaker, one becomes more helpless, more lazy, and also more indifferent. Will the Soviet Union last? a Soviet citizen has just demanded. Will General Electric and General Motors—are they "Capitalism," "Democracy"?—last longer than Hyde Hall, which, even in Republican America, was supposed to be still representing Feudalism? We have spent no one knows how many million years, as have the black widow spider, the hammerhead shark, the deadly amanita and the leaf-nosed bat, building up or assembling or creating—we do not even know how to put it—what we call our bodies and brains, our consciousness. Only now are we beginning a little to understand how these organs and members work. The process of finding out more is going to be very tedious. At least, that is how I feel toward the end of a fairly long life that has left me with the feeling—illusion?—that I have seen or sampled many kinds of experience, that I know what this planet is, what its climates in different places and at different seasons are, what its flora and fauna are, what both its more primitive men and more mechanized men are like—so that, not expecting any real novelty, I have no longer any curiosity beyond such as the satisfaction of which will keep me mildly amused while my faculties are gradually decaying. My young vision of New York State now hardly exists, though I do not think, as I did last year, that I shall sell my old place here. In spite of the encroachments of the highways and the element of impoverished ambitionless inhabitants, I have still, I think, just enough money to keep the old place going, and I am still as comfortable here as I can hope to be anywhere. That the old life is passing away, that all around me are anarchy and what seems to me stupidity, does not move me much any more. I have learned to read the papers calmly and not to hate the fools I read about. As long as my health holds out, I shall have to go on living, and I am glad to have had some share in some of the better aspects of the life of this planet and of northern New York.